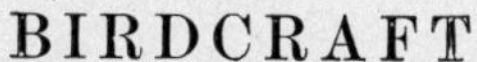

BIRDCRAFT

The laverock sings a bonnie lay
above the Scottish heather.
It sprinkles down from far away
like light and love together:
It drops the golden notes to greet
his brooding mate, his dearie,—
I only know one song more sweet,—
the wood-notes of the veery.

Henry van Dyke.

From "The Builders and Other Poems"

THE MACMILLAN COMPANY
NEW YORK · BOSTON · CHICAGO · DALLAS
ATLANTA · SAN FRANCISCO

MACMILLAN & CO., Limited
LONDON · BOMBAY · CALCUTTA
MELBOURNE

THE MACMILLAN COMPANY
OF CANADA, Limited
TORONTO

THE VEERY

BIRDCRAFT

A FIELD BOOK OF TWO HUNDRED SONG GAME, AND WATER BIRDS

BY

MABEL OSGOOD WRIGHT

AUTHOR OF "THE FRIENDSHIP OF NATURE," "TOMMY ANNE" "CITIZEN BIRD," "THE GARDEN OF A COMMUTER'S WIFE," ETC.

WITH EIGHTY FULL-PAGE PLATES BY LOUIS AGASSIZ FUERTES

NINTH EDITION

New York
THE MACMILLAN COMPANY
LONDON: MACMILLAN & CO., LTD.
1936

Set up and electrotyped. Published April, 1895. Reprinted January, 1896. Reprinted, with additions, and new illustrations, October, 1897; June, 1899; December, 1900; April, 1903; February, 1907; August, 1909; April, 1917; October, 1926; October, 1936.

· PRINTED IN THE UNITED STATES OF AMERICA ·

To J. O. W.

A RECORD OF HAPPY FIELD DAYS
ABOUT HOME

Fairfield, Conn.

"Thus on Earth's little ball to the birds you owe all, yet
your gratitude's small for the favours they've done.
And their feathers you pill, and you eat them at will, yes,
you plunder and kill the bright birds one by one;
There's a price on their head, and the Dodo is dead, and
the Moa has fled from the face of the sun!"

ANDREW LANG.

And the birds sang round him, o'er him,
"Do not shoot us, Hiawatha!"
Sang the Opechee, the Robin,
Sang the Bluebird, the Owaissa,
"Do not shoot us, Hiawatha!"

LONGFELLOW.

TABLE OF CONTENTS.

LIST OF PLATES.

Much of the technical excellence of these plates is due to the fine specimens of birds furnished the artist through the courtesy of the American Museum of Natural History, New York City. In this connection both illustrator and author wish to thank Dr. J. A. Allen and Mr. Frank M. Chapman of the department of ornithology in that institution.

The numerals on the plates indicate the approximate length of each bird, small fractions being avoided. The point of measurement being from the tip of beak over the back to the end of the tail, it must be remembered that this length is often variable according to the development of the tail.

LIST OF PLATES.

LIST OF PLATES.

PREFACE TO THE NINTH EDITION.

AN INVITATION.

More than twenty years ago this simple record was first sent forth with the hope that those who had never gone afield understandingly might be led out of doors and there enjoy what I had enjoyed, for in those days there were but few field aids to the identification of our common birds, and yet fewer available pictures of them.

Since then the scene has changed, and a great awakening to the value and beauty of bird life has swept the land. The Audubon movement has not only stimulated knowledge by its fine biographical bird leaflets adequately illustrated, issued by The National Association, but this knowledge has created the general desire to protect the bird.

Not only is the wild bird conceded to be an inheritance of the people, but the people have constituted themselves the trustees of its liberty.

Through the public spirit of one of these trustees, a woman, the name of *Birdcraft* has come to have a newer, more vital, meaning than as the title of this book, for on the twentieth anniversary of its writing a ten-acre tract of suitable wild land, containing trees, brush, and water, was bought and put into the writer's hands to be set apart as *Birdcraft Sanctuary*, a home perpetual, where wild birds might find safety and food the year round.

In the development one step led to another, and in two years such work as human hands may do has been completed. A high wire fence shuts out four-footed marauders, trails intersect the brush, a marshy spot is now a flower and fern edged pond, that not only delights the song birds but lures the remoter waterfowls, Herons, Black and Wood Ducks, to rest and feed.

This Sanctuary is the property of the Connecticut Audubon Society. At the entrance, where a gatepost of natural rock forms a shallow bathing pool, stands the warden's lodge, and opposite is a little museum, wherein the birds to be seen in Connecticut during the year are mounted against natural backgrounds in groups following the seasons of their appearance.

To this place you are welcome. You who have followed the birds through these pages may follow them here anew. A greeting, friends old and new, the greeting of Birdcraft Sanctuary and of Spring!

M. O. W.

OAKHAVEN,
FAIRFIELD, CONN.,
MARCH 21, 1917.

TO THE READER.

Do you want to know the birds and call them by their familiar names? You may do so if you will, provided you have keen eyes and a pocket full of patience; patience is the salt of the bird-catching legend.

The flowers silently *await* your coming, from the wayside wild rose to the shy orchid entrenched in the depths of the cool bog, and you may examine and study them at your leisure. With the birds it is often only a luring call, a scrap of melody, and they are gone. Yet in spite of this you may have a bowing and even a speaking acquaintance with them.

The way is plain for those who wish to study the science of ornithology and have time to devote to the pursuit; its literature is exhaustive, and no country offers a more interesting variety of species than our own. But for the novice, who wishes to identify easily the birds that surround him, to recognize their songs and give them their English names, the work at first seems difficult. There are many scientific terms, containing their own definitions, that lose force and exactness when translated into simpler language, requiring a dozen words to give the meaning of one. There is a comforting fact, however, for the novice, that while scientific nomenclature has been and is constantly changing, the common names, that science also recognizes, remain practically unchanged. Our Bluebird bears the same name as in Audubon's day, and the Meadowlark, who has been moved from one genus to another, is called the Meadowlark still.

In speaking of the common names of birds, I would draw a sharp line between the English names recognized by the text books and the American Ornithologists' Union, and the purely local titles. Local names, whether of flowers or birds, are often a hindrance to exact knowledge, because they frequently stand for more than one object. For example, I have heard the term Redbird applied alike to the Baltimore Oriole, Scarlet Tanager, and Cardinal; but a knowledge of the *recognized* common names of a bird will enable the student to find its species in any of the manuals.

Allowing that you wish to name the birds, do not be held back by minor considerations. You are not to be excluded from the pleasures of this acquaintance even if you are obliged to spend most of your life in the city. The bird-quest will lend a new attraction to your holidays, and you will be led toward the nearest park or along the front of river or harbour. Bradford Torrey gives, in his inimitable way, an account of the birds (some seventy species) which he saw on Boston Common, and Frank M. Chapman lists one hundred and thirty odd species which he has seen in Central Park, New York.[1]

The museums also are open to you, and their treasury of skilfully preserved birds offers the advantage of close inspection. The taxidermist's art has reached great perfection lately, and in the place of bird mummies, stuffed and mounted each in the stiff attitude of its neighbour, without the tribal marks of pose or expression, — as much alike as the four-and-twenty blackbirds that were baked in the pie, — we now see the birds as individuals in their homes. The American Museum of Natural History, New York, has sixty such bird groups which show the Chimney Swift, nesting on his little bracket, the Ruffed Grouse rustling through the leaves with her tiny brown chicks, the Baltimore Oriole and its swinging nest, or the Black Duck guarding its bed

[1] Mr. Chapman, Assistant Curator of the Department of Birds and Mammals of the Museum of Natural History, has recently completed an excellent Visitor's Guide to the Museum's Collection of Birds, found within fifty miles of New York City, in which all birds seen in Central Park are specially noted.

of marsh-grass. We Americans have not yet thoroughly acquired the habit of regarding the museums as great picture books, and yet such they are, and in this connection I wish to express my gratitude to Dr. J. A. Allen, Curator of the Department of Birds and Mammals of the American Museum of Natural History, for much valuable assistance and advice in connection with this book.

If you are not a dweller in a large city, but live in a suburban town with a few shrubs in your yard or a vine over your door, you have the wherewithal to entertain bird guests who will talk to you so cheerily that you will soon be led to discover that there is a lane or a bit of woods within walking distance, where you may hear more of such delightful conversation. Read the "Bird Songs about Worcester,"[1] by the late Harry Leverett Nelson, a graphic as well as charming account of the birds to be found in the neighbourhood of a rural city, and you will be encouraged.

And you who through circumstance, rather than choice perhaps, live in the real country and, as yet, feel the isolation more than the companionableness of Nature, who love the flowers in a way, but find them irresponsive, I beg of you to join this quest. You will discover that you have neighbours enough, friends for all your moods, silent, melodious, or voluble; friends who will gossip with you, and yet bear no idle tales.

If you wish to go on this pleasant quest, you must take with you three things,—a keen eye, a quick ear, and loving patience. The vision may be supplemented by a good field-glass, and the ear quickened by training, but there is no substitute for *intelligent* patience. A mere dogged persistency will not do for the study of the *living bird*, and it is to the *living bird* in his love-songs, his house-building, his haunts, and his migrations, that I would lead you. The gun that silences the bird voice, and the looting of nests, should be left to the practised hand of science; you have no excuse for taking life, whether actual or embryonic, as

[1] Boston: Little, Brown & Co.

your very ignorance will cause useless slaughter, and the egg-collecting fever of the average boy savours more of the greed of possession than of ornithological ardour.

Finally, whoever you are who read these pages, spare for me a little of your hoard of the same patience with which you are to study the birds, if, while striving to lead you through the wood-path, I often stumble or retrace my steps.

M. O. W.

STRANGERS AND PILGRIMS.

No matter how well one imagines he knows the birds of the neighbourhood, the day will surely come when a new note will fall upon the ear, or an unfamiliar shape be outlined against the horizon. It may be a broken scrap of song or merely a call, but from that moment until the bird is identified the listener knows no peace.

It is not that the novice can expect to discover new species in a well-known region, but there is always the chance that circumstances may cause a pair of birds to go outside the previous limit of the tribal breeding range, or that accident overtaking a migrating individual, it may linger and let its voice be heard far from its usual haunts. Then, too, foreign birds that have been liberated in given places with a view to their naturalization have a way of creating unexpected ranges for themselves in the new country.

The beautiful native Prairie Horned Lark, cousin of the Shore Lark that comes to us as a winter resident, is constantly extending its breeding range eastward. The most conspicuous difference between the Prairie Horned Lark and the Shore Lark is that the former has a *white* forehead and line over the eye instead of yellow, and that it is a trifle smaller.

This Lark is not mentioned in the 1895 edition of Stearn and Coues' "New England Bird Life," while the A. O. U. Check-list of the same year gives the eastern limit of its range as northeastern New York and western Massachusetts, yet 1905 finds it breeding freely in the farming region about Watertown, Litchfield Co., Connecticut.

The same Check-list speaks of the Carolina Wren as being "casual or rare in southern New England." Five years ago a pair of these Wrens nested and brought out two broods, quite close to my garden wall, in the dense brush made by the uprooting of some red cedars by a storm. Now there are several pairs in the neighbourhood and the powerful and spirited song of this Wren, that has some of the Cardinal's quality, is becoming a feature of the local music.

More than twenty-five years ago several pairs of English Goldfinches were set free near Hoboken, New Jersey. Now the bird is to be found in many places in southern New England, in the vicinity of Boston, and in Central Park, New York.

One bright cold afternoon toward the end of last March, being in a sheltered part of this park, I heard an exuberant and long-continued song, that suggested that of both the Pine Siskin and American Goldfinch, and yet belonged to neither. Many passers had stopped to listen to the music, but the bird kept well out of sight in some spruces.

Disobeying the sign to "keep off the grass" as is the bounden duty of a bird lover, I soon spied the bird performing gymnastics on a slender spray, singing lustily the while, and presently he dropped to the grass, even then raising his head and continuing the song at intervals. The bird was a fine specimen of the English Goldfinch in spring dress, the bill bounded with red at the base, the black crown and neck stripe, and black wings with their yellow band making a striking contrast to the whitish under parts and white tipped inner tail feathers which he showed as he turned and preened himself.

What a charming object was this little pilgrim singing in full bravery of plumage in our keen March air, while still our native Goldfinch wears his winter coat and muffles his voice to a call note or two.

I have seen these English Goldfinches three times in this neighbourhood in as many years. Once in a mixed flight of Sparrows and American Goldfinches, once in company with flocking Chipping Sparrows, and finally this summer, a solitary pair spent some time in the garden trees, reappearing in late September, and showing an absence of shyness that leads me to believe their nesting site was not far away.

For several years past inquiries have come to me by letter

and word of mouth as to the identity of "a speckled Blackbird, that is neither just like a Grackle or a Cowbird, and walks about the road and barnyard, but can't stand much cold." In some instances children have brought the bodies of these birds, evidently frozen and not starved to death, to the local school in the hope of having the name of a new bird written opposite their own on the blackboard.

This "speckled Blackbird" is none other than the English Starling, the companion of shepherds and their dogs in the pastures and hillsides wherever the flocks scatter. Well do I remember my first sight of a cloud of these Starlings circling about a vast flock of sheep on Salisbury Plains, close to Stonehenge, now lighting on the ground, and then on the back of the sheep, from which the birds would peck the ticks that burrow beneath the wool, while later in the day we found them sharing the roosting crannies in a church tower with the Rooks.

Sixty Starlings were set free in Central Park, New York, in 1890, and from this flock the birds have spread in all directions so rapidly that experts say in another twenty years their range will be bounded only by geographical conditions.

Here in Connecticut they were not conspicuous until 1900, but now they are a serious menace both to the summer resident birds, whose nesting sites they appropriate, and to the winter food supply of our most beneficial resident birds.

The Biological Survey at Washington is alive to the danger and is making an exhaustive study of the Starling as regards its feeding and other habits, with the view of devising means of curbing its increase.

Personally I have been watching the habits of the Starlings as individuals and in flocks for the past five years, limiting myself to a two-mile radius of home and I am appalled at the injury that they inflict, both upon birds, for the Starling is a great fighter armed with a strong bill, and on tree and bush fruits.

Beginning to mate, sometimes as early as February, the Starlings of Birdcraft Sanctuary and my own place often raise two broods a year, it being quite usual to see the first brood following the parents about and clamouring for food while they are busy with the second brood.

When the second family is on the wing, the two broods with the parents form a family flock in early June, when they spend the time in visiting cherry trees, berry bushes, and grain fields until August, when the general flocking takes place.

In the autumn they pillage the countryside of everything eatable, from grain gleaning to pepperidge berries and all other edible seeds that would form the winter food of Robins and Bluebirds. They also gobble the suet and other food put out on winter feeding shelves. At night they either take refuge in buildings or go in cloud-like flocks to the brushed edges of the marsh meadows, these roosts being often discovered by the fact that their droppings have seared the foliage, leaving the bushes leafless.

Connecticut has done wisely in placing the Starling on the list of *unprotected* birds, side by side with the English Sparrow, but a concerted country-wide effort must be made if the bird is to be kept in check.

If Starlings were but few in number, their melodious spring whistle, varied at times with a sort of muttered sound and some very startling ventriloquistic notes, together with the varied seasonal plumage, would make them interesting guests, but as conditions are they are another warning of the foolishness of importing birds to another habitat than their own. Nature resents this meddling and the innocent pay for the mistake of the rash.

Only a month ago over 500 Starlings were captured in the belfry of a near-by country church, by merely placing curtains behind the slat ventilation openings and dropping them after the birds had gone to roost at night, the condition of the tower being something beyond belief.

The range of many of our native birds has widened of late years, or perhaps there are more students on the watch for record keeping. The Black-crowned Night Heron was not recorded as a winter resident of Connecticut by two accepted authorities in a book of a few years ago, yet a small colony has wintered in my home grounds for five years, roosting in the thick spruces and going down to the marshes at ebb tide. Many people have seen these Herons and they have been photographed, a necessary condition when an amateur wishes to establish a new record.

The Evening Grosbeak, also a bird of the north, that not so long ago was considered as an irregular winter visitor within the borders of the North Atlantic states has made its way as far south as New Jersey, while a flock of 42 spent some time this winter in Birdcraft Sanctuary feeding upon the seed cases of the tulip tree and even displayed themselves in a row on a sweeping branch over the highway.

Thus it is plain to be seen that it is not wise to allow one's hope of identification of unknown birds to be bounded by old records, for many strangers and pilgrims visit us at their own sweet will, mingling the zest and quest of the unknown with the familiar.

INTRODUCTORY CHAPTERS.

THE SPRING SONG.

THE BUILDING OF THE NEST.

THE WATER-BIRDS.

BIRDS OF AUTUMN AND WINTER.

PLATE 1.

MEADOWLARK.

Length, 10.75 inches.

(See page 169.)

INTRODUCTORY CHAPTERS.

THE SPRING SONG.

What tidings hath the Swallow heard
  That bids her leave the lands of summer
For woods and fields where April yields
  Bleak welcome to the blithe newcomer? — BOURDILLON.

THE trees are leafless, and there are snow patches in nooks and corners; the air is laden with chilly gusts, but at noon a little softness creeps into it; the days, though gray, hold twelve hours of light, and the vernal equinox is at hand.

Come to the window, my friend, you who are going to spend some days, weeks, or months upon the bird-quest. You say that you see nothing but the bare trees, not even "the sun making dust and the grass growing green," like sister Anne in the fairy tale. Open your window, or better still, go into the porch, for a procession is soon to pass, and you must hear the music. Listen! on the branch of the oak where the leaves still cling is the bugler, the Song Sparrow, calling through the silence, "They come! They come! They come! Prepare the way."

Then presently, instead of tramping feet, you will hear the rustling of the innumerable wings of the bird army. Happy for you if it is a long time in passing and if a large part of it camps for the season. Usually it sends forward a few scouts, and then a company or two, before the brigade, clad in its faultless dress uniform, sweeps on, singing the greatest choral symphony of Nature, — the Spring Song.

There are many reasons, both of fact and of fancy, why it is best to begin the study of birds in the spring. The untrained eye becomes gradually accustomed to its new vocation before it is overtaxed. The matter of eyesight is of the first importance in the study of the living bird. Is your sight sufficiently good to allow you to exercise it in this way? The birds that you study will not be in the hand, but in the bush.

You may be accustomed to an out-door life, you may comprehend at a glance all the details of a landscape, or be able to detect a particular flower fields away; but in the quest of a bird which is oftentimes on the wing, your eyes will be obliged to distinguish certain details in a moving object backgrounded by a dazzling sky, and at the next moment refocus, to discover a bird, with perhaps very dull plumage, who is eluding you by circling in the black shadows of the pines. Thus you will be either peering into dim recesses or facing the strongest light twenty times to a single chance of seeing a bird in a clear light, with his plumage accentuated by a suitable background. If you squint and cannot face the sun, you must study birds in the museums, or learn to know them by their songs alone; a field-glass will lengthen the sight, but it will not give the ability to endure light.

Many people think that a bird wears the same plumage and sings the same songs all the year round, and expect to identify it by some easy and inflexible rule, which shall apply to all seasons and circumstances, but this is impossible.

When the birds come to us in spring they wear their perfect and typical plumage and are in the best voice, as befits those who are going courting. The male wears the most showy, or at least the most distinctly marked coat, and is generally slightly larger than the female, except in the case of Owls and a few others, where the female is the larger. In many families there is very little variation between the colouring of the male and female, and at a short distance you would probably notice none, except that the female is the paler of the two. But sometimes the difference is so marked that the novice invariably mistakes the female for a bird of another species; hence the importance of describing the plumage of both sexes.

The Scarlet Tanager has a green mate (there is great wisdom in this — a brilliant brooding bird would betray the location of the nest); the female Hummingbird lacks the ruby throat of her spouse; and the wife of the sleek black, white, and buff Bobolink wears sober brown. When the birds arrive in the spring, these colour distinctions are marked; but after the nesting time, which occurs mostly in May and June, a fresh complication arises. The young birds on leaving the nest, though fully grown perhaps and capable of strong flight, often wear hybrid feathers in which the characteristics of both parents are mingled. Soon after this time the summer moulting takes place, for the majority of birds moult twice a year. August is the time of this moulting. The jubilant love-song ceases, and the birds, dishevelled and moping, keep well in the shelter of the trees or retreat to the woods, as they are weakened and their power of flight is diminished. After the moulting comes another disturbing element, not only for the novice, but for those well versed in bird ways; with many birds the colours of the spring plumage are either wholly changed or greatly modified, and though the song may be in a measure renewed for a brief season, it is infrequent and not always true. The young birds are now associating with the old and adding their attempts at warbling, so that I think the snares that lie in the way of beginning the study of Song-birds after midsummer are quite evident.

The male Bobolink, after moulting, becomes brown like the female; the American Goldfinch, a late moulter, turns a dull olive; but the Bluebird's new feathers are rusty; many Warblers lose their identifying bands and streaks while the Baltimore Oriole keeps his flaming feathers.

After this moulting the bird's life as an individual ceases for a season; he is no longer swayed by sex, but by the flocking impulse of self-preservation, and in this case it is not always birds of a feather that flock together.

In the early spring, when the relaxing touch of the sun is

felt, the second moulting occurs, and the feathers that have borne the wear and tear of winter give place to the fresh new coat, and the bird throat swells with the Spring Song.

From a residential standpoint, we have four distinct grades of birds to consider:—

I. The summer residents: Those birds which, coming to us in the spring, rear their young, and after shifting about somewhat in late summer, retreat more or less southward for the winter.

II. The residents: Comprising those species which are represented by individuals all the year round.

III. The winter residents: The birds who are inhabitants of boreal regions, breeding beyond the northern border of the United States, coming only to us in winter, and retiring northward at the time of the general upward migration.

IV. The migrants: Birds that are with us for a few weeks in spring, en route from the south to their more northern breeding haunts, and are also visible for a similar period during the return trip in autumn. We may class with these the casual visitors that appear for a brief visit either summer or winter.

The two movements of bird life in spring and fall are known as the great migrations, some birds being plentiful in spring and quite rare in the autumn, and *vice versa*, as the path chosen for the upward and downward trip may not be the same. The individuals belonging to these classes will be specified in turn, and they are mentioned here to show you that if you do not begin the bird-quest in spring, in time to meet the army of migrants, you may miss some of the most interesting species.

Conspicuous among the birds that lodge with us in April and May, letting us hear their song for a brief period, is the great Fox Sparrow, the White-throated and White-crowned Sparrows, the group of lovely Warblers, and, best of all, the Hermit Thrush, whose heavenly notes of invocation, if once heard, are never forgotten.

If you are ready for this quest when the sun crosses the equinox the 21. of March, you will be in good time, and your labours will be lightened by studying the birds as they come one by one, hearing each voice in a solo, before all have gathered in late May and individual notes blend in the chorus. In this locality there is very little general upward movement before the vernal equinox, for the weather is too capricious. A few Song Sparrows and Bluebirds begin to sing, but the Yellowbirds that have wintered with us are still wearing their old coats, and have not broken into song. Last spring (1894) I noted in my diary the return of the Song Sparrows March 5, but the flocks of Bluebirds and Robins did not come until the 13. when a flock of a hundred or more Fox Sparrows also arrived, and the White-throated Sparrows followed them.

The birds oftentimes arrive singly or by twos or threes, and then again suddenly in great flocks. One afternoon there may not be a White-throat in sight, the next morning they will be feeding upon the ground like a drift of brown leaves. Almost all birds migrate at night, and every dawn will show you some new arrival, pluming and drying his feathers in the first rays of the sun. Birds who depend upon insect diet, like the Phœbe, the commonest of the fly-catchers, may arrive too soon, before insect life has quickened, and suffer much through their miscalculation. Often the appearance of individuals of a species does not indicate the beginning of the general return, as they may be birds that have not gone far away, but have merely been roving about all winter.

From the last of March until the first of June the spring migration is in full swing, some of the earlier birds to arrive will have passed on, before the Tanagers and Black-polls, and other late Warblers, appear. The last week of May the Spring Song is at its height; let us look at the order in which the singers begin and end their daily music.

You must be up in the long twilight that precedes dawn, if you wish to hear the little precentor — the Chipping Sparrow — give the signal on his shrill pitch pipe. Then the Song Sparrow sounds his reveille of three notes and a roulade — "Maids, maids, maids, put your kettle-ettle on." The Robin answers with his clarion notes, and the Bluebird, mildly plaintive, seems to regret that the quiet night is past, and sighs — "Dear, dear, think of it, think of it." Then the various Swallows begin their twitterings, and the Chimney Swift redoubles his winged pursuit of insects, and the Purple Martins, rising in pairs, coquette in mid-air, and their cheerful warble seems to drop from the clouds. As it becomes light, the Phœbe joins his "Pewit, phœbe-a," with the Wood Pewee's — "Pewee, pewee peer," and the Field Sparrow whistles and trills somewhat in the key of the Chipping Sparrow. Then up from the meadow wells the song of the Bobolink, our only bird that rivals the English Lark in singing and soaring, pouring out its delicious melody with virile fervour, while in the same field the Meadowlark rings his bell-like — "Spring o' the year, spring o' the year!" and the Indigo Bunting lisps from the briars.

One by one, the Oriole, the Song and Wood Thrushes, the Mourning Dove, Catbird, Towhee, Wrens, Warblers, Chat, and the obstreperous Vireos chime in. These are the birds that you may hear in your garden and the near-by meadows. Down in the lowlands the Red-winged Blackbird "flutes his okalee," the Crows keep up an incessant cawing, and in the woods between these lands and the marshes, the Herons cry; while from the marshes themselves the Snipe call. The flocking Sandpipers "peep" from the beach edge, and the migrating Ducks call as they settle in the flags.

Above the inland woods the Nighthawk, the Whip-poor-will's kinsman, skirling, circles a few times before hiding from day. There are Hawk cries, as Cooper's Hawk (the dreaded chicken-killer) bears a tender morsel to her nestlings already well fledged, who are in the top of the tall hickory, and the Quail whistles "Bob-white! Poor Bob-white!" the Ruffed Grouse clucks henlike, and the Woodcock calls like his brother Snipe.

It is in these woods, within sound of running water, that you may hear the Veery, though he is not so much the bird of dawn as of twilight, and in this same spot some day the Hermit Thrush may give a rehearsal for your private ear, of the music with which he will soon thrill the northern woods.

This is the Matin Song. When it ceases, you must watch for the individual birds as they go to and fro, feeding or building, or perching on some favourite twig to sing, either to their mates or from pure exultation. From nine o'clock in the morning until five in the afternoon, the principal singers are the Bobolink, Meadowlark, Vireos; the Redstart, who declares that every morsel he swallows is "Sweet, sweet, sweeter!" the Black-throated Green Warbler, who flashes his yellow feathers calling, "Will you co-ome, will you co-ome, will you?" the sprightly Maryland Yellow-throat, who almost beckons as he dashes about laughing, "Follow me, follow me"; the Baltimore Oriole, who alternately blows his mellow horn or complains querulously; and the Song Sparrow, who sings equally at all times.

Towards five o'clock the Evensong begins, and the Purple Finch, perching in the elm top, warbles in continuous bursts — "List to me, list to me, hear me, and I'll tell you, you, you," each peal being more vigorous than the last. The Wood Thrushes take up their harp-like "Uoli Uoli-, aeo-lee-lee," the Vesper Sparrow tunes, the birds of morning follow, one by one; but there are new voices that we did not hear in the matinal that continue after the chorus is hushed — the Rose-breasted Grosbeak, the Veery, and the Whip-poor-will.

The Veery rings his echo notes in the morning also, but his evensong is the best; and, as the dusk deepens, his notes have a more solemn quality. The Grosbeak has a sweet, rounded, warbling song that it is difficult to render in syllables intelligently, but when you hear it in the twilight you will know it, because it is unlike anything else. The Mockingbird is not heard freely as a night singer in this latitude, but further south he gives his best song only to the night wind; not his mocking, jeering ditty of squeaks and catcalls, but his natural heart-song; and when you hear it, you may listen for the martial note of the Cardinal, who seems to tell the hours, adding to each — "All's well." Then the Whip-poor-will calls, and the Owls answer, hooting, laughing, purring, according to the specific note.

When you go through garden, lane, and wood, on your happy quest, circling the marshes that will not yield you foothold, remember that if you wish to hear the Spring Song and identify the singers, you must yourself be in tune, and you must be alert in keeping the record, lest the troop slip by through the open doorway of the trees, leaving you to regret your carelessness all the year.

As you listen to the song and look at the birds, many will disappear, and you will know that these are the migrants who have gone to their various breeding haunts; and that those who are busy choosing their building sites, and are carrying straw, clay and twigs, are the summer residents. Then you must glide quietly among the trees to watch the next scene of the bird year — the building of the nest — which is the motive of the Spring Song, and you will feel that in truth —

> "Hard is the heart that loveth nought
> In May."

PLATE 2.

RUBY-THROATED HUMMINGBIRD.

Length, 3.75 inches.

(See page 194.)

THE BUILDING OF THE NEST.

Know'st thou what wove yon woodbird's nest
Of leaves, and feathers from her breast? — EMERSON.

MAY and June are the nesting months. Some impatient Bluebirds and Robins begin in April, and the lonely Owls and larger Hawks breed even in February and March, while, on the other hand, the Goldfinches and Cedar Waxwings wait until July; and other birds, who raise several broods in a season, like the Robins, Sparrows, Swallows, and Wrens, continue laying through July and straggle into August, but the universal song and nesting belong to May and June.

In early May the singing is wildly spontaneous, the birds are unguarded in their movements and constantly show themselves; but when they have mated, a sense of responsibility comes over the gay minstrels, and they become more wary. The soberly clad wife cautions secrecy; there is so much to discuss that must be whispered only in the echoless depths of the branches, for the great question of the season, the location of the nest, is to be settled, and quickly, too.

There are many things that the bird couple have to consider: the home must be within convenient distance of the proper food supply; there must be some protection from sun and rain, even if it is only a few leaves, or a tuft of grass; and then loom up the enemies to be avoided, — birds of prey, squirrels, snakes, and man. Of the four, the birds seem to dread man the least, and are constantly appealing to him, and taking him into their confidence as a protector against the others. Poor little birds! they do not realize that man with all his higher intelligence is really the most relentless of all. The other enemies kill for food only, man kills for food casually, for decorative feathers wantonly, and for scientific research plausibly, with the apology that the end and aim is knowledge. Are not the lives of hundreds of song-birds a high price for the gain of a doubtful new species, which only causes endless discussion as to whether it really is a species or merely a freak? One ornithologist proudly makes the record that, in the space of less than three weeks, he shot fifty-eight Rose-breasted Grosbeaks, to ascertain their average article of diet, and this slaughter was in the breeding season! There is also the stubbornly ignorant farmer, who measures only by dollars and cents and sets his hand against all birds, because half a dozen kinds in the excess of their friendliness invite themselves to supper in his berry patch, and think that no perch is so suitable for their morning singing as a cherry tree in June.

Now is the time to study all the best attributes of bird life, the period when we may judge the birds by our own standard, finding that their code of manners and morality nearly meets our own. We see them as individuals having the same diversity of character as people of different nations, and it is in the homes that we can best see their ruling instincts. Each bird now has a mind of his own and develops his own ideas. He is master of many arts.

If you wish to see all this, habit yourself in sober colours, wear soft, well-tried shoes, and something on your head that shall conceal rather than betray your presence, — Mrs. Olive Thorne Miller's leaf-covered hat is a clever invention. Do you realize how large you appear to the bird, whose eyes have very many times the magnifying power of our own? Walk gently but naturally, do not step on dry branches, but at the same time avoid a mincing gait. Have you not noticed in the sick-room, that a light easy tread is far less distracting than a fussy tiptoeing? Do not make sudden motions, especially of the arms, — a writer has said that birds are much more afraid of man's arms than of man himself.

Go through the lanes where the bushes hedge and the trees arch, thread between the clumps of crabs and briars that dot waste pastures, watch every tree and vine in the garden, skirt the hay meadows (their owners will hardly let you tramp through them), for there will be Bobolinks in the timothy. Best of all, swing a hammock in the old orchard, and, lying in it, you will see and hear so much that, wondering greatly, you will agree with Burroughs when he says, "I only know that birds have a language which is very expressive and which is easily translatable into the human tongue."

After watching the skill that builds the nest, it is difficult to overestimate the individual beauty of some of the structures. Comparatively few, outside of the charmed circle, know the diversity of form and materials shown in nest building, and the wonderful adaptability of both, by the bird, to its special needs.

The length of time which a nest remains in use varies with different birds. Burroughs says in the chapter on Birds' Nests, in his perennial "Wake Robin,"[1] "The birds may be divided, with respect to this and kindred points, into five general classes. First, those that repair or appropriate the last year's nest, as the Wren, Swallow, Bluebird, Great-crested Flycatcher, Owls, Eagles, Fish Hawks, and a few others. Secondly, those that build anew each season, though frequently rearing more than one brood in the same nest. Of these the Phœbe-bird is a well-known example. Thirdly, those that build a new nest for each brood, which includes the greatest number of species. Fourthly, a limited number that make no nest of their own, but appropriate the abandoned nests of other birds. Finally, those who use no nest at all, but deposit their eggs in the sand, which is the case with a large number of aquatic fowls."

Birds' nests are often regarded as merely aggregations of sticks and straws twisted together more or less carelessly; on the whole, rather monotonous, dirty affairs. I know an observant farmer who understands all the weather signs and a great deal of woodcraft, and spends his year in the pasture, field, brush lot, and woods; but whose ideas of birds' nests are purely conventional. He does not call any structure

1 "Wake Robin," by John Burroughs, Houghton, Mifflin & Co., Boston and New York.

a nest, unless it follows the pattern of a Robin's or Sparrow's. I asked him one day if there were many kinds of nests in his neighbourhood. "Wall," he said, leaning on his axe (for it was the wood-chopping season) and giving a reminiscent gaze through the brush, "there's plenty o' birds, but, bless yer, not half on 'em makes any reg'lar sort o' nests. Sparrers and Robins does, an' Catbirds an' Crows; but Swallers ony makes mud-pies, an' Humbirds jest sets down right whereever they see a round o' moss on a branch, and the warmth o' them makes the moss grow up a bit, but I don't call that a nest. The Hangbird (Oriole) he strings up a bag in a tree, an' them Red-eyed Warblers (Vireos) hooks a mess o' scraps in a twig fork, but those ain't real nests: an' treemice (Nuthatches) don't have none at all, jest stuffs a few feathers in a hole, I seen one to-day;" and after turning over his wood he produced an upright branch containing the feather-lined bed of the White-breasted Nuthatch.

Spend a month on the bird-quest, or a week even, and your eyes will be opened to the possibilities, and you will become alive to the fact, that the feathered race has its artisans the same as the human brotherhood. Weavers whose looms antedate all man's inventions, masons, carpenters, frescoers, decorators, and upholsterers, its skilled mechanics, and shiftless, unskilled labourers, and its parasitic tramps, who house their young at the expense of others. As for varied materials, — hay, sticks, feathers, hair, moss, bark, fur, hog-bristles, dandelion-down, mud, catkins, seedpods, lichens, paper, rags, yarn, and snake skins, are only a part of the bird architect's list of usable things.

You must not hope to identify all the nests possible to your locality in a single season, or even in three or four, but be always on the watch. If you fail to see the birds build, which is the easiest and surest way of knowing the nest, when the autumn comes and the leaves fall away many nests will be revealed in places where you never thought they existed, and you will learn where to look another season. If these nests are of marked types, you can identify them even in the autumn, and it will give you a new interest in the waning season; something to look for in the naked woods, a motive for winter walks. Though many of the frailer structures melt away or are torn down by high winds, the more carefully woven ones often remain over the winter.

On looking out one morning last January, after a night when a light, thawing snow had been followed by a sharp freeze, I was surprised and fascinated by the appearance of an Oriole's nest which hung from an elm near the house, and which had been invisible before. Its gray pocket was brimful of soft snow, which was oozing out of the top like foam, while the outside was coated with thin ice, which accentuated the woven strands and hung down in fantastic icicles scintillating in the sun.

Another winter day I was attracted by seeing a field-mouse run from a tuft of grass at the root of a small bush, and I found there a nest, presumably that of a Song Sparrow, containing two Sparrow eggs and one belonging to the Cowbird. The nest had evidently been abandoned on account of the alien egg, and it made a convenient hiding-place for the mouse, who had nibbled at the eggs and found their contents dried away. In the autumn and winter you may appropriate the nests you find, and examine and pull them apart with a freedom which, if indulged in during the spring or early summer, would give many a bird the heart-ache and an added distrust of bipeds.

Do you remember the January entry in Thoreau's journal? "Another bright winter's day, to the woods to see what birds' nests are made of."

Now if you are interested, awake, and clear-eyed, go out as I have said, and I will lead you, figuratively, telling you what you may find as a foretaste. Begin near at home; go through the garden first, then to the nearest field and the bit of marsh-bordered wood. Do not go further than where you may walk without ceremony or fuss. Never make a laborious tour of the bird-quest, or think that you must live in a tent remote from people, in order to name the majority of our every-day birds.

My first tramping-ground was the garden, enclosing eight acres of varied land, flowers, brush, open, plenty of trees, deciduous and evergreen, and a little pool of clear water. During the seasons of which I have the record forty species of birds have nested within its borders, and oftentimes many pairs of the same species; for example, as last year, when the garden sheltered five pensile nests of the Red-eyed Vireo. These forty nests were located in the following manner: —

Robin: In vines, hedge, and trees.
Wood Thrush: Spruces, bushes.
Catbird: Syringa bushes, and other shrubs.
Bluebird: Hole in old tree and bird-house.
Wren: Little houses and in outbuildings.
Yellow Warbler: Apple tree and elder bushes.
Maryland Yellow-throat: Tall grass and bushes.
Chat: Barberry bush.
Redstart: Spruces.
Tanager: Swamp oak.
Barn Swallow: Hay loft.
Purple Martin: Bird-house.
Red-eyed Vireo: Sugar-maple, apple tree, and birches.
White-eyed Vireo: Beech.
English Sparrow: Everywhere, until banished.
Purple Finch: Old quince-hedge.
Goldfinch: Sugar-maples.
Vesper Sparrow: Smoke-bush.
Grasshopper Sparrow: Under small spruce.
Song Sparrow: In many places, — hedge, bushes, ground.
Chipping Sparrow: High in evergreens, also in shrubs.
Field Sparrow: Meadow-sweet bush.
Towhee: On ground under a wild grape tangle.
Cowbird: Eggs found in the nests of a dozen different birds, particularly the Song Sparrow's.
Orchard Oriole: Old apple tree.
Baltimore Oriole: Elms on lawn.
Crow: Top of spruce.
Kingbird: In pear tree.
Phœbe: On beams in shed, also on bracket supporting the porch.
Chimney Swift: In brick-chimney.
Hummingbird: Cedars, elm, beech, and high in a spruce.
Yellow-billed Cuckoo: Wild tangle of vines, etc.

Flicker: Sassafras and hickory.
Hairy Woodpecker: Hickory.
Mourning Dove: White pines.
Quail: Under a thick, wild hedge.
Screech Owl: Hollow sassafras.
Barred Owl (only once): In a sycamore.
Cedar-bird: Old cherry tree.

You may add to these, as nests perfectly possible to find, those of the birds of marshy-edged meadows, — the Bobolink, Meadowlark, and the Red-winged Blackbird; the Rose-breasted Grosbeak, nesting in bushy pastures; the White-bellied Swallow of bird-boxes and hollow trees; the Bank Swallow, who burrows holes in railroad cuts, river and other sand-banks, where you may also discover the Kingfisher's home. In the river and creek marshes you will find the torch-shaped nests of the Long-billed Marsh-wren and the tussock nests of the Sharp-tailed Finch and the Seaside Sparrow. In swampy woods you may discover a heronry, or at least some single nests of the Green Heron, or the familiar Black-crowned Night Heron; and, perhaps, in some great tree leaning over the water you will see the huge platform-nest of the Osprey. The Marsh Hawks, Least Bittern, and Marsh Owls choose similar locations, and in the heart of the fresh-water marshes the Clapper and Virginia Rails, the Spotted Sandpiper and Woodcock, breed, though the latter more frequently nests in dry woods near a swamp.

Inland woods, especially if traversed by a stream, will yield countless nests: on the ground, the Veery's, the Oven-bird's hut, and the Ruffed Grouse's heap of leaves; above, in the trees, nests of the Blue Jay, Yellow-throated and Warbling Vireo, and the White-breasted Nuthatch. In drier woods the Blue-winged Warbler builds upon the ground; and the Black-throated Green Warbler nests in the hemlocks; while in high rocky woods you will see the eggs of the Whip-poor-will and Nighthawk, lying in depressions of the ground, and with your glass discern the nests of Hawks and Owls in the tree tops.

"I am poorly situated; there are no birds in my vicinity except Robins and Wrens," you say. Nonsense! it is impossible. You make me feel as Dean Hole, the genial ecclesiastical rose-grower did when certain lazy amateur gardeners, after admiring his rose garden, said that they could not grow roses because their soil was unsuitable, exclaiming, "Oh, what a garden yours is for roses! Old Mr. Drone, our gardener, tells us he never saw such soil as yours nor so bad a soil as ours for roses." And the Dean dryly exclaimed, "Herein lies a fact in horticulture, — Mr. Drone always has a bad soil."

Get the best possible results from your limited area, and if it is anything better than a back yard, you need not be discouraged. The difficulty with us Americans is that we are accustomed to a limitless extent of country, and scramble carelessly over it, in our amateur scientific investigations, as well as in other ways, instead of thoroughly studying *home* first. If the English naturalists ranged as wildly as we do, they would exhaust the island, and fall off the edge in a month. White, of Selborne, has left us a book that is classic, from his knowledge of one county, and our Thoreau has given us the perfect literature of woodcraft from his intimate knowledge of a comparatively small area.

The first nest that you will probably find, and one that will confront you at every turn, will be the Robin's. Common, rough in structure, and anything but pretty, it is a type nevertheless; being partly made of sticks and lined with clay, it is a combination of carpentry and masonry. The Wood Thrush also uses mud in a similar manner, but builds more neatly. Sparrows you will find lodged everywhere, — in the hedge, under bushes, by thick grass tufts, — their individual nests being so much alike that it is difficult to distinguish them apart. Dried grass and fine roots are the chief materials used by them, with the exception of the little Chipping Sparrow, who combines horsehair and pine-needles with the grasses, which, together with its delicacy and small size, identify the nest.

Next comes the Catbird, with a twig lattice, and the Wren, with a feather-lined pile in the little house provided for her; or, lacking the house, she uses an old hat or boot leg, instead. The Thrasher chooses a stout bush, and tosses together a bunch of grape-vine bark, sedge grass, and strong tendrils, in a way to correspond with his *bravura* music. The Purple Finch sets his large, sparrow-like nest in a high bush; you must visit it often, for you will always hear good music close by.

The Flicker utilizes a soft place in the swamp maple, boring his nest hole with great accuracy; the Yellow Warbler and Hummingbird strip the soft wool that wrapped the big, juicy Osmunda ferns in their winter sleep. The Warbler mixes the fernwool with cobwebs and milkweed flax, taking it to the apple tree; while the Hummingbird bears his load to a mossed cedar branch, and rounds a two-inch nest, blending it with the branch until it looks merely as if lichens had encrusted a raised knot hole. Next you will admire the work of the weavers, — the Orioles and Vireos. The darned basket of the Orchard Oriole is, perhaps, set in the strawberry-apple tree, as if to catch its early fruit; he makes his beak point his shuttle; as Coues says, antedating Elias Howe, who invented a needle with the eye at the point; and the Baltimore Oriole treads flax from old milkweed stalks, gathering his string far and near. The Baltimore Oriole builds too well to work quickly; and the pouch, sometimes eight inches deep, swings freely and firmly from its branch, so placed as to be safe from above and below.

The Vireos make a little pocket (like a stocking heel set between the knitting-needles) which is fastened firmly in the fork of a small branch. Woven into it are papers, scraps of hornets' nests, and flakes of decayed wood. The Solitary Vireo adds hair and fur to his, and the Red-eyed Vireo, the wings of moths and other insects, cocoons, and snake skins. It was in the nest of this Vireo, that Hamilton Gibson found twisted a bit of newspaper, whose single legible sentence read: " . . . have in view the will of God."

To go into much detail now may confuse you wholly, and you will find that every bird has a description of its haunts, nest, and eggs, in its particular division; this sketch is only to show you the possibilities. There is one more nest that I must mention, — the prettiest thing that you may ever hope to find when on the quest, — the lace hammock of the Parula Warbler. You must search for it early in June, in remote but rather thin woods, but never very far away from running water; often it is on a branch that overhangs a stream. Sometimes it will be on a slender birch twig and sometimes on the terminal spray of the hemlock-spruce. It is suspended lightly, like a watch-pocket with the opening on one side, and made of a delicate lace-work from the gray-white *usnea* moss, that grows on old trees. The whole fabric swaying in the breeze is the work of the two little birds with slate-blue backs and yellow breasts, who are watching you so anxiously. No, you must not take it now; it will keep until they are through with it, for it is much more durable than it appears.

The building of the nest will raise many questions in your mind. Do both birds take part in building? Does the female select the site and do the work and the male simply supply her with materials? Very pretty tales are told of the rejection of unsuitable stuff by the particular wife of a non-discriminating spouse and the consequent squabble. Alack! did not the labour question, as well as that of the equality of the sexes, begin as near to Eden as the building of the nest? But in spite of this *there are still nests!*

PLATE 3.

WOOD DUCK.

THE WATER-BIRDS.

With mingled sound of horns and bells,
  A far-heard clang, the Wild Geese fly,
Storm sent from Arctic moors and fells,
  Like a great arrow through the sky. — Whittier.

When you think of the Water-birds, you say, perhaps, that they are uninteresting, have no song, and inhabit marshy and desolate places; the Gulls are picturesque, to be sure, but as for the others, Snipe, Rail, and Ducks, they are only Game-birds and so much food, of a variety that does not particularly suit your palate. This is because you have regarded them as mere merchandise, and have never seen or considered them as living birds, winging their way over the lonely marshes and wind-swept beaches, clad in feathers that blend in their hues the sky, the water, the mottled sands of the shore, the bronzed splendour of the seaweeds, and the opalescence that lines the sea-shell. Though in a sense they are songless, their call notes are keyed in harmony with the winds that they combat, and the creaking reeds that hide their nests, and their signalling cries rise as distinctly above the more melodious sounds of Nature as the whistle of the distant buoy sounding above the surf.

The very remoteness of the Water-birds gives them a charm for certain natures. They do not build in the garden and come about your door craving attention; you must not only go half-way to meet them, but all the way, and that too right cautiously. There is an invigorating spice of adventure when the bird-quest tends shoreward, whether it is the banks of a river or lake that furnishes shelter and sustenance alike to the nesting bird and the restless migrant; or the shore of the sea with its possibilities and changing moods,—the sea that stretches infinitely on, ribbed by light-guarded reefs, where the Gulls flock and the Petrels dash in the wake of cautious ships, its arms reaching landward until the bay, where the Wild Ducks float, laps the shore, where the Sandpipers patter; and creeping on through the land as a sluggish creek, traverses the marshes where the Rail clamours about his half-floating nest, and finally mingling with fresh downward currents loses its way among gaunt trees, where the Herons and Bitterns build, and is absorbed by some low, wood-girt meadow, where the last earth-filtered drops make mud, from which the Snipe and Woodcock probe their insect food, and give a deeper green to the coarse grasses where the Plover pipes.

The Water-birds have another claim also upon your attention; you may study them in autumn and winter, and they fill many gaps in the bird year by their presence at seasons when the Land-birds are few. The majority of Water-birds come to us as migrants, or as winter visitors: the Herons, Bitterns, several of the Rails, a few Plovers, and Sandpipers breed in our marshes, and the beautiful Wood Duck nests in the river copse. When these birds breed, however, the high tides and spring-flooded meadows render it very difficult to approach the nests, or to gain a satisfactory knowledge of the birds themselves, and the same difficulty obtains in watching the migrants on their upward course. But in autumn the conditions are changed, especially in seasons of summer drought, and as the Land-birds withdraw, one by one, you will have the leisure to go shoreward.

The Plovers, Rails, and Sandpipers begin to gather in early August, and from that time until the rivers and creeks are ice coated, the Water-fowls will be passing every day, and from twilight until dawn. Various Ducks will go over the garden itself, and next day you will find them feeding in the sluggish marsh pools, where you gathered the cat-tail-flags and rose-mallows, or else floating on the mill-pond in the place of the summer lilies.

The Gulls return to the bar and shore islands, from their breeding-haunts at the eastern end of the Sound. The old charcoal burner, coming down from the hills with his dusky load, after the first light snow, tells of the Wild Geese that passed over his clearing the night before, and settled on the Forge Pond, and that when long John Hunt went after them in the morning, his gun kicked and knocked him into the worse bog hole; whereupon the whole flock flew away, laughing fit to kill themselves; and adding with a hoarse chuckle, "Sarved him right, too; never gives nuthin' he gits to neighbours, allers sends 'em to N'York."

In November and December, the hardy but inedible Sea Ducks return from the north, and settle noisily in their winter quarters; and all through the fall the lighthouse-keeper sends ashore some of the rarer migrants that, dazed and storm-blown, have dashed to death against his tower; and, as a bird-lover, he will find you out. If, in the autumn or early winter, you should chance to spend a little time among the lakes, or along the real sea-coast, from Massachusetts southward to the Chesapeake, a new pathway of delight will stretch before you, — read of the Sea-birds that Celia Thaxter entertained at Appledore in her Island Garden. And now that many people take their outings about the eastern shore, overrunning the pleasant islands, you too, may see the summer nesting of the Gulls and Terns, birds that before you had considered mysterious wanderers from the north.

These Water-birds, that count space as nothing and distance the swiftest locomotive in their flight, ever on the wing from the very necessities of their existence, always bring with them some of the atmosphere of their native haunts. The Wild Ducks, hanging in the market-stall, still wear on their wings a patch of rainbow colour, as if stamped there by the sun and mist through which they took their first flight. Call these birds songless, give them any names you please, they will remain mysteries, coming out of the sky and disappearing again in its horizon, pushing on to an invisible haven; because their homes are so remote we do not realize that they are like other birds, and we forget, when the garden trees are full of nests and sway with ecstatic music, that the Water-fowl, hastening along at twilight, is swayed by the same longings, that they guide him surely to his journey's close.[1]

> And soon that toil shall end,
> Soon shalt thou find a summer home, and rest,
> And scream among thy fellows: reeds shall bend
> Soon o'er thy sheltered nest.— BRYANT.

[1] In this connection read "North American Shore Birds," by Daniel Giraud Elliott. A reference book for the naturalist, sportsman, and lover of birds. Illustrated. New York. F. W. Harper.

"Upland Game Birds," Edwyn Sandys and T. S. Van Dyke. Macmillan's Sportsman's series.

"The Water Fowl Family," by L. C. Sanford, L. B. Bishop, and T. S. Van Dyke, of the same series.

PLATE 4.

SNOWY OWL.

Length, 20–24 inches.

(See page 213.)

BIRDS OF AUTUMN AND WINTER.

Dimly I catch the throb of distant flails:
Silently overhead the Hen-hawk sails,
With watchful, measuring eye and for his quarry waits.
—LOWELL.

DURING the last week in August there is a decided stir among the feathered folk. The summer residents who have been moulting in seclusion for the last month, emerge from their retreats and are joined by flocks of others of similar species, who have summered further north and who will remain with us for several weeks before beginning their downward trip.

By calling certain species *resident*, it does not necessarily mean that the same individuals remain in one place for the entire year. Except in the breeding-season all birds rove about, even if they do not absolutely migrate, guided in their course by the food supply and the weather. The food supply is the more potent motive of the two, for many insect-eating birds like the Flycatchers and Vireos could winter with us in the protection of hedges and evergreens; but with the coming of frost their food is cut off. Even the seed-eating birds, like the hardy Goldfinches, Buntings, and Juncos, are often driven to begging about barns and granaries when a sudden snow-storm covers the low herbs and grasses upon whose seeds they subsist.

It is during the last week in August that the Baltimore Orioles gather, and pipe with an anxious note in their voices, as much as to say, "It is very pleasant here still, but we must be off before the leaves grow thin and betray us to our enemies." The Kingbirds swoop and call, going nearer to the house than usual. With September comes the first decisive gathering of the bird clans. The Swallows flock in the low meadows and on the edge of the beaches, flying and counter-flying, as if to strengthen their wings for the long journey; hordes of them wintering as far south as the Bahamas. The cheery Yellow Warblers disappear from the orchards, and the Veery comes from the moist woods and scratches in the shrubbery.

Now you may look for the numerous Warblers as they pass; but you must be alert, for they go silently and may only stop for a day. The length of time that migrating birds remain varies greatly with different seasons; during some autumns they linger, and then again, without any apparent reason, they hurry along, arriving and departing sometimes the same night, so that you will be unconscious that they have passed at all.

The most conspicuous summer residents that slip away during September, are the Baltimore Orioles, Veeries, Chats, Wood Thrushes, Flycatchers, Rose-breasted Grosbeaks, and Bobolinks. The Chimney Swifts go in the wake of the Swallows, and closely resemble them in habit if not in anatomical structure. We miss these birds of the air sadly, for their beautiful flights are the great feature of early September. The voiceless brown Bobolinks are driven from the shelter of the reeds and marsh-grasses by the gunners, and in early evening, if you go down the lane, their clinking, metallic call can be heard as they fly over. The Wood Thrushes leave quietly; gathering for a week or so in low trees, at this season their only note is a dry chirp resembling the shaking of peas in a sieve. The last of the month the Chickadees emerge and become prominent, and the Juncos arrive in straggling flocks.

The Robins flock in great numbers, and occasionally give a sweet, reminiscent song; the Bluebirds are legion and bustle about, calling, as Burroughs says they do in autumn, "Bermuda! Bermuda!" The Goldfinches are no longer yellow, but you can always distinguish them by their dipping flight. Purple Grackles and Red-winged Blackbirds are also gathering, and the Wrens are peeping in and out, but they have forgotten how to scold. The scanty music is furnished chiefly by the faithful Song Sparrow, the

Purple Finch, and the Chicadee; there are individuals of every species who do a little autumn singing, but it is heard only from solitary voices.

Meanwhile, the tiny Ruby-crowned Kinglet, and the Myrtle, Palm, and Bay-breasted Warblers make us a visit, and the Brown Creeper, Black and White Warblers, and White-breasted Nuthatches circle the trees.

By the first of October, the Blue Jays have returned from the deep woods where they nested, and are in full scream, as is their wont. Hermit Thrushes come and go, together with the Thrashers. The Tanagers disappear, and the Vireos one and all are packing their belongings. The lively Red-eyed Vireo, who has preached and laughed at you all summer from the maples, is taking a farewell peep under every bit of loose bark, determined not to leave one insect behind. You miss the Catbirds also, and in looking for them you will find an occasional Pine Finch or Winter Wren. Quail and Ruffed Grouse (Partridge) scramble furtively along road-sides and through the stubble fields, and the Osprey fishes more boldly.

All the while the various Warblers are trooping by, young and old together; if you have not recognized them in spring, you will be sadly puzzled now. The White-throated Sparrows hop along the paths, giving a few sweet notes,—"Pé-peabody-peabody-peabody,"—but without the springtime fervour, and the rarer White-crowned Sparrows show themselves warily. In fact, the greater part of this family are on the move, and even the ranks of Song Sparrows are thinning. The Black-throated Green and the Black-throated Blue Warblers come about the spruces again; the Phœbes vanish and the trim Towhee no longer hops jauntily among the briars. If there is an early frost the flocks go quickly, but otherwise all the birds linger. We have Hummingbirds here in the garden through October, unless the weather is very gusty; for I think that all birds dread wind more than cold.

The third week of October sees the last of the Golden-crowned Thrushes and Maryland Yellow-throats, the Fox

Sparrows pay a flying visit, and the Red-breasted Nuthatches settle down. Even if there has been no hard frost, November is sure to bring it, and then in the afterglow, the illusive Indian summer, we begin to realize that the song-birds have left us. Grackles we have and Meadowlarks, but the Robins and Bluebirds are diminishing, and after the middle of November the birds that you see may safely be called *winter residents.*

The Blue Jay becomes very conspicuous now, and in late November walks you will constantly see his pointed crest, while his harsh notes no longer jar upon your ear, but sound companionable. Most likely he is nutting, and jeering and laughing at the squirrels who are filling their paunches under the same tree. If, however, "he laughs best who laughs last," the squirrels have decidedly the best of it, for they frequently find the holes where the Jays hide their plunder and rob them.

Golden-crowned Kinglets, with their dainty little heads on one side, peep into every crevice in the apple trees, giving a shrill, wiry call, the Winter Wrens are settled in their old quarters about the woodpile, Pine Warblers come in bustling flocks, White-throated Sparrows appear at rare intervals, and three, at least, of the Woodpeckers.

If December is moderately snowy and not too cold, you will see a distinct change even among the winter residents. The Horned Larks become quite tame, and together with the Meadowlarks keep near the upland farms, and if the rivers are free from ice the Kingfisher still constitutes himself their guardian. The Tree Sparrow takes the place that the Chipping Sparrow filled in summer, resembling it both in appearance and note, and the Cedar-birds come from their warm coverts and feast upon the remaining berries which are now completely ripe and soft.

The Shrike is in his element seeing his victims afar through the leafless trees, the Hawks grow bold and circle over the meadows by the hour, and the Barred Owl, with strange blue-black eyes, leaves the wood with the Great Horned Owl, to forage in the brush and in open pastures.

If you hear a snapping noise in the pines do not think that it is merely the cones springing open, for you will find a small flock of Red Crossbills, whose warped beaks seem particularly adapted to tearing the scales from the cones and liberating the pungent seeds. Middle December is the time for the showy Pine Grosbeaks, whose stout bodies and brilliant colouring at once reveal their identity; they are sometimes abundant here but usually straggle about in pairs; and great flocks of the hardy American Goldfinches may be seen if seed-bearing plants are not buried up by the snow. The Crows are very hungry and prowl around the stacks of dry corn stalks, going to the shore for clams and drift scraps, and returning at night to their inland cedar roosts. This is the season that you may successfully give them poisoned corn, thus justly killing some of these cannibals who create such havoc every spring among the nests of our Song-birds.

An occasional Purple Finch flies out of the evergreens, though it is a difficult bird to recognize at this season, and the Pine Siskin constantly flits in and out, swinging itself under the cones and terminal sprays like an acrobat, and this is the time for Snow Buntings and the little Redpoll Linnets. If there are severe storms in the month, accompanied by north-east gales, many of these birds appear on the very crest of the storm, and when it ceases troop from the evergreens in a half-famished condition, searching for bare places where a few seeds may be found. The Redpoll feeds in the same localities and in the same manner as the American Goldfinch, and, having a similar call note, it is quite easy, at a little distance, to mistake one for the other.

Now you may catch a glimpse of the great Snow Owls. You will be more likely to find them back of the shore, along the line of salt marshes and woody stubble, than further inland. The marshes do not freeze so easily or deeply as the iron-bound uplands, and field-mice are more plentiful in them. This alert and powerful Owl is so fleet of wing that he can follow and capture a Snow Bunting or a Junco in its most rapid flight if his appetite is whetted. Woodpeckers have mostly drifted southward, and this is the time of greatest hardship for all birds that depend in any way upon insect food. The Robins leave, except for a few individuals; the Quails come from the brush and feed with the Meadow and Horned Larks. The four resident Hawks — the Sharp-shinned, Cooper's, the Red-tailed, and Red-shouldered — are now the only inhabitants of the woods and remote pastures; there is something invigorating in the way in which they sail through the lonely air. Food is very scarce, mice are snowed under, rabbits do not venture far from their burrows, and it is too early for young chickens. Besides, the farmer's wife, knowing Hawk ways, keeps her poultry safely guarded in a sunny place in view of the kitchen window. Alas! for the flocks of Snow Buntings that have been tempted too far afield. Every time a Hawk swoops, and dropping suddenly wheels back to its perch, there is one Bunting less to return to its boreal birthplace. The Shrike drops on his prey with the thud and click of the guillotine; the Hawk flashes through the air with the curving sweep of the scimiter.

The Brown Creeper is seen daily winding about the tree trunks; if it is severely cold and there is much ice he only comes at mid-day and works on the sunny side of the tree, while his friends, the Chickadees, call encouragingly to him. January, with us, is the month of all the year that comes the nearest to being birdless; there are days when not even a Crow is seen; then a mild streak follows, and the murmurings of the Chickadees, Bluebirds, and Goldfinches give cheer, and if you tie some bits of fat meat or well-covered bones to the branches of a tree in a sheltered spot you will be surprised at the number of visitors that will come to dine.

With February the days begin to lengthen visibly, and a reaction sets in. There is a return movement among the Robins, who have gone but a short distance southward, and the Buntings travel in large flocks. Late in the month a thaw brings the Kingfisher back, and at any time you may expect to hear the Song Sparrow in his old haunts, — in fact, you may have heard him early in the month, or in January even, but now it is his spring song, only needing companionship and the mellowing effects of mild weather to bring it to perfection.

The Snow Owls are thinking of going northward, unless barred by an early March storm, and the Meadowlarks that have braved the winter sing a full month before the migrating flocks arrive. When March comes in, even if it does roar like a lion, a single day may change the character of the bird life about you and you will imagine that the Snow Owls, Shrikes, Pine Finches, and Horned Larks are under orders to vanish before the spring flocks of Fox Sparrows, Robins, and Bluebirds can appear. But when March comes the ear is listening for the Spring Song and the winter-birds are quickly forgotten, unless you happen to have a stuffed Owl to preside in solemn silence in your library, performing its mission of looking wise quite as well as a piece of bric-à-brac as it did in life. Is not the Owl's general immobility the reason why it was chosen for the pet of the Goddess of Wisdom? Doubtless her ancient ladyship knew that her protégé would never take the trouble to contradict her and never express a decided opinion, and thus would pass for the incarnation of knowledge.

Winter is the only season when you may point a gun at a bird, and then never at a Song-bird, but you may do these a favour by shooting some of their enemies, the bad English Sparrows, and one or two Hawks and Owls. Yet you must spare both Hawks and Owls with these exceptions, since Dr. A. K. Fisher has given conclusive evidence of their value to agriculture.

Never shoot even a Game-bird, or Wild Duck, merely for the sake of killing, and remember when on the bird-quest to keep your hands free from all destruction of life, so that you may answer the question, —

"Hast thou named all the birds without a gun?"

in the affirmative, as far as the familiar birds of field and garden are concerned, and if the Warblers and Sparrows puzzle you, the aid offered by the museums will still make the gun needless.

HOW TO NAME THE BIRDS.

PLATE 5.

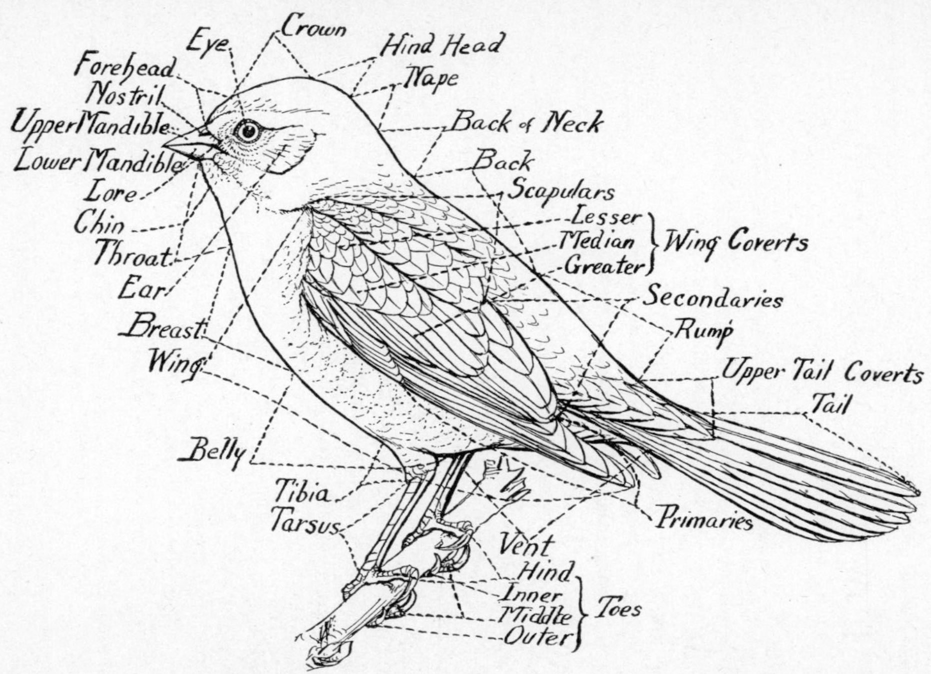

MAP OF THE BIRD.

HOW TO NAME THE BIRDS.

In studying the birds as you see them about you, try to acquire the habit of gauging the size, general colour, and poise at a glance, gaining the details, if possible, afterward. Impress upon yourself the location in which you saw the bird, its occupation, its method of feeding, whether, if upon the ground, it walked or hopped. Was it dashing through the air or skimming low over the meadows, uttering a twittering cry and turning and curving sharply as it caught insects in its wide mouth? If so, you must look for it in the Swallow Family.

Was it a brown or olive-backed bird somewhat of the build of the Robin but smaller, with a light-coloured breast more or less speckled, scratching among the bushes for the insects upon which it feeds? You must look for it in the Thrush Family, and if you do not place it there search among the Ground Warblers. Or was it a tiny olive-gray bird that caught your eye as it peeped about the twigs of the orchard trees in the autumn, turning its head and looking at you sidewise, showing every now and then its gold and scarlet crest? Then you must look among the Kinglets.

If you keep a note-book and pencil in your pocket when you are on the bird-quest, many particulars can be jotted down to refresh your memory when consulting the reference book. In rapidly gauging the size of a particular bird do not think in inches, but compare it mentally with some bird that is familiar to you. Say to yourself, Is it as large as a Robin, a Bluebird, or a Chippy?

Read the Synopsis of Bird Families[1] to gain an idea of their groupings, and if you fail to locate your bird in this way go through the Key[2] very slowly, not jumping hastily at conclusions, but following every reasonable clue. It is impossible to make such a key absolutely trustworthy, when it is necessarily based upon the more superficial qualities, and is arranged to guide those who rely upon impressions of colour gained from a bird, perhaps many feet distant.

In condensing the attributes of each bird into a reference table to precede its biography, its length in inches is given as a means of comparison, especially in referring to the illustrations; for in adapting the bird portraits from many sources it has been impossible to grade them according to a mathematical scale. In these tables I have endeavoured to give only such broad descriptions of plumage as shall be recognizable with a field-glass, noting the difference in colouring between male and female when it is at all marked, and giving when possible the accentuated value of the song and call notes in syllables. Not that any literal meaning may be attributed to them, but that the *sound* of these syllables, when repeated aloud, may aid in identifying the song with the singer. Critics who do not understand the motive of this syllabication, call it nonsense, and consider it merely a sentimentalist's attempt to make the birds talk. I only know that it has been a great help to me, and that it has aided many people who depend even more upon the ear than the eye in their study of birds. Thoreau and Emerson understood it thoroughly, and Burroughs has formulated much of the language, so that it does not lack champions.

The seasons of bird migration, or residence, are in accordance with records of this part of New England (southern Connecticut), both from the notes of Rev. James Linsley, Mr. C. K. Averill of Bridgeport, and others, and also from my own diaries. Allowance must therefore be made by those living further north or south, as in the spring migration birds will arrive in Delaware two weeks earlier than in

[1] Page 43.   [2] Page 281 (1).

Connecticut, and in Maine not for a week or two later. The breeding-haunts are indicated, and the nest and eggs mentioned, when they are either accessible to the student, or, when belonging to northern latitudes, of special interest. The range of the bird for the year is taken from the Check-list of the American Ornithologists' Union, which is the acknowledged authority. The nomenclature is also that of the A. O. U. Check-list, the *first* English name and the Latin title being according to its tenets. In some cases I have added one or more English names, because they are universally understood and are more or less used in the manuals and state publications.

In modern science, classification follows the method of natural evolution, grading from the lowest forms to the highest. Under this system the Diving Water-birds should head the list, and the Thrush Family of Song-birds end it. Some time ago a different system obtained, that of beginning with the highest orders and descending in the scale, and the birds in this book are so arranged. The reason for doing this is that it presents the Song-birds first, and it is to these that you will be first attracted, and, finding many of them familiar, you will be led by easy stages to the Birds of Prey and the Water-birds, which probably you have had less chance to know. If, however, you prefer to habituate yourself to the more modern method, all that you have to do is to begin at the end of the book and work backward.

The two hundred birds chosen for description from the A. O. U. list of over nine hundred species of North American Birds are selected as being those which will be the most likely to interest bird-lovers living in the temperate parts of the country, and especially in the Middle and Eastern States. If birds are included that are rarer (in other localities) than species that are omitted, it is owing to marked characteristics or some interesting traits of the particular birds.

The mazes of classification are omitted. As a novice who wishes to recognize the birds by sight, you have no need of their services beyond learning the English and Latin names of the birds, and that of the order and family to which they belong; then you must buy a good manual to answer all further queries; either Ridgway's,[1] Coues's,[2] or Chapman's[3] will serve your purpose. If you live or journey west of the Mississippi, the books of Mrs. Bailey[4] and Mrs. Wheelock[5] are indispensable. It is the same as when beginning the study of history: you first wish to learn the name of a character, for what he was famous, and how he appeared; then with a distinct realization of the man's personality in your mind, you take an interest which, at first, would have been impossible, in looking into his ancestry, and finding precisely what union of races and families produced his particular type.

Inverted evolution, or working from effect to cause, is the simplest way to interest popular attention in any branch of science. If people accept a tangible fact and go no further, they have at least gained some information; if they possess the thinking-faculty, and desire to find the causes, they are one step on the right road. Of course this method, if method it can be called, lies open to the charge of superficiality, and to the saying that "when science and sentiment meet, sentiment loses its case." There is, of course, a species of maudlin sentiment that is the proverbial cloak of inaccuracy, the variety that weaves touching but perfectly impossible tales and fables about natural facts. This is the sentiment that originated the story of the self-sacrifice of the Pelican in feeding its young from the blood of its own breast. Whereas the Pelican belongs to a class of birds who, after taking their food into the crop and partly digesting it, bring it up again to feed their offspring. The act of pressing the bill against the distended crop to dislodge the food, sometimes irritates

1 "A Manual of North American Birds," Robert Ridgway.

2 "Key to North American Birds," Dr. Elliott Coues, Boston: Estes & Lauriat.

3 "Hand Book of the Birds of Eastern North America," Frank M. Chapman, New York: D. Appleton & Co.

4 "Manual of Birds of the Western United States," by Florence Merriam Bailey.

5 "Birds of California," by Irene Grosvenor Wheelock.

the skin; hence the conclusion was drawn that it drew its own blood.

There may be also in the study of birds a sentiment that is born of fact and accuracy, provable by all scientific requirements, which will render the bird-quest a recreation, and not a mental discipline; being a bridge where those who can go no further, may rest and enjoy intelligently the beauty and music of the bird world. Of course a little learning *may* be a dangerous thing, but it is only so when we overestimate the extent of our limited scope, and try to speak a language of which we only know the alphabet.

Nature is to be studied with the eyes of the heart, as well as of the microscope, and ever so scanty a knowledge of our feathered brothers helps us to feel that the realms of Nature are very near to the human heart and its sympathies, and that "the truth of Nature is a part of the truth of God: to him who does not search it out, darkness; to him who does, infinity."

SYNOPSIS OF BIRD FAMILIES.

SYNOPSIS OF BIRD FAMILIES.

LAND-BIRDS.

ORDER PASSERES: PERCHING BIRDS.

SUB-ORDER OSCINES: SINGING BIRDS.

THE birds of this Order have the most highly complex vocal organs, the term *Oscines* being derived from the Latin, signifying those birds whose songs were regarded in past times as augural.

Family Turdidæ: Thrushes. Page 57.

7 Species.[1]

Birds of moderate size and stoutish build, bills of moderate length, sexes of nearly similar plumage. Melodious singers, feeding chiefly on the ground. The American Robin and the Bluebird belong to this family. The true Thrushes vary through browns and olives on the back, with light breasts more or less spotted, and tails that are wider at the tip than at the base. Insectivorous birds, also casual fruit-eaters. Hoppers.

Family Sylviidæ: Kinglets. Page 68.

2 Species.

Very small insectivorous birds, feeding in the trees. General tone of plumage olivaceous, with highly coloured crown patch. Song, during the spring migration, rich and powerful for such small birds. Seen here only in autumn, winter, and early spring.

[1] Number of species described.

Family Paridæ: Nuthatches and Titmice. Page 71.

4 Species.

Birds seen creeping conspicuously about tree trunks, especially in autumn and winter, frequently walking head downward. The Nuthatches have compactly feathered bodies, straight bills, are varied grayish above, with somewhat ruddy breasts. The Titmice are alert, sprightly little birds, with gray, white, and black feathers, one having a crest and the other a black cap and white cheeks. They feed also about trees.

Family Certhiidæ: Creepers. Page 75.

1 Species.

This bird is slender, with a long, sharp bill, much mottled, brownish plumage and a long tail. It is seen creeping *spirally* about trees in fall and winter.

Family Troglodytidæ: Wrens, Thrasher, Catbird, etc. Page 76.

8 Species.

Insectivorous birds and highly accomplished singers. The Wrens are all small, and more or less barred and washed with browns, while the tail is usually held erect. The Catbird (which really belongs to a sub-family) is dark slate with a black cap, the Mockingbird gray and olive, and the Thrasher is like a great red-brown Thrush with speckled breast, and a long tail with which he continually beats the air.

Family Motacillidæ: Pipits, etc. Page 87.

1 Species.

American Pipit, Titlark. Brownish bird, with long, pointed wings, slender bill, and outer tail-feathers white; seen in stubble fields as a migrant in late fall and spring. Peculiar, wavering flight.

Family Mniotiltidæ: Wood Warblers. Page 88.

30 Species.

Beautifully plumed, graceful birds, which, with the exception of a few species, are practically unknown or rather unnamed by people in general. These Warblers inhabit the woods, feeding among the trees, or, in some species, upon the ground. They comprise both migrants and summer residents; of small size, bills slender, shorter than the head, wings pointed and usually shorter than the tail. All but a few Ground Warblers have brightly coloured or much varied plumage, ranging through all shades of olive, yellow, red, orange, brown, and black. They have sweet, lisping songs, which are neither full nor varied. The well-known Yellow Warbler belongs to this class; also the Black and White Warbler. The exceptions to this rule are the Ovenbird, Water Thrush, and the Louisiana Water Thrush, which are Ground Warblers, having sober, Thrush-like plumage and exquisite voices, and the Chat, which has brilliant green and gold plumage and a clear, loud voice, mocking and whistling by turns.

Family Vireonidæ: Vireos. Page 116.

5 Species.

Birds of small size, bills hooked at tip — shorter than the head. Sexes alike in colouring; the plumage (remaining quite constant at all seasons) is generally olivaceous above and whitish or yellow below. One species has red and one white eyes. All are musical and persistent singers of a colloquial type, feeding and singing in orchard or forest trees, according to the species. A family easily confused with the Warblers, unless its superior vocal abilities are remembered.

Family Laniidæ: Shrikes. Page 122.

1 Species.

Carnivorous birds, bold, handsome, and quarrelsome, bills sharply hooked at end; general colour gray and black, bristles at nostrils, and muscular feet. In winter and early spring they may be seen perching in the bare trees, where they are on the watch for small birds, upon which they prey.

Family Ampelidæ: Waxwings, etc. Page 124.

1 Species.

Birds of six or seven inches in length, stout-bodied, head with a conspicuous crest; beautifully soft, quaker plumage, tail tipped with yellow, *red wax-like* tips to the wing coverts, straight black bill. Sexes similar; a resident bird.

Family Hirundinidæ: Swallows. Page 125.

5 Species.

Birds of the air in the fullest sense. "Bill flat, broad, triangular." Mouth opening to below the eyes; long, strong wings, small feet, which are seldom used; broad head and stout neck; the tail more or less forked. Sexes similar; song, a pleasant, twittering warble. The plumage in some species is dull, but in others beautifully iridescent above and ruddy below. All insectivorous birds and summer residents.

Family Tanagridæ: Tanagers. Page 131.

1 Species.

A brilliantly coloured family undergoing great changes of plumage during the year, the colours of the sexes being wholly different, the males having much red about them. Bill short, the long, pointed wings exceeding the tail in length.

Family Fringillidæ: Finches, Sparrows, etc. Page 133.

28 Species.

The largest family of North American Birds, comprising one-seventh of all our birds. These birds are true seed-eaters, though they feed their young largely on an insectivorous diet.

"The bill approaches nearest the ideal cone, combining strength to crush seeds with delicacy of touch to secure minute objects." (Dr. Coues.) The family contains birds, of every size and colour, sexes either similar or unlike,—Finches, Buntings, Linnets, Grosbeaks, Crossbills, and Sparrows, whose traits it is impossible to describe in general terms.

Family Icteridæ : Blackbirds, Orioles, etc. Page 165.

8 Species.

Forming a link between the Finch and Crow families and containing, beside Blackbirds and Orioles, the Meadowlark, Bobolink, and Cowbird. Sexes unlike. All species but the Orioles have large, muscular feet adapted to walking, and feed on or near the ground. They are both seed and insect eaters, and vary much in size and colour. The predominating hues are black, white, orange-red, and what Dr. Coues calls a "niggled pattern" of brown in the Meadowlark. Musically the species are divided, half being highly vocal and half casually so.

Family Corvidæ : Crows, Jays, etc. Page 177.

3 Species.

The Crows are large black birds, having bills as long as the head, stout feet suitable for walking, pointed wings longer than the tail, appearing saw-toothed in flight. Gregarious; sexes alike. The Jays are a great contrast to the Crows, being crested and having conspicuous plumage in which blue predominates. Both Crows and Jays are partly carnivorous, and though having harsh voices, moderate them to a not unpleasing song in the breeding season.

Family Sturdidæ : Starlings. Page 180.

1 Species.

Family Alaudidæ : Larks. Page 181.

1 Species.

True Larks, kin of the European Skylark, and not to be confused with Meadowlarks or Titlarks. Our species, a Shore Lark, seen here only in the fall and winter, is highly musical in the breeding-season. It has very long, straight hind claws, long, pointed wings, and two slender, feathered ear tufts that give it the name of Horned Lark.

SUB-ORDER CLAMATORES : SONGLESS PERCHING BIRDS.

Birds with but poorly developed singing apparatus, the vocal muscles being either small or few.

Family Tyrannidæ: Tyrant Flycatchers. Page 182.

8 Species.

Insectivorous birds of small and medium size, with or without erectile crests, having broad bills tapering to a sharp point, and large mouths. Colouring ranging from brown to olive-gray, with yellow washes on the breast. Usually having harsh voices, one or two species, however, possessing plaintive call notes. To be distinguished from other birds of a general, similar appearance, who pursue insects upon the wing by the "habit of *perching* in wait for their prey upon some prominent outpost, in a peculiar attitude, with the wings and tail drooped and vibrating in readiness for instant action; and of dashing into the air, seizing the passing insect with a quick movement and a click of the bill, and then returning to their stand." (Dr. Coues.)

ORDER MACROCHIRES: WHIP-POOR-WILLS, SWIFTS, ETC.

Family Caprimulgidæ: Whip-poor-wills, Night-hawks, etc. Page 190.

2 Species.

Medium-sized, heavy birds with long wings, short, thick heads and gaping, bristly mouths, taking their insect food on the wing (the Whip-poor-will is strictly nocturnal in habit). When at rest they either perch *lengthwise* on a branch or sit on the ground.

Family Micropodidæ: Swifts. Page 193.

1 Species.

The bird known commonly as the Chimney Swallow, but which is in reality a Swift and closely allied to the Night-hawk, being a nocturnal as well as diurnal feeder.

Family Trochilidæ: Hummingbirds. Page 194.

1 Species.

Very small birds, with long, needle-like bills, small feet, iridescent green plumage (ruby throat in male), and restless, darting flight. Feeding among flowers.

ORDER PICI: WOODPECKERS.

Family Picidæ: Woodpeckers. Page 196.

5 Species.

Birds of small and medium size, feeding as they creep around the branches and trunks of trees. They are of stocky, compact build, with strong, straight bills (one species has a slightly curving bill), mottled and variegated plumage, and red markings about the head. To be distinguished from other creepers by their superior size, and the fact that they seldom, if ever, walk head *downward*.

ORDER COCCYGES: CUCKOOS.

Family Cuculidæ: Cuckoos. Page 202.

2 Species.

Medium-sized tree-birds, with softly-tinted gray and brownish plumage, most noticeable at the time of apple blossoms, when they feed upon the nests of the tent-caterpillar.

Family Alcedinidæ: Kingfishers. Page 204.

1 Species.

Common birds of streams and ponds. Head crested, long bill. Lead blue plumage above, light breast banded with blue. Seen perching on stumps and dead trees over the water watching for fish.

ORDER RAPTORES: BIRDS OF PREY.

Family Strigidæ: Barn Owls. Page 206.

1 Species.

Family Bubonidæ: Horned Owls. Page 207.

7 Species.

Stoutly-built birds, varying in length from eight inches to two feet, with and without feathered ear-tufts (horns), and having mottled loose plumage, feathered disks around the eyes, hooked beaks, and muscular feet. The family comprises both diurnal and nocturnal species.

Family Falconidæ: Hawks, Eagles, etc. Page 215.

8 Species.

Diurnal Birds of Prey, with mottled and streaked plumage, no horns or eye disks; of graceful build, and dashing, rapid flight. The family includes the Osprey and the American Eagle.

ORDER COLUMBÆ: PIGEONS.

Family Columbidæ: Doves and Pigeons. Page 225.

2 Species.

Wood Doves, with delicately-shaded, and often glossy plumage, small heads and full breasts, long, pointed wings, and soft, cooing voices. Often seen feeding on the ground like the domestic Pigeon.

ORDER GALLINÆ: GALLINACEOUS BIRDS (Birds scratching on the ground like barnyard fowls).

Family Tetraonidæ: Grouse, Partridges. Page 227.

2 Species.

Comprising our two most familiar Game-birds, the Ruffed Grouse (Partridge) and the Quail, birds with mottled feathers of varied browns, the Partridge having feathered legs. The female rears the young, who leave the nest when hatched, following her as a brood, after the manner of chickens.

ORDER LIMICOLÆ: SHORE-BIRDS (Waders).

Family Aphrizidæ: Turnstones. Page 231.

1 Species.

Small Shore-birds (8 inches long) with pied plumage, seen turning over stones on rocky beaches, in search of marine insects, etc.

Family Charadriidæ: Plovers (Popular Game-birds). Page 232.

6 Species.

A large and important family of Shore-birds, frequenting both fresh and salt water. They have Pigeon-like bills *which are never longer than the head.* In size they vary from small to medium (7 to 12 inches); the plumage undergoes many variations owing to season and age, but the sexes are nearly alike. The neck is short, the head bullet-shaped, and the body usually stout; the wings are longer than the tail. They are generally seen in flocks during the migrations, as the majority of species breed far north. They fly and run with great rapidity, and inhabit dry uplands, as well as the vicinity of ponds, and the seashore. They all have pleasing call notes, and one species has a melodious, piping whistle.

Family Scolopacidæ: Sandpipers, Snipes, etc. Page 236.

11 Species.

Another large family, inhabiting inland meadows as well as salt marshes and the seashore, including Woodcock and Snipe, both well-known Game-birds (that probe for their food in the mud with their bills), and the less familiar Sandpipers. *Bills not Pigeon-shaped; slender, usually longer than the head.* Plumage mottled and streaked with neutral tints and sober colours. Voices peculiar, varying according to the species.

Snipe are among the most delicately flavoured of Game-birds, and Sandpipers comprise the smallest of the Waders. The Snipe group may be easily distinguished from the rest by the plain, unbarred tail. The Tattlers are a long-legged, noisy species, *not probing for their food in the mud,* but picking it up in the vicinity of flats and sand bars.

ORDER PALUDICOLÆ: RAILS, GALLINULES, COOTS.

Family Rallidæ: Rails. Page 245.

5 Species.

"Birds of medium and small size, generally with compressed body and large, strong legs, enabling them to run rapidly and thread with ease the mazes of the reedy marshes to which they are almost exclusively confined; while, by means of their long toes, they are prevented from sinking in the mire or floating vegetation. . . . The head is completely feathered; the general plumage is ordinarily of subdued and blended coloration, lacking much of the variegation commonly observed in Shore-birds; the sexes are usually alike, and the changes of plumage not great with age or season. The food is never probed for in the mud, but gathered from the surface of the ground and water." (Coues.)

ORDER HERODIONES: HERONS, ETC.

Family Ardeidæ (Marsh Birds). Page 250.

5 Species.

Long-legged, long-necked, long-billed birds, often beautifully crested in the breeding-season, and having broad, generous wings. They nest in trees in swampy places. Their voices are harsh, and they undergo great changes of plumage, and must be recognized by the novice more by general shape than detailed colour description. They may often be seen standing on one leg on the edge of ponds or swamps in the attitude of the Storks of Andersen's "Fairy Tales."

ORDER ANSERES: LAMELLIROSTRAL SWIMMERS.

Family Anatidæ: Ducks, Geese, etc. Page 255.

16 Species.

Stoutly-built birds of rivers and seashore, with varied and beautiful plumage of a type familiar to every one. "Body full, heavy, flattened beneath, neck of variable length, head large, eyes small. . . . Wings of moderate length (rarely very short), stiff, strong, pointed, conferring rapid, vigorous, whistling flight; a Wild Duck at full speed is said to make ninety miles an hour. . . . Legs short, knees buried in the general integument, toes palmate." (Coues.)

ORDER TUBINARES: TUBE-NOSED SWIMMERS.

Family Procellaridæ: Shearwaters, Petrels, etc. Page 268.

1 Species.

The various Petrels are comprised in this family; they are off-shore birds of Gull-like appearance. Dr. Coues says of one group, that their "flight is peculiarly airy and flickering, more like that of a butterfly than like ordinary birds; they are almost always seen on the wing, appearing to swim little if any, and some, if not all, breed in holes in the ground like Bank Swallows."

ORDER LONGIPENNES: LONG-WINGED SWIMMERS.

Family Laridæ: Gulls and Terns. Page 269.

7 Species.

Off-shore birds, breeding on the coastwise islands. The Gulls are large and stout, with hooked bills, large feet, and strong wings that make their flight even and steady, and not impulsive and dashing like the Terns'. They both dive for their food and glean it from the surface of the water. The Terns are more slender, have greater rapidity in flying, and *forked tails;* the tails of the Gulls are never forked.

ORDER PYGOPODES: DIVING BIRDS.

Family Alcidæ: Auks, etc. Page 275.

1 Species.

Our species, the Dovekie or Sea Dove, is an off-shore bird seen usually about lighthouses and flying in the wake of vessels. It is a rather small-sized, dusky bird, white below, with a clumsy, awkwardly-shaped body, and long wings.

Family Urinatoridæ: Loons. Page 276.

2 Species.

Stout divers with long bodies, legs set very far back, bob-tailed, long twisting necks, and plumage which is more or less spotted above and plain below. We see them only in the migrations, as they breed in the far north.

Family Pygopodes: Grebes. Page 277.

2 Species.

Very dexterous diving birds of lakes and rivers, as well as of salt water, variously crested in the breeding-season; their bodies are held upright by the posterior position of the legs; they are practically tailless, and, though smaller, bear a close resemblance to the Loons.

BIRD BIOGRAPHIES.

PERCHING SONG-BIRDS.

PERCHING SONGLESS BIRDS.

BIRDS OF PREY.

PIGEONS, QUAILS, GROUSE.

SHORE AND MARSH BIRDS.

SWIMMING BIRDS.

PLATE 6.

1. AMERICAN ROBIN.

Length, 10 inches.

2. WOOD THRUSH.

Length, 7.50–8 inches.

PERCHING SONG-BIRDS.

ORDER PASSERES: PERCHING BIRDS.

SUB-ORDER OSCINES: SINGING BIRDS.

FAMILY TURDIDÆ: THRUSHES.

Wood Thrush: *Turdus mustelinus.*

PLATE 6. FIG. 2.

Length: 7.50–8 inches.

Male and Female: Above tawny, deepest on head, tail olivaceous. Sides of throat light buff, middle of throat, breast, and belly white; sprinkled on sides with heart-shaped or triangular dark-brown spots. Whitish eye ring, bill dark brown, feet flesh-coloured.

Song: A melody in which some notes have the effect of a stringed accompaniment. The syllables are uttered deliberately, about four seconds apart—"Uoli—a-e-o-li, uoli—uoli—uol—aeolee-leé!"

Season: Early May to October.

Breeds: Northward from Virginia, Kentucky, and Kansas.

Nest: Of small twigs with a mud lining, sometimes saddled upon the boughs of evergreens not far from the trunk, or in small trees and bushes.

Eggs: Four usually, similar in colour to the Robin's, but smaller.

Range: Eastern United States to the Plains, north to southern Michigan, Ontario, and Massachusetts, south in winter to Guatemala and Cuba.

Next to the American Robin, the Wood Thrush is the most widely known of its tribe. He is an exquisite vocalist, the tones having a rare quality of rolling vibrance, and often as he utters his placid notes, each one full and deliberate, the song seems like the music of a flute and an æolian harp strung in the trees. "Uoli," he begins, and after pausing continues, "Aeolee-leé" (the last syllable having the harp quality), "Uoli-uoli—aeolee-lee." First softly, then modulating, reiterating sometimes for an hour together; but compassing in these few syllables the whole range of pure emotion.

The Wood Thrush is called shy by many writers, but here in Connecticut it is both abundant and sociable, feeding about the lawn in company with Robins, though it keeps more in shelter, skirting the shrubbery, as it scratches. Two pairs nested last season in the spruces below the lawn. Their nests so closely resemble the best efforts of the Robin, and the eggs being of a like colour, that I had mistaken them until I saw the Thrushes in possession. These nests were made wholly of sticks, and lined thinly with clay, but two others that I found in the woods showed more varied materials. One was placed, some six feet from the ground, in a cedar bush close to a pool. The mud used to line the nest was full of Sphagnum, and of the water-soaked seed vessels of the sweet-pepper bush, which, mingled with dry beech leaves, made the nest very picturesque, while the mud was barely visible through the bedding of the runners of *Potentilla,* to whose stems some identifying leaves still clung.

The second nest was in a laurel bush on the top of high rocks in Samp-Mortar woods. It was beautifully stuccoed with lichens and lined with the hair-like roots that cover the surface of leaf mould.

The Wood Thrush builds the middle or last of May, and as it comes often the very first day of the month and continues singing well into July, it gives us a goodly season of song. Wood Robin is one of its local names, but this is used, somewhat at random, for other Thrushes.

Wilson's Thrush; Veery: *Turdus fuscescens.*

Frontispiece.

Length: 7–7.50 inches.

Male and Female: No eye ring. Above evenly olive-brown, with a tawny cast. Throat buff, flecked on the sides with fine arrow-shaped brown spots. Breast and under parts white. Bill dark above, lower mandible light. Feet light.

Song: Ringing, echo-like. Professor Ridgway indicates it thus: "Taweel 'ah—taweel 'ah, twil-ah, twil-ah!"

Season: Early May to October.

Breeds: According to Coues, in the northerly part of its range, but it also breeds freely in our river groves and in the more southern portion of the Middle States.

Nest: Built either upon or near the ground, of sticks and twigs like that of the Wood Thrush, but lacking the mud.

Eggs: Like Robin and Wood Thrush, of a greenish blue, but smaller than either.

Range: Eastern United States to the Plains, north to Manitoba, Ontario, Anticosti, and Newfoundland.

The Veery, the most slender and graceful of the Thrushes, is with us all the season, but it is so shy and elusive in its ways of slipping through the trees and underbrush in swampy woodlands that it seems scarcely an actual presence. Change a word in Wordsworth's verses on the Cuckoo and the description is perfect:—

> "O *Veery!* shall I call thee bird,
> Or but a wandering voice?"

When it first arrives, and before mating, the Veery is seen frequently in the garden, prying under dead leaves and in low bushes like all its insect-eating kin, but when it retires to the woods to nest all but the voice seems to vanish. That wonderful, haunting voice! It was a woodland mystery to me not so very long ago; a vocal Will-o'-the-Wisp. Leading on and on, up and down river banks, into wild grape tangles and clinging brush, then suddenly ceasing and leaving me to return as best I might.

There came a time, however, when a few pairs, mating before they left the garden in the spring, surprised us by singing while in view, and the same season we took a leisurely drive through the country to see the orchards in bloom, and stopped for the night at a hospitable farmhouse in a hollow that winds between banks clad with laurel and hemlocks up to the old village of Redding Ridge.

We were told that the woods were full of birds "that sang all night," so we walked up the lane road, the soft light coming partly from the setting sun and partly from the high May moon.

The waterfall resounded from where the hills dropped suddenly to the hollow. A single Whip-poor-will darting from the woods almost brushed my face and uttered his mournful call in my ear. Above the waterfall was a chain of ponds, and sitting on the rail of a separating bridge we listened and waited. A fox crept down to the water to drink, and as the wind blew toward us he did not suspect our proximity and lapped at leisure, the clear moonlight showing his shabby, faded spring coat.

Suddenly from the woody banks the Veeries began their song. They had been singing by twos and threes ever since sunset, but now the sound was as of a full chorus compared to the humming of a few voices. From all sides the notes rang: "Taweel 'ah, taweel 'ah!" and then a tone lower: "twil-ah, twil-ah!" no two birds seeming to sing precisely at once but continually echoed themselves and each other. Why is not this bird called the Echo Thrush? The name would reveal its identity to any one who had ever heard the song.

The music lasted until after nine o'clock, when it died away in a whisper like a benediction of the night and the Whip-poor-will was left as sentry for the midnight hours.

Gray-cheeked Thrush: *Turdus aliciæ.*

Length: 7.50–8 inches.

Male and Female: No eye ring. Head and back uniform olive-brown. Throat buff and slightly speckled; sides dull grayish white, the specks running into a wash. *Cheeks gray;* bill slender.

Song: In tone like other Thrushes, but differently accented — "Wee-o, wee-o, tit-ti wee-o!" (Torrey.)

Season: May, remaining a week or so; return migration in October.

Breeds: Northward from northern New England; and var. bicknelli in New York and New England.

Nest: In bushes made of moss, twigs, and grass.

Eggs: 4, greenish blue, speckled with brown.

PLATE 7.

OLIVE-BACKED THRUSH.

Length, 7-7.50 inches.

Range: Eastern North America, west to the Plains, Alaska, and eastern Siberia, north to the Arctic coast, south in winter to Costa Rica.

This Thrush is one of the rarest in southern New England. It is a near relative of the Olive-backed Thrush, from which it differs in having gray sides to the head and in being somewhat larger. A few of the Gray-cheeked Thrushes come to the garden and lane every spring and fall; but even these migratory visits are very irregular. Bradford Torrey, whose White Mountain experience has brought him into intimate contact with Bicknell's Thrush (as those individuals which breed in the mountains of New York and New England are called) during its season of song, says that ". . . while the Gray-cheek's song bears an evident resemblance to the Veery's, . . . the two are so unlike in pitch and rhythm that no reasonably nice ear ought ever to confound them."

The song is one of the most infrequent sounds in this locality; but I have heard it three times in the lane, and have come within identifying range of the singer, attracted and aided by Mr. Torrey's description and syllabication.[1]

Olive-backed Thrush: *Turdus ustulatus swainsoni.*

Plate 7.

Length: 7-7.50 inches.

Male and Female: *Yellowish eye ring.* Head and back olive-brown, deepest on wings and tail. Buff breast and throat, deepening in colour on the sides and speckled everywhere but on the throat with arrow-shaped blackish spots. Dark bill; feet pale brown.

Song: Of the same quality as the Wood Thrush's, but less inspiring, and tinged with melancholy.

Season: Arrives in May, often in company with White-throated Sparrows, passes on in early May, and returns in October.

Breeds: In mountainous parts of southern New England and northward.

Nest: In low trees and bushes, like that of Wood Thrush minus the mud.

Eggs: 4-5, greenish blue, freely spotted with brown.

Range: Eastern North America and westward to the upper Columbia River and East Humboldt Mountains, straggling to the Pacific coast.

[1] "The Foot-Path Way," Houghton, Mifflin & Co.

The early ornithologists were rather mixed as to the identity of the Hermit, Gray-cheeked, and Olive-backed Thrushes. Samuels calls the latter the least common of New England Thrushes, while Nuttall confused the Hermit with the Wood Thrush.

The Olive-backed Thrush comes quite freely to the garden, rather early in the spring migration, at the time when the other migratory Thrushes and northern-breeding Sparrows appear, and hops about quite sociably, but seldom gives any other sound than its liquid call note. Its identification is easy, owing to the even olive colour of its back, and it entirely lacks the tawny warmth of its kin. This colour difference of the Thrushes is tritely summed up on page 60 of Stearns & Coues's "New England Bird-life": "The Wood Thrush is tawny, turning to olive on the rump. The Hermit is olive, turning to tawny on the rump. The Olive-back is entirely olive. The Veery is entirely tawny." When seen feeding with the Wood Thrush along the garden edges, this colour difference appealed to me very plainly, as well as the greater slimness of the Olive-back.

Mr. Nehrling says that this Thrush, in company with the Veery and Wood Thrush, is killed in great hordes, by the miserable pot-hunters about New Orleans, on its return in the fall migration; so that even sober plumage is no protection, and the fact that our country is not wholly birdless goes far to prove the wonderful power that Nature uses in her struggle with the destructive side of man.

Hermit Thrush: *Turdus aonalaschkæ pallasii.*

PLATE 8. FIG. 1.

Length: 7–7.25 inches.

Male and Female: Above olive-brown, *reddening on the rump. Yellowish eye ring.* Throat, sides of neck, and breast washed with buff and thickly sprinkled with brown arrowheads growing larger on belly. Under parts white. Bill blackish above, lower mandible light; feet light brown.

Song: Flute-like, ascending. "O spheral, spheral! O holy, holy! O clear away, clear away! O clear up, clear up!" (Burroughs.)

Season: Comes in the migrations before other northern Thrushes.

PLATE 8.

1. HERMIT THRUSH. 2. GOLDEN-CROWNED KINGLET.

Length, 7–7.25 inches. Length, 4 inches.

Breeds: From mountainous parts of southern New York and New England northward.

Nest and Eggs: Similar to those of the Veery.

Range: Eastern North America, wintering from the Northern States southward.

Burroughs says: "If we take the quality of melody as a test, the Wood Thrush, the Hermit Thrush, and the Veery Thrush stand at the head of our list of songsters." One may be very familiar with the songs of two of this trio without ever having identified the third, or at least without having heard it sing.

At the first glance the Hermit closely resembles the Wood Thrush, but a good field-glass will enable you to see the colour distinction of the back, and also that the Hermit has a more yellowish throat and that the breast spots are more acute. Its rarity differs very much according to location. It is comparatively common in the northeast, and Dr. Warren says that in Pennsylvania it is, with the exception of the Robin, the commonest of the Thrushes and breeds occasionally in some of the higher mountain districts. Here, as well as in many of the Middle States, where it is only a migrant, its full song is seldom heard. I have not found it a shy bird, not more so than the Wood Thrush, but it doubtless becomes shy in its breeding-haunts.

I made its acquaintance, several years ago, in the lane back of the garden, and had watched its rapid, nervous motions during many migrations before I heard it sing. This spring, the first week in May, when standing at the window about six o'clock in the morning, I heard an unusual note, and listened, thinking it at first a Wood Thrush and then a Thrasher, but soon finding that it was neither of these I opened the window softly and looked among the nearby shrubs, with my glass. The wonderful melody ascended gradually in the scale as it progressed, now trilling, now legato, the most perfect, exalted, unrestrained, yet withal, finished bird song that I ever heard. At the final note I caught sight of the singer perching among the lower sprays of a dogwood tree. I could see him perfectly: it was the Hermit Thrush! In a moment he began again. I have never heard the Nightingale, but those who have, say that it is the surroundings and its continuous night singing that make it even the equal of our Hermit; for, while the Nightingales sing in numbers in the moonlit groves, the Hermit tunes his lute sometimes in inaccessible solitudes, and there is something immaterial and immortal about the song. Presently you cease altogether to associate it with a bird, and it inspires a kindred feeling in every one who hears it.

Mrs. Olive Thorne Miller tells delightfully of her pursuit of the Hermit in northern New York, where it was said to be abundant, but when she looked for him, he had always "been there" and was gone; until one day in August she saw the bird and heard the song and exclaims: "This only was lacking. . . . This crowns my summer."[1]

Among many local names this bird has received, that given by the early settlers in the Adirondack region is the most appropriate; they call it the Swamp Angel.

American Robin: *Merula migratoria.*

PLATE 6. FIG. 1.

Length: 10 inches.

Male: Above olive-gray, head black, wings dark brown, tail black with white spot on two outer quills. Entire breast brick-red. Throat streaked with black and white. White eyelids. Bill yellow, dusky at tip; feet dark.

Female: Paler throughout, resembling the autumn plumage of the male.

Song: A vigorous interrogative melody, cheerful but somewhat lacking in variety. "Do you think what you do, do you think what you do, do you think?" Call note, "Quick! Quick!"

Season: Present all the year. The migratory flocks come in March and leave in October and early November.

Breeds: From Virginia and Kansas northward to the Arctic coast.

Nest: On a horizontal branch, in a tree crotch, hedge, or strong vine. Made of small sticks, plastered more or less and lined with mud.

Eggs: 4, of the peculiar green-blue, known by the name of the bird.

Range: Eastern North America to the Rocky Mountains, including eastern Mexico and Alaska. Winters from southern Canada and the Northern States (irregularly) southward.

[1] "Little Brothers of the Air."

In early March the Robins come flocking from the South, and those seen before this time are usually the roving winter residents. At first they sing most freely at noon or late in the afternoon, when their notes mingle with the peeping of the marsh-frogs, but with milder weather the Robin becomes the bird of dawn, whose persistent, regular melody unites the whole chorus.

From this time until late July, at morning before twilight and at intervals all through the day, he sings, varying the accentuation of the melody, even while its range remains the same. At dawn he says, "Cheerily, cheerily, cheer up, cheer up!" While one who sings every afternoon in the apple tree by my window says plainly, "Do you think what you do, do you think what you do, do you thi-n-k?"

Wilson Flagg, who is always unique if sometimes inaccurate, writes, "There is no bird that has fewer faults than the Robin, or would be more esteemed as a constant companion." Passing over his habit of helping himself to the ripest cheek of cherry or strawberry, which is a trifling harm when compared with his good reputation as an insect destroyer, and which from a bird's standpoint of course is not a fault at all, — he has two radical defects that detract from the pleasure of his society. He is extremely and unnecessarily noisy in his cries of alarm when any one approaches his nest, not only in this way calling attention to its location, but setting the entire bird colony in an uproar. His sharp, useless call, given vehemently, often without cause, reminds one of the silly housewife who ran down the village street crying, "Fire! Fire!" — because the damper being closed, her stove smoked.

It is very aggravating to be thus interrupted while watching the movements of some rare or shy bird. One day I had almost located a Hummingbird's nest when a Robin cried, "Quick! Quick!" and the Hummers took the hint.

His other fault is untidiness and general disorder in nest-building. If Robins build about the porch or in an arbour, they invariably make a litter and exercise little of the precaution, used by so many birds, in removing the excrements of the young from the nest. In the choice of a nesting location they are often extremely stupid. The nest being a combination of clay and sticks, is a rather bulky and weighty affair, yet the birds frequently build it in a spot so exposed that a heavy summer shower will reduce it to pulp; or on so slender a branch that the weight of the growing young cause it to tip over.

Twelve pairs of Robins, that I know of, nested this season in various parts of the garden, some huddled close to the house, or in fruit trees, others in the evergreens, but in addition to these homes I found five nests, some containing eggs, which, though of the season's building, had been abandoned through hopeless faults of location and construction, and the Robin does not lightly abandon its nest after the eggs are laid, like some other Thrushes and many Warblers.

But with the list of the Robin's shortcomings before us, the cheery sound of his piping effaces them all, and awakens memories that go back to the very dawn of life. He was the first bird, probably, that we learned to call by name, and every spring he returns as the marshal of the feathered hosts and well sustains the honour.

The American Robin is an entirely different species from the English Robin Redbreast; the latter is a smaller bird of more compact build, with a brilliant red breast, in form resembling our Bluebird.

Bluebird: *Siala sialis.*

PLATE 9.

Length: 6.50–7 inches.

Male: Azure-blue above. Wings blue with some dark edgings. Breast brick-red, lower parts white. Bill and feet black.

Female: Dull blue above. Breast paler and more rusty. Young with speckled breast and back.

Song: A sweet plaintive warble, seeming to say, "Dear! dear! *think* of it, *think* of it!" Burroughs says it continually calls "Purity, Purity"; in either case the accent is the same.

Season: A resident species, though the majority come early in March and retire to the South in late October.

PLATE 9.

BLUEBIRD.

Length, 6.50–7 inches.

Breeds: All through its range.

Nest: Hardly to be called a structure as it is usually merely a lining in a decayed knot hole, a bird-house, or the abandoned hole of the Woodpecker.

Eggs: 4–6, pale blue, shading sometimes to white.

Range: Eastern United States to the eastern base of the Rocky Mountains, north to Manitoba, Ontario, and Nova Scotia; south in winter, from the Middle States to the Gulf States and Cuba. Bermuda, resident.

The Bluebird is the colour-bearer of the spring brigade, even as the Song Sparrow is the bugler. There may be snow on the ground, and the chimney nightly tells the complaint of the wind. All other signs fail, but when we see the Bluebird in his azure robe and hear his liquid notes (he is April's minstrel), we know that spring is close at hand, for in autumn and winter the blue coat is veiled with rusty-brown, as if the murky storms had cast their shadows upon it. The Bluebird's note is pleasing and mellow, mingling delightfully with the general spring chorus, but in itself it ranks more with the music of the Warblers than with its own Thrush kin. It has a rather sad tone, a trifle suggestive of complaint or pity. Heard at a distance it has a purling quality. Uttered close at hand, as when the birds go to and fro about their nests, it sounds as if their domestic arrangements were being discussed with the subdued, melancholy voice so often assumed by unwilling housewives. Then the male will fly off on a marketing expedition, murmuring to himself, "Dear, dear, *think* of it, *think* of it!" In fact, these birds seem to be practical, every-day sort of little creatures, and very seldom exhibit any tokens of affection after the nesting season begins. Yet the Bluebird is one to which romance strongly attaches us, its notes recall the first thrill of early spring, and we cannot disassociate him from blooming orchards. In the autumn he is one of the latest to call to us, the last leaf (so to speak) on the tree of beautifully coloured Songbirds, from which the Oriole, Tanager, Rose-breasted Grosbeak, and Cardinal have dropped away.

One of the finest bird eulogies in any language is Burroughs's chapter on this bird in "Wake Robin"; it has even a greater charm than Michelet's rhapsody on the Nightingale. One paragraph quoted will lead the reader to search out the whole.

"When Nature made the Bluebird she wished to propitiate both the sky and the earth, so she gave him the colour of one on his back and the hue of the other on his breast, and ordained that his appearance in spring should denote that the strife and war between these two elements was at an end. He is the peace-harbinger; in him the celestial and terrestrial strike hands and are fast friends."

FAMILY SYLVIIDÆ: WARBLERS, KINGLETS.

SUB-FAMILY REGULINÆ: KINGLETS.

Golden-crowned Kinglet: *Regulus satrapa.*

PLATE 8. FIG. 2.

Length: 4 inches.

Male: Flame-coloured crown spot edged with yellow and enclosed by black line. Above olive-green and yellowish olive, which is more decided on wings, rump, and tail. Under parts yellowish gray. Whitish line over eye. Bill and feet black.

Female: Crown yellow, no flame colour or black line.

Song: A sharp call and a few notes. Mr. Brewster gives them as,— "Tzee-tzee-tzee-tzee, ti-ti-ter-ti-ti-ti-ti!"

Season: A fairly constant winter resident.

Breeds: From northern New England northward.

Nest: Bulky for the size of the bird. A ball of hair, moss, etc., often lined with feathers, placed on the high bough of an evergreen.

Eggs: 6–10, white, thickly speckled.

Range: North America generally, migrating south in winter to Guatemala.

The dainty little Golden-crowned Kinglet shares with the Winter Wren and Hummingbird the distinction of being one of the three smallest birds in the United States. It is ranked as a winter resident, for, coming from the north with the Ruby-crowned species, it lingers well into the winter, passing southward in rigorous seasons, for a time in January and February, but returning very early in March en route to its northern breeding-grounds.

It has a decided preference for evergreens and searches tirelessly by the hour for insects in the rough bark, but it is so very small and restless that it may easily escape notice. My first discovery of the bird in the garden was in December, while looking in the spruces for the source of what I supposed to be the wiry note of some belated insect. A gleam of sunlight shooting through the branches, touched the flaming crown of the Kinglet, who was quite close and eyeing me inquisitively.

The bird has been known to breed in Worcester County, Mass., and the nest is described by Mr. Brewster, who says that in one nest the outer walls were made of soft green mosses and lichens; near the top were feathers of the Ruffed Grouse, Hermit Thrush, and Ovenbird, ranged quills down so that they made a tent-like protection for the eggs. In the two nests which contained eggs, they were so numerous as to be piled in two layers, one above the other.

It would be interesting to know how the tiny birds manage to hatch such a quantity of eggs: whether they are turned and stirred up daily in order to bring all equally to the warmth of the body, or if perhaps the top row hatches first and the young birds, by their warmth, aid in bringing out their brothers and sisters.

Ruby-crowned Kinglet: *Regulus calendula.*

Length: 4–4.50 inches.

Male: Vermilion spot on crown (which, however, does not always appear until the second year). Ash-gray head, back olive-gray, yellowish on tail. Wings brownish olive with yellow and white edgings. Breast and under parts yellowish gray. Edges of eyelids white. Bill black, feet dark brown.

Female: Lacking the red head spot.

Song: A thin, metallic call note, like a vibrating wire. Song full, varied, and melodious; often heard here in the spring migration.

Season: In the migrations April–May and October–November.

Breeds: Mostly north of the United States.

Nest: Very rare, only six known. Of matted hair, feathers, moss, etc. Bulky, globular, and partly pensile.

Eggs: Marked "unknown" in Coues's "Key to North American Birds," but have been more recently found. Dirty cream-white, deepening at larger end to form a ring. Some specimens are spotted.

Range: North America, south to Guatemala, north to the Arctic coast.

In late autumn, even after a light November snow, these cheery, sociable, little birds come prying and peering about the orchard or garden fruit trees, examining every twig or nook which may conceal insects with profound interest. They remain at the most only a few weeks, but make us a similar visit in April on the return trip. I only know its call note, though its full song is often heard in the spring migration, and is said to be rich and sweet. Mr. Nehrling,[1] who has heard it sing in central Wisconsin and northern Illinois, speaks of the "power, purity, and volume of the notes, their faultless modulation and long continuance." Dr. Coues says of it, "The Kinglet's exquisite vocalization defies description."

It is a very valuable bird to the agriculturist, coming when most insect-eaters have passed on, and does prodigious work among all classes of fruit trees, by killing grubs and larvæ.

The Kinglets have been, in common with many other attractive birds, recklessly killed for millinery purposes, but the present law in many States prohibits the sale of stuffed song-birds for such use, and this, together with the increase of public opinion against this vandalism, is not without effect; for I have never seen so many of these little sprites as during the past December.

[1] "Our Native Birds of Song and Beauty," Henry Nehrling, Milwaukee.

FAMILY PARIDÆ: NUTHATCHES AND TITMICE.

SUB-FAMILY PARINÆ: TITMICE.

Tufted Titmouse: *Parus bicolor.*

Length: 6–6.50 inches.

Male and Female: Crested, with black spot on brow at base of crest. Above ash-gray, wings and tail darker. Sides of head dull white. Under parts whitish with brownish wash on sides. Bill lead-black, feet lead-colour.

Song: A persistent whistle, which Mr. Nehrling translates as "Hee-dle-dee-dle-dee-dle-dee," and at other times "Peto-peto-peto-daytee-daytee!"

Season: Straggling to southern New England in early April or May in company with many of the Warblers.

Breeds: In all parts of range.

Nest: Sometimes in bird-boxes, otherwise in the abandoned holes of Woodpeckers, etc., lined with hair and feathers.

Eggs: 6–8, white, spotted with reddish-brown and lilac.

Range: Eastern United States to the Plains, but rare towards the northern border, being a straggler merely to southern New England.

The Tufted Titmouse is quite rare here, but is a summer and, perhaps, winter resident in southern New York; and whenever it is seen, it is sure to be recognized.

In shape it has all the jaunty pertness of the Blue Jay, but with an added air of confidence and sociability. During the winter they travel about in flocks searching for food, and when insects fail they content themselves with nuts and hard seeds which crack readily, after the fashion of the Nuthatches. They pair in April, and Mr. Nehrling says that they grow silent as the nesting time approaches, and very stealthy in their movements; a pair occupied a Bluebird house, which he had placed on the edge of the woods near his home in Texas, and then shifted to a Wren box to raise the second brood.

Montague Chamberlain, who heard these Titmice singing in the South in January, thinks that their song sometimes takes the high key of the Baltimore Oriole, and that among other colloquial expressions they frequently said, "Whip-

Tom-Kelly," but he gives them the name of Peto, from their most characteristic note.

Chickadee; Black-capped Titmouse: *Parus atricapillus.*

PLATE 10. FIG. 2.

Length: 5.50 inches.

Male and Female: No crest. Above gray with a brownish tinge. Crown and nape, and chin and throat black; sides of head white. Below white, shading to light gray with brown wash. Wings and tail gray with white edgings. Bill and feet lead-black.

Song: Cheerful, conversational. "Chickadee-dee-dee-dee!" varied in winter with "Day, day, day!" and a whistle "Pè-we, pè-we."

Season: A resident.

Breeds: Nearly throughout its range.

Nest: Made of all sorts of soft material, — wool, fur, feathers, and hair, placed in holes in tree stumps.

Eggs: 6–8, white, thickly sprinkled with warm brown.

Range: Eastern North America, north of the Potomac and Ohio Valley.

This hardy little fellow, always cheery and lovable, is a familiar figure in our light woods and garden trees in autumn and winter, seeming, by his good-nature and energy, to be trying to console us, in a measure, for the loss of the tree-haunting summer Warblers.

The Chickadee adapts himself to all surroundings and to all circumstances, suiting his appetite to what he can find, when insects fail, taking kindly to seeds, berries, cone-kernels, and crumbs.

In the winter of 1891–92, when the cold was severe, the snow deep, and the tree trunks often covered with ice, the Chickadees repaired in flocks daily to the kennel of my old dog Colin and fed from his dish, hopping over his back and calling "Chickadee, dee, dee," in his face, — proceedings that he never in the least resented, but seemed rather to enjoy.

Taking a hint from this, I made a compound of finely minced meat, waste canary seed, buckwheat, and cracked oats, which was scattered in a sheltered spot from which the snow had been swept. This bird-hash was rapidly con-

1. YELLOW WARBLER.

Length, 4.75–5 inches.

2. CHICKADEE.

Length, 5.50 inches.

sumed, and I was convinced during that season that it was a food suited to the needs of all our winter-birds, both seed and insect eaters finding in it what they required.

The Chickadee breaks the silence of many winter days with his jovial notes, and fairly begs for companionship:—

> Chic-chicadeedee! saucy note
> Out of sound heart and merry throat,
> As if it said, "Good day, good sir!
> Fine afternoon, old passenger!
> Happy to meet you in these places,
> Where January brings few faces."—R. W. EMERSON.

FAMILY PARIDÆ: NUTHATCHES AND TITMICE.

SUB-FAMILY SITTINÆ: NUTHATCHES.

White-breasted Nuthatch: *Sitta carolinensis.*

PLATE 11. FIG. 1.

Length: 5.50–6 inches.

Male and Female: Body flat and compact. Above slate-blue. Top of head and nape black. Wings slate, edged with brown. Outer tail feathers brownish with white bars. Belly white, rusty toward vent. Bill dark lead-colour, feet dark brown. Female paler with colour boundaries less distinctly marked.

Song: A call, "Quank-quank-quank!" and a few other notes.

Season: A common resident, roving about all winter.

Breeds: Freely in all parts of range.

Nest: In tree holes, which it excavates with great patience, and lines with feathers, moss, etc., after the fashion of Titmice.

Eggs: Often 10, white, speckled with red and lilac.

Range: Southern British Provinces and eastern United States to the Rocky Mountains.

This Nuthatch, who is our most conspicuous bird-acrobat, persistently walking head downward and performing various tortuous feats while he searches for food, is a resident of the eastern United States, only leaving the most northerly parts of his range for a short time in winter.

He appears to migrate in spring and return in autumn, but in reality only retreats to the woodlands to breed, emerging again when the food supply grows scant in the autumn.

The Nuthatches are great friends of the Kinglets and Titmice, and often travel in flocks with them. They pass for being shy, but are not so in reality, but merely elusive because of their restless habits, which seldom allow them to stay in one spot long enough to be examined. In fact "tree-mice," the local name our farmers give them, is quite appropriate.

This species has a particularly adroit way of knocking off bits of decayed or loose bark with the beak, to obtain the grubs or larvæ hidden beneath. They never suck the sap from trees, as is sometimes supposed, but are wholly beneficial to vegetation.

Red-breasted Nuthatch: *Sitta canadensis.*

Length: 4.50–4.75 inches.

Male: Above lead-coloured, brownish on wings and tail. Crown and sides of neck black. White stripe over eye, meeting on brow. Under parts rust-red. Bill dark lead-colour, feet lead-brown.

Female: Paler, crown and back of one colour.

Song: Note — "Day-day-day-dait!"

Season: A winter resident in Connecticut, but seen most frequently in early spring and late autumn.

Breeds: Chiefly north of the United States.

Nest: In holes, like the White-breasted species.

Eggs: Very heavily speckled with red-brown.

Range: North America at large, migrating south in winter.

This species, like the preceding, and the whole family, in fact, walk head down around the trunks of trees, and often roost in this singular fashion. Their bright colouring makes them particularly noticeable among the leafless trees. They come about the garden every spring, but more particularly in late November, when I have noted them in numbers on Thanksgiving Day in 1888–89–91–92. They search the bark of the orchard trees, at this time, with all the care of the Kinglets; notwithstanding, this species does not seem to be considered by some authorities a common bird in Connecticut.

1. WHITE-BREASTED NUTHATCH.

Length, 5.50–6 inches.

2. BROWN CREEPER.

Length, 5.50 inches.

Mr. Averill, of Bridgeport, says, "Abundant in September and October, 1888. Not seen at any other time by me." Dr. J. A. Allen writes, in his "Revised List of the Birds of Massachusetts," "Winter visitant. Not generally common." In New York State it seems to be plentiful only in the migrations, but Bradford Torrey, in his essay on "December (1888) out of Doors," says, "Throughout December, and indeed throughout the winter, Brown Creepers and Red-bellied Nuthatches were surprisingly abundant. Every pine wood seemed to have its colony of them."

On October 18, of the past autumn, half-a-dozen pairs appeared in the spruces in the garden and remained all winter, and on January 1 I saw five at one time feeding in the old apple tree, where meat had been placed for their benefit.

FAMILY CERTHIIDÆ: CREEPERS.

Brown Creeper: *Certhia familiaris americana.*

PLATE 11. FIG. 2.

Length: 5.50 inches.

Male and Female: Above brown and ashy-white striped, the brown being of several shades, growing more red on rump. Tail pale brown. Throat, breast, and belly grayish white. Slender, curving bill, black above, yellowish below. Feet brown.

Song: Wild and sweet, but difficult of syllabication. Call note short and lisping.

Season: Winter resident, common from September to April.

Breeds: Locally in Massachusetts, but usually further north.

Nest: *Tucked into a crevice* between loose bark and the trunk of the tree, and composed of moss, sticks, and soft bark.

Eggs: 4–8, cream-white (sometimes having a pink tinge), spotted with brown.

Range: North America east of the Rocky Mountains, breeding from the northern and more elevated parts of the United States northward. Migrating southward in winter.

The Brown Creeper is one of the *tree-trunk birds* that, together with Woodpeckers and Nuthatches, are chiefly to be seen when prying their food from the crevices of the bark. The Creeper is the most difficult to observe of them all, for his colouring is a mixture of browns and grays that blend perfectly with the background upon which he rests. He has also a peculiar spiral motion when creeping, which renders it particularly uncertain at what point he will reappear. If, however, you chance to see him with a glass at short range, his markings will surprise you by their richness; and his sharp, curving bill (very much like a surgeon's needle) completes his identification, as it is unlike the bill of other tree-trunk birds.

The protective plan of his colouring is carried out in his nest-building instinct, the nest being practically unfindable unless the bird is seen coming from, or going to it. Mr. William Brewster thus describes the location of a nest which he found near Lake Umbagog: [1] "... I shortly detected the sweet, wild song of the Brown Creeper, and, looking more carefully, spied a pair of these industrious little gleaners winding their way up the trunk of a neighbouring tree. ... I instituted a careful search among the dead trees that stood around, and at length detected a scale of loose bark, within which was crammed a suspicious-looking mass of twigs and other rubbish. A vigorous rapping upon the base of the trunk producing no effect, I climbed to the spot and was about to tear off the bark, when the frightened Creeper darted out within a few inches of my face, and the next moment I looked in upon the eggs." He says of its song: "It consists of a bar of four notes, the first of moderate pitch, the second lower and less emphatic, the third rising again, and the fourth abruptly falling, but dying away in an indescribably plaintive cadence, like the soft sound of the wind among pine boughs. I can compare it to no other bird voice that I have ever heard."

FAMILY TROGLODYTIDÆ: WRENS, THRASHERS, ETC.

Mockingbird: *Mimus polyglottos.*

PLATE 12.

Length: About 10 inches.

Male and Female: Gray above, wings brown-gray, white spot on outer edge. Tail brownish gray, three outer quills white. Breast grayish white. Bill and feet black. Female smaller, paler.

[1] Bulletin Nuttall Club, IV., 1879.

PLATE 12.

MOCKINGBIRD.

Length, 10 inches.

Song: Natural love-song, a rich, dreamy melody. "Mocking" song distinctly different, — an imitation of the notes of all the birds of field, forest, and garden broken into fragments.

Season: A chance visitor, under which circumstances it is a summer resident.

Breeds: All through the South, and casually as far north as Massachusetts.

Nest: Loosely made of leaves and grass, rags, feathers, etc., bulky and poorly constructed, never far from the ground.

Eggs: 4–6, bluish green, heavily spattered with shades of brown.

Range: United States south into Mexico. Rare from New Jersey, the Valley of the Ohio, Colorado, and California northward.

The Mockingbird, commonly known in this part of the country as a cage pet only, does not properly belong among the birds of the Middle or Eastern States, but as there are many records of its nesting in these latitudes, and as it is a conspicuous and interesting bird, it is safe to include it.

Escaped individuals are often seen in our city parks, one having lived in Central Park, New York, late into the winter of 1892–93, a season which is remembered as being very cold and stormy. Venturous pairs of Mockers have reared their young as far north as Arlington, near Boston, and they are noted as "rare summer visitants, occasionally breeding, particularly in the Connecticut Valley," by Dr. J. A. Allen. Stratford, Conn., also has one breeding-record of long standing.

The Mockingbird is very valiant in the care of its young, and particularly winning and sociable in its relations with man, which friendliness is illy rewarded by the theft of its nestlings, that they may be sold at home and abroad. In addition to this, all through the South these birds are wantonly shot by man and boy because they consume berries and small fruits.

As a cage bird it retains its nocturnal habits, often singing and fluttering in the middle of the night; it also shows many intelligent traits and marked preferences for certain individuals.

The power of song varies greatly in different individuals, some become vocal jugglers, and others retain many of their thrilling, wild notes, which are to be much preferred. The pathetic quality of its native night music inspired Walt Whitman with the theme of one of his best poems, — that of the Mockingbird searching for his lost mate, singing and calling in his loneliness: —

"But soft! sink low;
Soft! let me just murmur,
And do you wait a moment, you husky-noisèd sea;
For somewhere, I believe, I heard my mate responding to me.
So faint — I must be still, be still to listen;
But not altogether still, for then she might not come immediately to me."

Catbird: *Galeoscoptes carolinensis.*

PLATE 13.

Length: 8.50–9 inches.

Male and Female: Above clear, deep slate. Under parts lighter gray. Crown and tail black. Vent rust-red. Bill and feet black.

Song: A brilliant recitative, varied and inimitable, beginning, "Prut! Prut! coquillicot! really, really, coquillicot! Hey coquillicot! Hey! Victory!" Alarm cry, "zeay! zeay!" like a metallic mewing.

Season: Early May to October and November.

Breeds: From Gulf States northward to the Saskatchewan.

Nest: In bushes, of the type of the nests of the Thrushes, but without clay.

Eggs: 4–6, clear green-blue.

Range: Eastern United States and southern British Provinces, west to, and including, the Rocky Mountains; occasional on the Pacific coast. Winters in the Southern States, Cuba and Middle America to Panama. Accidental in Europe.

Next to the Thrushes, no bird would be so much missed from the garden as the (to my mind misnamed) Catbird. For it is as a garden bird that it is best known here, although Wilson Flagg considers it more frequently a tenant of woods and pastures. I have found it nesting in all sorts of places, from an alder bush, overhanging a lonely brook, to a scrub apple in an open field, but never in deep woods, and it is when in its garden home, and in the hedging bushes of an ad-

PLATE 13.

CATBIRD.

Length, 8.50–9 inches.

joining field, that it develops its best qualities,—"lets itself out," so to speak. The Catbirds in the garden are so tame that they will frequently perch on the edge of the hammock in which I am sitting, and when I move they only hop away a few feet with a little flutter. The male is undoubtedly a mimic, when he so desires, but he has an individual and most delightful song, filled with unexpected turns and buoyant melody. The length of the song varies greatly, sometimes lasting almost uninterruptedly for an hour. One strain is used as an introduction and as a constant refrain, Prut! Prut! coquillicot! The ejaculation "prut! prut!" turns into the shrill "zeay! zeay!" when he is really alarmed or angry.

His song is only second, in its colloquial variety, to that of the Brown Thrasher, and it is sometimes for a moment difficult to distinguish between the two. He is particularly successful in imitating the whistle of the Chat (itself a mimic and ventriloquist), and has several times lured me by it, through bushes and briars, only to mock at me and call, "Hey Victory," in my face.

That the Catbird is a fruit thief, its best friend cannot deny; but during the breeding-season it feeds largely upon insects, and particularly upon many highly injurious kinds then in the moth stage; seizing them adroitly in the air and when near the ground, after the manner of Flycatchers.

I kept a Catbird (that had fallen from the nest) in a cage for many months, and became greatly attached to him. He was perfectly fearless and would fly about the room freely, and run about the floor with the rapidity of a mouse. Frequently he would perch on my head, or flit up and dexterously knock the ashes off O——'s cigar to attract his attention. He had a great dislike of newspapers, and if O—— tried to read, when he was at liberty, he would invariably perch on the top of the sheet, thus bending it over and stopping the proceedings, and then utter a triumphant "Zeay, Z-e-a-y!"

It seems strange that there should be any difference of opinion about this merry, friendly bird. Mr. George H.

Ellwanger, near whose window one sang early every morning, writes: "Nothing could be more delightful than his opening matin song, begun in a dulcet undertone; did I not know from experience his long-drawn *crescendo* and the frenzy of the *finale*—a perfect Hungarian 'Czardus'! Pelting him with stones, a pile of which I keep within reach, stops him, as it does my morning nap."

Granting this even, it simply proves the wit of Nature, to set this merry, rippling jester, this whirlwind of delightful mockery, as a foil, a companion to the Thrushes with their spiritual melodies. Was it not by the rendering of such contrasts that Shakespeare mirrored Nature in every phase?

Brown Thrasher: *Harporhynchus rufus.*

PLATE 14.

Length: 11 inches.

Male and Female: Above reddish brown, darker on wings. Beneath yellowish white, with brown, arrow-shaped spots on breast and sides. Wings with two whitish bands. Tail very long. Female paler. Bill black, lower mandible yellow at base; feet light.

Song: Bravura style, with frequent colloquial strains.

Season: Last week in April to early October.

Breeds: From the Gulf States northward.

Nest: In low shrubbery or thickly leaved tree, a boldly made structure of grape-vine, bark, grasses, twigs, and rootlets. In sandy localities, generally on the ground.

Eggs: 4, green, sometimes paling to white, thickly speckled with brown.

Range: Eastern United States, west to the Rocky Mountains, north to southern Maine, Ontario, and Manitoba, south to the Gulf States, including eastern Texas. Accidental in Europe.

Song Thrush, Red Thrush, Brown Mockingbird, Mavis, are four of the local names for this most exultant and (quantity and quality considered) dashing of our song-birds. He arrives from late April to early May, and, after a week or so of almost uninterrupted music, settles down and prepares his nest.

It is impossible to mistake the Thrasher. The brilliant

PLATE 14.

BROWN THRASHER.

Length, 11 inches.

rust-red which covers his entire back, his habit of twitching and thrashing his tail when feeding on the ground, and his bold, swinging flight are certain marks of identification. His song is heard early in the morning from the bushes of some pasture or thickly brushed waste, but later in the day he usually perches on the topmost twig of a tree, and with swelling breast and drooping tail pours forth his freest music; and under no circumstances does he sing when near his nest.

The song has the same colloquial quality as the Catbird's, without its extreme rapidity, and one frequently detects in it the pauses peculiar to the Wood Thrush. I have tried in vain to reduce it to syllables, and find the result is misleading; but the song is always bold and ejaculatory, as Thoreau describes it: "Upon the topmost spray of a tree sings the Brown Thrasher, or Red Mavis, as some love to call him,— all the morning glad of your society (or, rather, I should say, of your lands), that would find out another farmer's field if yours were not here. While you are planting the seed he cries, 'Drop it, drop it,—cover it up, cover it up,— pull it up, pull it up, pull it up.'"

A different mood, that of a reflective shoemaker whom Wilson Flagg knew, wove the song into other words, but with the same accented value: "Look up, look up!—Glory to God, glory to God!—Hallelujah, Amen, Videlicet!"

The Thrasher is something of a fruit thief, and I encountered one this June, in a very picturesque attitude, swooping directly toward me, wings extended, while from his beak, hanging by their twin stalks, were a pair of luscious, ripe cherries. His fruit and corn eating proclivities are much exaggerated, however, and are inconsiderable, in view of his usefulness as an insect-destroyer. The Thrasher's period of song ends with June, or, at the latest, during the first week in July, and Mr. Bicknell says that it does not seem to have a second singing period after the moulting.

FAMILY TROGLODYTIDÆ: WRENS, THRASHERS, ETC.

Sub-family Troglodytinæ: Wrens.

Carolina Wren: *Thryothorus ludovicianus.*

Length: 6 inches.

Male and Female: Chestnut-brown above, wings and tail barred with clear brown. Whitish stripe over eye. White chin. Under parts buffy. Bill straight and dark, same length as head. Feet dusky flesh-coloured. Female smaller.

Song: A joyful melody, — "Sweetheart, sweetheart, sweet!" Also many varied mocking notes.

Season: A rather rare summer visitor north of New Jersey, yet breeding sparingly in New England as far as Massachusetts.

Breeds: Through range, but seldom in the northern portion. Raises two broods.

Nest: Builds a large nest in tree-holes and bird-boxes as well as in the undergrowth of wild places.

Eggs: 6–7, white, spotted with purple and reddish brown.

Range: Eastern United States (rare toward the northern border), west to the Plains. Breeds frequently in southern Connecticut.

The Carolina is the largest of our Wrens and is also the best vocalist, its melodies (for it sings several) having called up many eulogies. In addition to this, it is a great mocker, with an especial fancy for weird and unusual sounds. When in full song it perches on the top of a bush or small tree, raising its head and dropping its tail in Cat-bird fashion.

It is a winter resident in some of the Middle States, and is said by Dr. Warren to be abundant in southwestern Pennsylvania. Though much more shy than its smaller kin, it builds like them about outhouses and in various odd nooks, and has the House Wren's habit of prying and peeping. It collects its food chiefly from the bark of trees, except in autumn when, like many other insect-eaters, it feeds upon berries.

Dr. Shoemaker, a Western bird-lover, wrote a song beginning, —

PLATE 15.

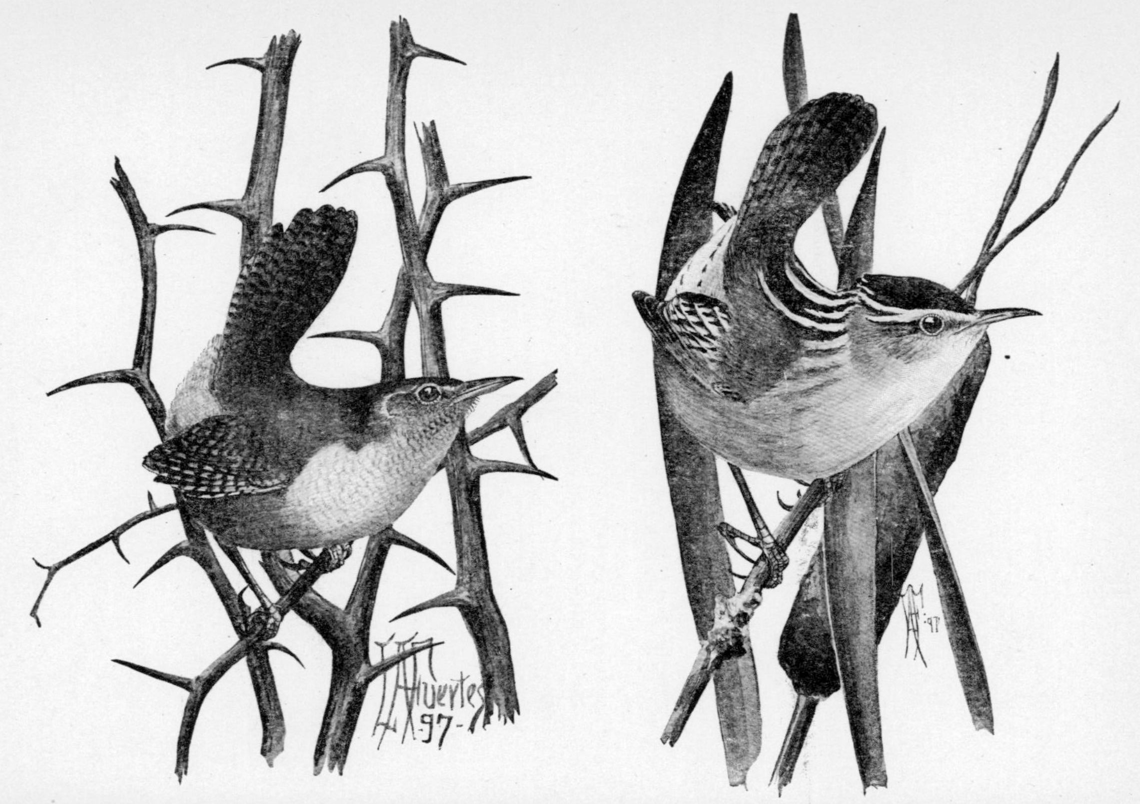

2. LONG-BILLED MARSH WREN.

"There is a little bird that sings —
Sweetheart — sweetheart — sweet!"

without knowing that it was the Carolina Wren, whose notes his accurate ear interpreted in syllables.

House Wren: *Troglodytes aëdon.*

PLATE 15. FIG. 1.

Length: 4.50–5.25 inches.

Male and Female: Dark brown above, minutely barred with blackish. Under parts gray with brownish wash and faint bandings. Fairly long tail. Bill black above, lower mandible light; feet brown.

Song: A merry roulade, sudden, abruptly ended and frequently repeated.

Season: Middle of April to October.

Breeds: Locally through range. Frequently rears three broods a season.

Nest: A loose heap of sticks with a soft lining, in holes, boxes, etc.

Eggs: 6–10, cream-colour, so thickly spotted with brown that the whole egg is tinged.

Range: Eastern United States and southern Canada, west to Indiana and Louisiana.

The House Wren is a bird who has allowed the word *male* to be obliterated from its *social* constitution at least. We always speak of Jenny Wren; always refer to the Wren as *she*, as we do of a ship. It is Johnny Wren who sings and disports himself generally, but it is Jenny, who, by dint of much fussing and scolding, keeps herself well to the front. She chooses the building-site and settles all the little domestic details. If Johnny does not like her choice, he may go away and stay away; she will remain where she has taken up her abode and make a second matrimonial venture. In fact, a little exhibition of independence of this kind took place in our barnyard last spring.

Jenny makes herself as much at home about the wood-shed and outhouses as the mouse does in the granary, and when she slips in and out of the woodpile she seems like a mouse masquerading in feathers. Raise her suspicions or her anger, however, and there is no mouse-like meekness about her; she becomes a tiny shrew, almost thrusting her bill in your face as she pierces your ears with her persistent, "Chit-chit-chit-chit!"

Forgive her for this; it is merely a bad habit, not really an attack, and even while she scolds, her mate is off perching on the pointed top of the clothes-post, head raised high as if he would allow no unnecessary curve in his neck to impede his outburst of sparkling song. "Foive notes to wanst," was the Irish labourer's comment upon this song. "Foive notes to wanst," it is, and I defy any one to render this *appoggiatura* into intelligible syllables.

The Wrens are a most particular bird about the care of their nest, and, though inhabiting pent-up places, their homes are singularly free from vermin. Its industry is very great in collecting the insects upon which it feeds, both itself and the young, and oftentimes it seizes small butterflies when on the wing. Usually, as many as twenty pairs of these Wrens build in the garden bird-boxes and about the barn and sheds. One nest, last year, was placed in an old leather mitten which was left on a shelf in the tool-house; the birds going in and out through the wrist, and, after stuffing the thing entirely full of sticks, to give stability, they lined a little depression with soft duck feathers.

Winter Wren: *Troglodytes hiemalis.*

Length: 3.90–4.10 inches.

Mal^ and Female: Colour very similar to House Wren, but the under parts rusty, dimly and finely barred with dark. Tail and bill short, the latter dark, and slender; feet dark.

Song: Strong, and very musical; not often heard here. Call note, "tr-r-r-r-r-r."

Season: Winter resident, arriving often in October. A summer resident of northern New England.

Breeds: Northern New England, northern portions of New York State, and Pennsylvania northward.

Nest: In odd nooks, crevices, logs, etc. Of twigs mixed with moss, hair, and feathers.

Eggs: 5–8, pure white, finely dotted with purple and brown.
Range: Eastern North America generally, wintering from Massachusetts southward.

The Winter Wren is one of the group of tiny birds that enliven December, January, and February. It is more common than it appears to be, for it is the most retiring and shy of its family. Though it will sometimes nest near dwellings, it prefers seclusion, and especially the proximity to running water. Mr. Otto Boehr writes of the breeding-habits of this Wren in Sullivan County, Penn.: "We found his nest but once. It was built on the side of a mossy log that laid across a small run in a dark, rocky place. The nest was composed entirely of moss, with the entrance at one side near the bottom; it contained six eggs, which resembled those of the Chickadee. The eggs were fresh; time, July 4."

Burroughs considers that its song is surpassed by very few, being of a gushing, lyrical character, uniting brilliancy and plaintiveness.

Short-billed Marsh Wren: *Cistothorus stellaris.*

Length: 4.50 inches.
Male and Female: Above brown. Crown and part of back streaked with black and white. Wings and tail barred. White line over eye. White beneath, washed with rusty across breast and along sides. Very short bill, dark above, light below; feet brown.
Song: "'Che, 'chet, de-de-de-de-de!"
Season: Early May to late September.
Breeds: In all but most southerly parts of its range.
Nest: Among the grasses of marshy meadows; it is made of grass and always softly lined; closed over the top, with the entrance at one side. It may be either suspended between rushes, or be placed on the ground in a tussock, away from the water.
Eggs: 6–9, pure white.
Range: Eastern United States and southern British Provinces, west to the Plains. Winters in the Gulf States and southward.

The Short-billed Marsh Wren is a bird of moist meadows and reedy places. As a summer visitor it is erratic and irregular, being locally fairly plentiful during one season, and the next rare, but abundant in some adjoining place. It is very adroit in eluding the curious, by disappearing in the long grass, and not emerging until it is a long distance away, very much as many of the Ducks escape notice by diving, and swimming under water.

This bird, as well as the next species, has a peculiar habit of building several nests every season. Samuels relates that these are built, it is believed, to secure protection for the female; so that when people search for the nest near where she is sitting, the male will lure the hunter to an empty nest. Its haunts, in this vicinity, are similar to those chosen by the Red-winged Blackbird.

Long-billed Marsh Wren: *Cistothorus palustris.*

PLATE 15. FIG. 2.

Length: About 5 inches.

Male and Female: Above clear brown. Whitish line over eye. Neck and back streaked sparingly with white. Wings and tail brown, the latter barred. Below, white, washed with pale brown. Bill nearly as long as head. Dark above; lower mandible light. Feet brown.

Song: Suggestive of the House Wren, but less agreeable, and at times quite harsh.

Season: Summer resident. Early May to September.

Breeds: Throughout summer range.

Nest: Along river borders. Made of sedge and grasses suspended between tall reeds, above tide level. Rather bulky, with entrance on one side.

Eggs: 6–10, chocolate-brown.

Range: Eastern United States and southern Canada. In winter from the Gulf States south.

These Wrens have all the alert ways and nervous habits of the family. They inhabit marshy and reedy river wastes, and often build their torch-shaped nests in little colonies. They are abundant summer residents all along the Housatonic River, from Stratford upward, following the course of tide rivers in preference to smaller streams. It is not an easy nest to find, even if you know where to look, and you should either go upon your search at high tide in a duck boat, or else at very low water, wearing seven-league boots. I could relate an amusing tale of an ardent female wearing rubber boots on the bird-quest, who, approaching the reeds from the land side, on seeing one of the coveted nests a little beyond, lost her head completely, and, forgetting in her enthusiasm to pick her way from hummock to hummock, straightway found herself in two feet of hidden water, and, when she finally extricated herself, the boots were left behind as a tribute to the tenacity of the mud, and their own generous size.

FAMILY MOTACILLIDÆ: WAGTAILS; PIPITS.

American Pipit, Titlark: *Anthus pensilvanicus.*

Brown Lark.

Length: 6.25-6.75 inches.

Male and Female: Above dark olive-brown. Tail and wings brown-black, the tail shorter than the wings, several outer tail feathers partly or wholly white. White eye ring and line over eye. Underneath whitish with washes of various shades of brown. Bill dark; feet brown.

Song: A hesitating querulous note.

Season: Abundant on salt marshes in migrations, April, May, October, and November.

Breeds: Only in high latitudes, sub-Arctic regions, and in Rocky Mountains, etc.

Nest: Close to ground, of grass, moss, or lichens.

Eggs: 4-6, chocolate-colour, marked and scratched with black.

Range: North America at large, wintering in the Gulf States, Mexico, and Central America. Accidental in Europe.

The Titlark may be recognized by its very uncertain, wavering flight, seldom remaining long in one spot, but moving on and hovering and wheeling about the place where it intends next to alight. I have seen them frequently in the fields, on late October mornings when everything was white with hoar frost and they were gleaning a breakfast, uttering their thin notes and scattering irregularly, only to gather immediately on some convenient fence-rail, or telegraph wire. They also flock in the autumn ploughed fields, searching out the newly uncovered grubs and larvæ. When on the ground they resemble the Water Thrushes and they are continually jerking their tails about, a habit which has given them, together with these Thrushes, the title of *Wagtails.*

FAMILY MNIOTILTIDÆ: WOOD WARBLERS.

Black and White Warbler: *Mniotilta varia.*

PLATE 16. FIG. 1.

Length: About 5 inches.

Male and Female: Above striped black and white. White stripe on top of head, bordered by black stripe. White stripe over eye. Black cheeks and throat, separated by a black line. Breast white in middle, black stripe on sides. Wings and tail black; wings with two white cross-bars and some white edgings, tail with white markings on outer quills. Bill and feet black. Female paler stripings, less distinct. *Strong resemblance to the Downy Woodpecker.*

Song: Feeble and lisping, "Weachy, weachy, weachy, 'twee—'twee, 'twee 'tweet."

Season: April to late September.

Breeds: From Virginia and southern Kansas northward.

Nest: Low down, either on a stump or the ground, composed of bark, grass, leaves, hair. Very difficult to find.

Eggs: 4-5, white, dotted thickly with red and brown.

Range: Eastern United States to the Plains, north to Fort Simpson, south, in winter, to Central America and the West Indies.

The Black and White Warbler is one of the most familiar and sociable of the Warblers. At first you will doubtless think it a small Woodpecker, as it is seen principally scrambling around tree trunks searching for the insect food upon which it, together with the entire family of Warblers, subsists.

During the past four years this Warbler has not varied a week in the dates of his first and last appearance in the garden. He has come to a certain gnarled old apple tree, his favourite resort, twice on May 2, once May 1, and once April 29, and has invariably been last seen, in the same locality, between September 25 and October 2.

1. BLACK AND WHITE WARBLER.

Length, 5 inches.

2. MYRTLE WARBLER.

Length, 5.50 inches.

The Creeper, when at rest, is not at all graceful, but it is most interesting to watch its zig-zag course from the tree trunk out to the angles of the crooked branches, picking up insects which are invisible to us, with its slender, sharp bill. In watching the manœuvres of all bark-feeding birds, you must keep in mind that the eyes of birds are powerful magnifiers, and that to them objects appear twenty-five times as large as they do to us.

Worm-eating Warbler: *Helmitherus vermivorus.*

Length: 5.50 inches.

Male and Female: Head yellowish brown, black stripe on each side of crown, also back of eye. Above greenish olive. Under parts buffy. Bill and feet light.

Song: Similar to that of Chipping Sparrow, — "trrrr-rrr-rrr," — from which Mr. Ridgway says that "it is difficult sometimes for the most critical listener to distinguish it."

Season: Rare summer resident in southern New England.

Breeds: In all parts of its United States range, but casually in the northerly sections.

Nest: On the ground in woods, and in swamp tussocks, or in a ground hollow like the Ovenbirds, and composed chiefly of leaves.

Eggs: 4–5, clear white, specked with reddish brown.

Range: Eastern United States, north to southern New York and southern New England, west to eastern Nebraska and Texas, south, in winter, to Cuba and Central America.

This compact, soberly clad Warbler is not at all common north of New Jersey, and, even where it is plentiful, it is very likely to escape notice; for its colouring is such as to make it blend with the ground upon which it nests, or with the branches and trunks of trees where it frequently creeps and circles in feeding, after the manner of the Brown Creeper. Its nest seems also to be well concealed, and generally in remote places, for the descriptions of it are infrequent.

Blue-winged Warbler: *Helminthophila pinus.*

Length: 4.75 inches.

Male: Above olive-green. Wings a slatish blue with white bars; tail plain slate. *Forehead and under parts clear yellow*, dark stripe through eye. Bill bluish black.

Female: Paler throughout, with a general olive cast.

Song: Sharp and metallic, drawling and continuous.

Season: May to September. A common summer resident.

Breeds: Throughout range.

Nest: On or near the ground; sometimes in the centre of a plant tuft. Made of grass, etc., and rather deep and bulky.

Eggs: 4–5, white, with reddish dots.

Range: Eastern United States, from southern New York and southern New England southward; in winter Mexico and Guatemala.

The name of this bird is misleading to the novice, as the blue of the wing is dull and inconspicuous, and not *blue* at all in the sense in which this colour distinction is applied to the Bluebird and Jay. It is well to remember the fact that only two or three of our New England birds are "true blue," and that the term, when applied to the Warblers especially, simply means either a bluish gray, or slate, which seems barely different from plain gray at a short distance.

These Warblers are not a bird of gardens and open places, preferring well-brushed woods, but come frequently into the orchard in the blossoming time, and search the trees carefully for insects, as they feed almost wholly upon spiders, larvæ, and beetles, such as are found in bark, bud, or flower. They are very beautiful birds, with brilliant plumage, and dainty little tricks and manners, and are usually seen consorting in pairs.

Golden-winged Warbler: *Helminthophila chrysoptera.*

Length: About 5 inches.

Male: *Yellow crown and wing bars.* Above bluish gray. Chin, throat, and eye stripe black. Throat divided from sides of head by white line. Below ashy white, tinged with yellowish. Bill and feet blackish.

Female: Olive above. Below dusky, eye stripe gray.
Song: An insect-like sound, "zee-zee-zee!"
Season: May and September.
Breeds: North from northern New Jersey and northern Indiana, and southward along the Alleghanies to South Carolina.
Eggs and Nest: Same as last species.
Range: Eastern United States, north to southern New England, southwestern Ohio, and southern Minnesota.

The Golden-winged Warbler seems to be considered rare, or only locally common, in many parts of its range. It comes about the orchard sparingly in May, but has a habit of retiring very suddenly into dense underbrush, which renders its identification difficult. Its name also is very delusive; for, if you go out to search for a gorgeous bird with canary-yellow wings, you will never suspect this bird, with small golden splashes on the *wing coverts only*, of being the Golden-winged Warbler.

All Warblers depend upon their markings rather than song for their identity, which renders the majority of the tribe of greater interest to the scientist than to the novice.

In fact, until you have named four or five of the commonest species as landmarks, you will be considerably confused, and feel oftentimes inclined to scold the brilliant beauties, and tell them that they are bores, like gaily dressed people who have no conversational ability; and also that fine feathers do not make fine voices, but quite the reverse. Then some gloomy recess in the pines will be lighted by the flitting birds, like sun motes filtering through the branches, and all is forgiven, and you will say, "I *know*, at least, that these are *Warblers*," which, after all, is something.

Nashville Warbler: *Helminthophila ruficapilla.*

Length: About 5 inches.
Male and Female: No bars on wings or tail. Clear yellow below. which remains constant all the season. Above olive-green, brightening on the rump and shoulders. Slate-gray head and neck, obscure chestnut spot on poll; wings and tail brownish. Bill and feet dark. Female dull olive.

Song: Feeble — "Que-ar-Que-ar-Que-ar," a note which Audubon says sounds like the breaking of twigs.

Season: Summer resident, perhaps, from late April to September and October, but only plentiful as a migrant.

Breeds: From New England northward.

Nest: On the ground, sometimes in mossy banks. Nest made of fibres, pine-needles, etc., with a lining of the softer grasses and hair.

Eggs: 4, blush white (if fresh), thickly speckled.

Range: Eastern North America to the Plains, north to the Fur Countries. Mexico in winter.

This brilliant Warbler is a common summer resident from Massachusetts northward, but I think irregularly so in this part of Connecticut. It visits us freely, however, in May or sometimes the last week in April, and usually appears in greater numbers on its return trip in the fall. They are shy birds, prying about the borders of woodlands, and here, in the fall migration, they haunt a belt of wild hemlocks that border the rocky banks of a stream; Dr. Warren says that in the southward migration in Pennsylvania, they are seen in small parties feeding among the willows along the banks of streams and ponds.

The name "Nashville" was applied to this Warbler by Wilson, who discovered it near Nashville, Tenn., but it is another case of a poor name for a beautiful bird, and, like so many other titles, unsatisfactory in the extreme. The accepted English name of a bird should embody some of its personal attributes, as the Latin title frequently does; *ruficapilla*, from *rufus*, red, and *capilla*, hair, signifies that the bird has red markings on his head. Why is Nashville given as an English equivalent? The American Ornithologists' Union has a magnificent chance to show its inventive ability in such cases, and then, perhaps, the Wood Warblers, as a family, may be better known by the masses.

Parula Warbler: *Compsothlypis americana.*

Blue Yellow-backed Warbler.

Length: 4.50 inches.

Male and Female: Above slate-blue, triangular spot of greenish yellow back of shoulders. *Chin and throat yellow.* Wings brownish with two white bars; two white spots on tail. Belly white, reddish brown band across breast. Markings of under-parts variable. Bill black above and flesh-coloured below. Feet light. In spring the female closely resembles the male, but lacks the brown wash on breast.

Song: Shrill wiry — "Chirr-rirr-irr-reeh." (Nehrling.)

Season: April to October.

Breeds: Eastern United States and northward.

Nest: In swamps where the *usnea* moss is plentiful, or, at least, never far from water. Nest a delicate structure of filmy moss, suspended from a slender branch.

Eggs: 4–5, with reddish spots.

Range: Eastern United States, west to the Plains, north to Canada, and south in winter to the West Indies and Central America.

In early May, before the apple trees are in bloom, if you look up among their branches you will see this airy little bird flitting in and out, pausing every moment, head down in Titmouse fashion, then raising its head again to utter its chirping song, and, lifting its wings, seems half to fly, half to be blown from branch to branch.

This is the bird that awakened Burroughs, when a boy, to the unfamiliar birds that lodge in very familiar woods. He writes, under title of "The Invitation," in "Wake Robin": "Years ago, when quite a youth, I was rambling in the woods one Sunday with my brothers, gathering black birch, wintergreens, etc., when, as we reclined upon the ground, gazing vaguely up into the trees, I caught sight of a bird that paused a moment on a branch above me, the like of which I had never before seen or heard of. . . . How the thought of it clung to me afterward! It was a revelation. It was the first intimation I had had that the woods we knew so well, held birds that we knew not at all."

So it is with each one of us. Some day a bird absolutely new and unknown flies through the orchard or sings above the familiar footpath through the woods, which, though it is meant to be a "short cut" to somewhere, is often rendered a loitering-ground by the magic of these very bird voices that speak so directly to us.

A special gift of sight is needed to search out these tree-flitting Warblers, but in this case the nest of the Parula will tell you of its whereabouts if you are so lucky as to find it. No other bird of our fauna builds a structure akin to its swinging, eery, moss nest, and the day you find it must be noted with red ink in your journal. (See Building of the Nest, p. 20.)

Yellow Warbler: *Dendroica æstiva.*

Summer Yellowbird.

PLATE 10. FIG. 1.

Length: 4.75–5 inches.

Male and Female: Above rich olive-yellow, brightening on the rump; breast and under parts golden-yellow. Breast streaked with cinnamon-brown. Wings and tail olive-brown edged with yellow. Bill lead-coloured; feet light brown. Female darker with streaks on breast faintly marked or absent.

Song: Rapid warble, "Sweet-sweet-sweet-sweet-sweet-sweeter-sweeter?" Seven times repeated.

Season: First week in May to middle September.

Breeds: In all parts of its North American range.

Nest: In the crotch of some terminal branch of a fruit tree, or stout shrub, made of the frayings of milkweed stalks lined with fern wool and hair.

Eggs: 4–5, greenish or grayish white, spotted and blotched with lilac tints and red-browns.

Range: North America at large, except southwestern part, south in winter to Central America and northern South America.

In early May, often on May-day itself, if the weather is clement, when the marsh-marigolds are vanishing from the swamps, and the cherry trees are in bloom, the Yellow Warblers descend upon the gardens and orchards.

They come like whirling leaves, half autumn yellow, half

green of spring, the colours blending as in the outer petals of grass-grown daffodils. Lovable, cheerful little spirits, darting about the trees, exclaiming at each morsel that they glean. Carrying sun glints on their backs wherever they go, they should make the gloomiest misanthrope feel the season's charm. They are so sociable and confiding, feeling as much at home in the trees by the house as in seclusion.

This bird is one of the particular victims which the Cowbird (see page 167) selects to foster its random eggs, but the Warbler puts its intelligence effectively to work, and builds a floor over the unwelcome egg, and repeating the expedient, if the Cowbird continues her mischief, until sometimes a three-story nest is achieved. In spite of the Warbler's seeming preference for man's society, it builds also in lonely fields and byways. The most beautiful nest that I have found, and which is now before me, was set in the crotch of an old elder bush, about six feet from the ground, by the side of the marsh lane. The outside is composed of glistening milkweed flax, which forms a felt-like case, and likewise lashes the nest to its support. The interior, to the depth of an inch, is made of the wool from the stems of young ferns, matted into a material resembling soft sponge; and inside this, to give shape and stability, are woven a few horsehairs. The Yellow Warbler sings from its arrival until July, but has no second song period.

Black-throated Blue Warbler: *Dendroica cœrulescens.*

Length: About 5 inches.

Male: Above bluish slaty, rather than blue; lighter on forehead. Black throat, extending along sides of body. White spot on wings; outer tail feathers, white spotted. Beneath white. Bill and feet dark.

Female: Entirely different. Greenish olive above, light yellow underneath, wing spots smaller.

Song: A plaintive strain, not particularly noticeable. Call note, "Z-ip, z-ip."

Season: Early May to September in northern New England. Here as a migrant in May and October.

Breeds: From northern New England and New York northward.
Nest: Close to the ground in bushes.
Eggs: Typical Warbler's eggs.
Range: Eastern North America to the Plains. West Indies in winter.

Again we find the term *blue* used in reference to a Warbler which is of an inconspicuous, dull slate colour. This Warbler is likely to be one of the most difficult of its tribe to identify, as its plumage, being wholly devoid of yellow, is not easily seen among the trees.

All authorities agree that its favourite nesting-haunts are near swampy ground and in laurel thickets, especially in those parts of Connecticut where it breeds. Mr. Averill notes the bird as a "tolerably common migrant," but I can find no breeding-record for it in this vicinity. Still, I think that they sometimes breed here, for I saw a pair on May 30, in the laurel glen near Aspetuck, who were evidently collecting building-materials; for the male bird had the dry tendrils of a small vine in his beak.

Myrtle Warbler: *Dendroica coronata.*

Yellow-rumped Warbler.

Plate 16. Fig. 2.

Length: 5.50 inches.
Male: Slate colour, striped and streaked with black. *Crown, sides of breast, and rump yellow.* Below whitish; upper breast black. Two white cross-bars on wings; tail with white spots. *In winter*, brownish olive; yellow of rump constant, but lacking on crown and breast. Bill and feet black.
Female: Resembling the *winter* male.
Song: A few notes only — "Twhip-twéeter-twéeter."
Season: Most plentiful Warbler in the migrations, and also a *winter resident.*
Breeds: From the northern United States northward.
Nest: In low shrubs, particularly evergreens.
Eggs: 4–6, the usual Warbler variety.
Range: Eastern North America chiefly, straggling, more or less commonly, westward to the Pacific; winters from the Middle States and the Ohio Valley, southward to the West Indies and Central America.

In the spring and fall migrations, and particularly in the spring, this is one of the most conspicuous of the smaller migrant birds. In autumn it grows more sociable, and in winter it comes freely about the barn and sheds in search of food, often in the company of Juncos, Tree Sparrows, and Titmice, individuals of this species, wintering as far north as Massachusetts; a few, according to Dr. Allen, remaining at Cape Cod.

In winter it forsakes its usual insect diet for such berries as it can find. Dr. Warren says that in Pennsylvania the berries of the poison-sumach (*Rhus venenàta*) are a favourite article of its food, during the early winter, and these Warblers congregate in considerable numbers where the bush is abundant.

Speaking of the baleful poison-sumach, with its scattering clusters of whitish berries, it is well for the amateur ornithologist to be on the watch for it, as its poison is so insidious that it affects many people through substantial clothing. It may be easily distinguished by the fact that the flower clusters come from the leaf axils, and the berries are whitish and semi-translucent, while the harmless species of sumach bear their flowers in terminal spires, which turn to sticky, opaque berries of a rich, brilliant red. Hamilton Gibson's clever jingle will prove a talisman, against either poison-sumach, or the commoner poison-ivy (*Rhus toxicodendron*) to those who will memorize it: —

"Berries red,
Have no dread!
Berries white,
Poisonous sight!
Leaves three
Quickly flee!"

Magnolia Warbler: *Dendroica maculosa.*

Black-and-Yellow Warbler.

Length: 4.75–5 inches.

Male and Female: Above, back dark olive, crown a bluish ash, bordered by white lines, and these framed in black, extending across forehead and sides of head. Wings dark, bars white, and small spots of white on tail. *Rump and under parts rich yellow*, the latter streaked with black across the breast and along the sides. Bill and feet dark.

Song: Not particularly distinguishable.

Season: Migrant, common the middle of May.

Breeds: Breeding from northern New England, New York, and Michigan, to Hudson's Bay Territory.

Nest and eggs: Warbler type.

Range: Eastern North America to the base of the Rocky Mountains; in winter, Bahamas, Cuba, and Central America.

The Magnolia Warbler is one of the most gaily dressed of all his dainty family, and is quite easily identified by his distinct markings. It is only a migrant here, lodging with us a while in May, and passing through in autumn. But be sure to look for it in *May*, for in October it wears the duller travelling cloak with which Nature protects so many of her feathered children in their journey through the leafless trees.

Chestnut-sided Warbler: *Dendroica pensylvanica.*

Length: About 5 inches.

Male and Female: Top of head yellow. Black stripe running through the eye, and a black spot in front of it. Back and wing coverts streaked black and yellow. Throat and breast white, with *chestnut stripe* starting at the black mustache and extending down the sides. Belly black; feet brown. Female less highly coloured.

Song: "'Che-'che-'ch-'chéea."

Season: First week in May to September. Also very plentiful in migrations.

Breeds: From central Illinois, and probably northern Georgia northward.

Nest: In bushes and low trees; when in the latter a forking branch is chosen. Nest on general plan of the Yellow Warbler's, but coarser and less woolly.

Eggs: Some simply speckled; others prettily chained with chestnut.

Range: Eastern United States and southern Canada; west to the Plains. Visits the Bahamas and Central America in winter.

A most abundant and sociable bird in the spring migration, the Chestnut-sided Warbler becomes shy and retiring in the breeding-season, and in the fall journey keeps well in the protection of the trees.

During the second week of May, 1892, after a storm which had lasted three days, a perfect swarm of Warblers appeared in the garden, among the evergreens and on the walks, and, after arranging their wind-beaten plumage, dispersed to satisfy appetites that seemed to have been tried by a long fast. Upon going to the door about seven o'clock in the morning, I was greatly surprised to see a dozen or more of the Chestnut-sided Warblers, chiefly males, feeding eagerly upon some minute insects that they picked from the gravel, while among them were several Redstarts, moving backward and forward with the airy motion which is peculiarly theirs, and which seems as if they were propelled by a puff of wind rather than their own volition. The Warblers were so fearless, owing to their hunger, that they only moved a few yards away when I went out to see what they were eating. Upon scanning the gravel on the path, I found that it was literally plastered together by myriads of dead ants, which had been drowned out of their hills at the roots of some large trees, and washed down. The same condition obtained in other parts of the garden, and these ants, together with the abundant earth-worms and various seeds in the lawn and many low-flying insects, brought together such a carnival of migrants as I had never before seen outside of the cases of a museum, — Thrushes, Warblers, Flycatchers, and Finches of all descriptions, that seemed to have been swept into the garden shelter by the fury of the storm.

Bay-breasted Warbler: *Dendroica castanea.*

Length: 5.25–5.75 inches.

Male: Above streaked with black and grayish olive. Forehead, cheeks, and sides of head black, enclosing a chestnut patch. *Chin, throat, upper breast, and a streak along the sides dull chestnut.* Below buffy. White cross-bars on wings and white spots on tail. Bill and feet dark. Female with crown olive-green and chestnut striped with black.

Song: Not marked, insect like.

Season: A rare migrant here. Seen in May, and less frequently on the return trip.

Breeds: From northern New England and northern Michigan northward.

Nest: Large and rough, for so small a bird, made of tree moss and twigs, and fur-lined.

Eggs: Blue-green and spotted.

Range: Eastern North America, north to Hudson's Bay; winters in Central America.

This Warbler is an irregular migrant in the greater part of its range; sometimes it will not be seen at all in a locality where in previous seasons it was fairly constant. The chestnut colouring of the breast is the distinctive mark by which it may be recognized, and this dull red breast renders it conspicuous and more likely to be discovered than many plainer, though more common species. In full spring plumage the male looks, at a little distance, like a well-fed Robin in miniature.

The Bay-breasts seem, according to many authorities, to be very freaky and capricious as to the course of their migrations, and it is said they return to the South by a different route from that by which they travelled up in spring, no two people being able to agree with certainty as to the locations where they may be found. Dr. Allen, in his "List of Massachusetts Birds," says that they are common in both migrations, varying in abundance; while Mr. Minot says that as a rule these birds are rare in spring in eastern Massachusetts and are *never* seen in autumn, — the consensus of opinion being that in some seasons the birds take a westerly course in spring and an easterly in autumn, or *vice versa.* All of which goes to prove that you may have considered this Warbler an unknown bird in your locality, and some May morning in looking out your window you will find a little party of them almost peering in at you.

Black-poll Warbler: *Dendroica striata.*

Length: About 5.50 inches.

Male: Black cap, grayish white cheeks, general upper parts striped gray, black, and olive. Breast white, with black streaks. White spots on outer tail feathers; upper mandible brownish black, lower yellowish; feet flesh-coloured.

Female: Crown and back, olive-green, faintly streaked with black. Paler than male all through.

Song: Call note, "Screep,-screep." Torrey says that, short as the song is, it contains a perfect crescendo and a perfect decrescendo.

Season: Late May and late October. One of the latest arrivals among the migrants.

Breeds: From northern New England northward.

Nest: In evergreens. Nest large for the size of the bird, as Mr. Brewster notes several nests 5 inches across and 8 inches deep. They are made of terminal shoots of conifers, lichens, rootlets, and sedges, lined with grass panicles.

Eggs: Not especially marked.

Range: Eastern North America to the Rocky Mountains, north to Greenland, the barren grounds, and Alaska. South in winter to northern South America.

The jolly Black-poll has all the vivacity and activity of a Flycatcher, and, in fact, Dr. Coues gives it credit for many of the Flycatcher's attributes, and says that it catches insects on the wing with the same ease as the Wood Pewee.

Some authorities say that the Black-poll climbs and walks about the trees in the manner of the Black and White Warbler. I do not think that it does this; for I watched a number of them at short range last spring, and while the birds *seemed* to *creep*, they really *flew* about by means of a short and rapid flip of the wings.

Their call notes, which were the only ones I heard, were very weak and scarcely distinguishable from other wood sounds, and I have often mistaken them for the creaking of a branch. Audubon says: " . . . its notes have no title to be called a song. They are shrill, and resemble the noise made by striking two small pebbles together more than any other sound I know."

Blackburnian Warbler: ***Dendroica blackburniæ.***

Torch Bird.

Length: 5.50 inches.

Male: Black head, *striped with flame*, black wings and tail with white markings, black streak on throat. *Throat and breast flame-colour*. Lower parts yellowish. Bill and feet dark.

Female: Olive-brown above, entire breast yellow.

Song: A thin warble, with little variety, ending with a high Z—.

Season: A migrant here; seen occasionally through May, but is less uncommon in September.

Breeds: From the northern and more elevated parts of the eastern United States northward. Dr. Merriam says that a few breed in Connecticut, and Dr. Allen notes them as casual residents in Massachusetts.

Nest: Well concealed by bark and moss; built in small trees and bushes, preferably evergreens.

Eggs: 4–6, white, with lilac and chestnut shell markings, chiefly on the larger end.

Range: Eastern North America to the Plains; in winter south to the Bahamas, Central America, and northern South America.

Another Warbler, with a totally inadequate name. It should be called the Torch Bird, for half a dozen of them, as they flash about in the pines, raising their wings and jerking their tails, make the darkest shadows seem breaking into little tongues of flame. Look for them in the autumn, and you will find that even then their colours will vie with the most brilliant leaf tints. But because some one named Blackburn first discovered or reported the Warbler, it bears the name Blackburnian. Burroughs says: "The *burn* seems appropriate enough," . . . but ". . . the Orange-crowned Warbler would seem to be his right name, his characteristic cognomen."

Black-throated Green Warbler: ***Dendroica virens.***

Length: 5 inches.

Male: *Back and crown bright olive-yellow, sides and front of head clear yellow.* Entire throat and upper breast black, black continued in a stripe down the sides. Lower parts yellowish white. Wings and tail brownish, white wing bars. Bill and feet dark.

Female: Chin yellowish, throat dusky, below pale whitish. In autumn plumage the male resembles the female.

Song: Cheerful interrogative, "Will you co-ome, will you co-ome, will you?"

Season: A summer resident, also abundant in the migrations. Comes in April, retires to woods to breed in May, emerges in September.

Breeds: From New England, New York, and the higher parts of Pennsylvania northward.

Nest: At the forking of high branches; made of twigs, bark, grasses, and lined with hair, roots, down, etc.

Eggs: 4–5, white, sprinkled and veiled with brown-purple.

Range: Eastern North America to the Plains, north to Hudson's Bay Territory; in winter, south to Cuba and Panama. Accidental in Greenland and Europe.

You will have but little trouble in recognizing this brilliant and talkative little Warbler, which comes to us both as a summer resident and as a migrant. In late April I am always sure to see its green and gold feathers among the hemlocks on the east side of the garden, while it continually utters its anxious and persuasive notes, to which I eagerly respond. It repeats a little phrase that separates it from the indistinct songs of so many of its tribe: "Will you co-ome, will you co-ome, will you?" it says, giving a particularly emphatic pause on the last two syllables.

It has never nested in the garden, and only comes to it before the breeding and after the moulting season.

Pine Warbler: *Dendroica vigorsii.*

Length: 5.50–6 inches.

Male: Above bright yellowish olive, clear yellow below, dark streaks on sides. Yellow eye line; white bars on wings. White blotches on two outer tail feathers.

Female: Dull throughout, dirty white instead of yellow breast.

Song: A delicately trilled whistle. (Minot.)

Season: A locally common summer resident, May to October and November. Possibly a resident. Some remain in the Middle States all winter.

Breeds: All through its range, beginning in the Carolinas in March.

Nest and Eggs: No special marks of identification.

Range: Eastern United States to the Plains, north to Ontario and New Brunswick, wintering in the South Atlantic and Gulf States, and the Bahamas.

The Pine Warbler, the largest of the tribe, shares with the Myrtle and Palm Warblers the distinction of being one of the three hardiest of the tribe. Like so many of the family, they are most frequently seen in hemlock and pine woods, and also in parks and gardens where these conifers have been planted freely. This Warbler has none of the delicacy of shape or beauty of colouring belonging to his kin. Even the male in full plumage shows few dainty variations and blendings of colour, and it has a heaviness of build that is more Finch-like.

The best way to designate its song is to say that it has some of the qualities of a Sparrow's; remembering to keep in mind (as with all Warblers) that the notes are never clear and pure as in the case of Sparrows and Thrushes, but are half whispered, as if to save the strain on the vocal chords. This Warbler combines some of the traits of a Creeper and Flycatcher. It often circles about the tree trunks like the Nuthatch or Brown Creeper, sails into the air after insects, and then descends to the ground, all in the space of a few minutes.

Yellow Palm Warbler: *Dendroica palmarum hypochrysea.*

Length: 6 inches.

Male and Female: Chestnut crown, brownish, verging on olive above, with some dark streaks; rump and wing coverts yellowish. *Under parts clear yellow, with bright chestnut streaks on the sides.* Wings and tail dull, dark brown. Bill and feet dark. Female not essentially different.

Song: Unknown to me. It gives a few whispering notes as it feeds.

Season: A migrant, middle of April and October.

Breeds: Northward from Nova Scotia and New Brunswick.

Nest: On the ground, and very deep; made of weeds, grasses, and lined with moss, fine grasses, and hair.

Eggs: 2–4, rosy white, marked with brown spots at the large end.

Range: Atlantic States north to Hudson's Bay; winters in the South Atlantic and Gulf States.

This Warbler — only distinguishable by slightly superior size and a more evenly yellow breast from the Yellow Redpoll of the Interior and Western States — is a lover of cool, brisk weather, and is almost the first of its tribe to pass upward to its northern breeding-grounds. It spends a few early April days in the leafless roadside bushes, often appearing when the first hepaticas are in bloom, and leaving before the shadbush blossoms, and, though it feeds on the ground, it has the habit of making little sallies into the air like the Redstart and the Flycatchers.

It does not return in autumn until warm weather is a thing of the past, and is not at all abashed if a hard frost, or even a flurry of snow, overtakes it, seeming to partake of the nature of the Yellow-rumped Warbler, who is the winter companion of Chickadees and Kinglets.

Prairie Warbler: *Dendroica discolor.*

Length: 4.75–5 inches.

Male and Female: Colours much broken up. Upper parts olive-green or yellow, *chestnut-red streaks across back between the wings. Under parts beautiful yellow;* also yellow streak running from nostril back of eye, and two yellow wing bands. Sides of neck and body streaked with black; also black line through eye. Inner webs of outer tail feathers white. Female paler, and chestnut bars obscured.

Song: "Wee-wee-chee-chee-chee-chee!"

Season: Common May migrant; also probably breeds here.

Breeds: Through its United States range.

Nest: In small trees or low brush, scrub pines, etc. Cedar and grape-vine bark, feathers and fern down, elaborate and beautiful.

Eggs: 4, greenish white, wreathed on larger end with various browns.

Range: Eastern United States to the Plains, north to Michigan and southern New England; winters in southern Florida and the West Indies.

The diminutive Prairie Warbler, which may be known by the reddish streaks across its back, has a decidedly southerly range. It is quite abundant all through the Middle and Southern States, and fairly common along the Massachusetts seaboard — Massachusetts seems to be its usual northern breeding-limit, though Mr. Minot found a nest in northern New Hampshire.

Dr. Coues says that it is remarkable for its quaint and curious song. I have never heard its best musical efforts, for its notes seem to me harsh, like the familiar call of the Ovenbird.

Ovenbird; Golden-crowned Thrush: *Seiurus aurocapillus.*

PLATE 17. FIG. 1.

Length: 5.75–6.50 inches.

Male and Female: Olive-green above, white eye ring, two brown stripes on head, enclosing an orange crown. White below, with brownish spots in the centre of breast running into streaks on the sides. Brown bill, legs and feet flesh-coloured.

Song: Call note, "Teacher-teacher-teacher!" given in gradual crescendo. The love-song liquid like that of the Water Thrush, but seldom heard.

Season: May to October.

Breeds: Northward from Kansas, the Ohio Valley, and Virginia.

Nest: A ball of leaves and grasses on the ground with a side opening, hence the name Ovenbird, though the nest bears a closer resemblance to the earth huts the Italian labourers build.

Eggs: 4, cream-white, specked with brown-purple.

Range: Eastern North America, north to Hudson's Bay Territory and Alaska; in winter southern Florida, the West Indies, and Central America.

With the Ground Warblers we come again to birds with musical voices, who, even if they do wear more sober plumage, are a welcome change from the lisping prettiness of the previous groups.

If you wish to identify the Ovenbird, or Golden-crowned Thrush, as he is still called, you must trust to sound rather than sight, for you will hear far oftener than see him. On his arrival in the early part of May, he comes familiarly about the garden, sometimes in company with the Veery, and spends a week, perhaps, among the shrubs and evergreens, running out on the ground occasionally, with an alert air, as if looking for his mate.

PLATE 17.

1. OVENBIRD.

Length, 5.75–6.50 inches.

2. RED-EYED VIREO.

Length, 5.75–6.25 inches.

At this time the bird appears like a small, slender Thrush, with a little golden-brown streak on the crown. Suddenly from the pines comes the half-defiant call, "*Teacher*, TEACHER, TEACHER!" each syllable accented, and rattled off with increasing volume, and you are quite incredulous that so small a bird can utter such a sound. The notes are familiar to you; you have heard them a hundred times breaking the intense noon stillness of the woods, but you had supposed that they proceeded at least from a large Woodpecker; but no, it is the Ovenbird; and this call has given him a third name, — the Accentor. By the tenth of May they leave the garden and seek the lighter woods where, having paired, they go into deeper shade to build their homes.

Hickory, oak, and beech woods, with fern-grown banks sloping to a stream, are their favourite haunts, and on these banks, where the ground is covered with leaves in various stages of decay, they build their hut-like nests. While thus occupied, the males give, at rare intervals, an exquisite little serenade to their mates, which is wholly different from the shrill call notes. It is most likely to be heard when the bird is on the wing in the early evening, and somewhat resembles the music of the Louisiana Water-thrush. Many people who are familiar with its nest and haunts have never heard this love-song. The nest is extremely difficult to locate; settled as it is into a ground hollow and roofed over, it may be easily passed by as a bunch of huddled leaves. Sometimes you may see a bird alight on the ground and run nimbly toward such a tuft, and that will be the best method of finding the nest, which, though it is cleverly hidden, often holds the unwelcome eggs of the Cowbird. All the singing and calling is done from the trees; and, as you look up in the uncertain wood-light, the singers appear to be only dusky specks, like the few last year's leaves that still lodge there. But when the rare music is heard, the little brown mote is transfigured, and soars above the trees.

Water Thrush: *Seiurus noveboracensis.*

Water-wagtail.

Length: 5-6 inches.

Male and Female: Above, including wings and tail, plain olive-brown. Under parts sulphur-yellow, specked everywhere, except a space in the middle of belly, with dark brown. Spots small on throat, and growing larger below. Bill and feet dark.

Song: Liquid and Thrush-like.

Season: Early May, late August, and September.

Breeds: From northern New England northward.

Nest: In inaccessible swampy places, especially sphagnum bogs, upon the ground, or between old stumps; bulky; made of moss, roots, and grass.

Eggs: 4-6, white and thickly speckled.

Range: Eastern United States to Illinois, and northward to Arctic America; south in winter to the West Indies and northern South America.

The Water Thrush usually appears at the same time as the Ovenbird, but never ventures with it into the garden. He is a water-loving recluse, who seems to have learned his song from the brooks that tinkle and dance over the little pebbles, and is never content away from the voice of his teachers.

If you catch a glimpse of him, away he goes, running through the leaves and tangled underbrush, wagging or jerking his tail in a very knowing way, and few land-birds will lead you such an uncertain dance through bog and briars as he will, if you have the pluck to follow him.

Louisiana Water Thrush: *Seiurus motacilla.*

Length: 6-6.25 inches.

Male and Female. Peculiarly heavy, dark bill. Above grayish brown, with a brown crown and white line over the eye. Creamy white breast, sparingly streaked with brown. Legs lightish.

Song: A thrilling warble, interspersed with flute and water notes.

Season: Summer resident, arriving the last of April.

Breeds: Through its United States range.

Nest and Eggs: Like the last species, but often sunken in the ground.

Range: Eastern United States, north to southern New England and Michigan, casually to Lake George, west to the Plains; in winter, West Indies, southern Mexico, and Central America.

This Thrush, which, until comparatively lately, has been considered out of its range in New England, is a fairly common summer resident all through this section and as far north in the state as Saybrook. It differs chiefly from the Water Thrush in its superior size and heavier bill and the buff colouring of its lower parts; but its principal point of identification at long range is the greater richness and melody of its song.

The past summer, in late June, a male of this species spent an entire morning in a secluded part of the garden, in some bushes near the pool. It was after the breeding-season (unless this individual was either belated or about to raise a second brood), but the song retained all of its spring volubility. The song first attracted me, and, after crawling cautiously through the tall grass, I discovered the singer.

He was perching near by, in the lower branches of a scrubby arbor-vitæ. He did not sing continuously, but, after waiting a few minutes, took up his refrain. Drooping his wings, he threw back his head, his smooth throat swelling with pent-up music.

In a few minutes, he went down to the pool, took a few sips of water, and amused himself by running over the thick water-lily leaves, at the same time snatching insects from their edges. He next took a vigorous bath, sprinkling the water about with great force, and then retired into a clethra bush to plume himself. This completed, he sang once more, and he seemed to have a joyous yet serious message to impart, rather than a flood of gossip.

> In the swamp in secluded recesses
> A shy and hidden bird is warbling a song.
>
> *   *   *   *   *   *
>
> Sing on ! sing on, you gray-brown bird !
> Sing from the swamps, the recesses, pour
> Your chant from the bushes.
> O liquid and free and tender !
> O wild and loose to my soul !
> O wondrous singer !

—Walt Whitman.

Mourning Warbler: *Geothlypis philadelphia.*

Length: 5.25–5.50 inches.

Male: Decidedly marked *gray head* and *neck*, the feathers having black edges that give them a crape-like quality; the rest of upper parts yellowish olive. Throat and upper breast usually black, veiled with some ash-gray feathers. *Rich yellow lower breast and belly.* Wings and tail glossy olive-green. Upper mandible dark, lower mandible and feet flesh-coloured.

Song: "Let me see, let me see, let me see, do!"

Season: A rare migrant, — May and September.

Breeds: In the Berkshires, and from the mountainous portions of Pennsylvania, New England, New York, and Michigan northward.

Nest and Eggs: Like those of the Maryland Yellow-throat.

Range: Eastern North America to the Plains; Central America and northern South America in winter.

The Mourning Warbler is seen here only as a migrant, but its appearance is so marked that it deserves mention even when others of the same genus of equal rarity, but of less distinctive plumage, are omitted. Dr. Coues refers to it as resembling in its appearance and behaviour a gay and agreeable widow, who is conscious that her weeds are becoming. Its general habits, like its song, somewhat resemble those of the Maryland Yellow-throat, but though a Ground Warbler, nesting and spending much time in the bushes and tangles, it does its most vigorous singing in the tree-tops of woods where the underbrush has been left undisturbed.

Burroughs says: "The Ground Warblers all have one notable feature, — very beautiful legs, as white and delicate as if they had always worn silk stockings and satin slippers. High Tree Warblers have dark brown or black legs and more brilliant plumage, but less musical ability."

Maryland Yellow-throat: *Geothlypis trichas.*

PLATE 18.

Length: 5–5.50 inches.

Male: Above grayish olive on head, clearing to bright olive on rump. *Under parts, under wing and tail coverts, beautiful yellow,* grading to white in middle of belly. *Forehead and sides of*

PLATE 18.

MARYLAND YELLOW-THROAT.

1. Male. 2. Female.

Length, 5–5.50 inches.

head masked with black, separated by ash-white line from crown. Black bill; flesh-coloured feet.

Female: Smaller, and colours less distinct; *mask wanting*, as it is also in the young.

Song: "Follow me, follow me, follow me!"

Season: From May to September. Common summer resident.

Breeds: From Georgia northward.

Nest: Large and deep, sometimes partly roofed over; made of broad grasses, either on ground or in bushy tangles.

Eggs: 4–6, white, sparsely sprinkled with brown.

Range: Eastern United States, mainly east of the Alleghanies, north to Ontario and Nova Scotia; in winter, South Atlantic and Gulf States and the West Indies.

Next to the Yellow-Wood Warbler, this Ground Warbler is the best known and merriest of the entire clan, and easily identified by his mask, yellow throat, and distinctive song.

Early in May you will see a flash of yellow among the white flowers of the dogwood (*Cornus florida*), or quivering in the willows, and a bright eye peers through the black mask and a sweet, persuasive voice calls, "Follow me, follow me, follów!" If you wisely accept the invitation, you will become so well acquainted with all of his little innocent airs and graces that before the summer has passed you will recognize his plainer, maskless mate, and perhaps note the plumage development of the young.

In following this Merry Andrew across some old pasture or along a thickly shrubbed fence, you will also discover his nest. The nest that I have now before me was found not far below the garden wall, in an old meadow, where a tangle follows the watercourse, and was lodged between tall weeds and grasses at a little distance from the ground. It is of a long cup-shape, the form of the little baskets in which strawberries used to be sold, and which were called *pottles*. It is quite bulky, made of wide grass-blades and leaves, and very thick at the bottom, the nest being shallow in the interior and lined with vanilla grass. This nest is not roofed over, but shows a tendency to it by being higher and slightly curved on one side, as if the bird had intended to form a roof and then changed its mind.

Yellow-breasted Chat: *Icteria virens.*

PLATE 19. FIG. 1.

Length: 7.50 inches.

Male and Female: Olive-green above; *brilliant yellow throat, breast, and wing linings.* Whitish belly, white line over eye, and white spot beneath. Brownish glaze on wings and tail. Strong, curving, blue-black beak. Feet lead-coloured.

Song: A varied whistle, with a decided ventriloquistic quality, interspersed with mocking syllables.

Season: Common summer resident. May to September.

Breeds: All through its summer range.

Nest: Bulky, made of leaves, bark, and dead twigs, lined with grasses; placed in briary and inaccessible bushes.

Eggs: 3–4, often of unequal size, white, mottled with buff and spotted with red and lilac.

Range: Eastern United States to the Plains, north to Ontario and southern New England, south, in winter, to eastern Mexico and Guatemala.

A bird easily recognized by its large size and brilliant colour. The Chat has reversed the motto so often preached at children, and is *heard* more than *seen.* When seen, however, it is the picture of healthy, well-groomed beauty, with a voice at once powerful and melodious, and a reputation for shyness of disposition, which trait takes the form of a bewitching elusiveness that it seems to know is very attractive.

Its call notes, and the mocking gibes which it utters from the bushes to the distraction of the bewildered passer-by, are wholly different from the fervent spring song. Then it yields to an ecstasy of feeling, and soars singing into the air, trailing its long legs behind like a Heron, and looking, it must be confessed, very foolish; but after a few weeks it abandons its aerial gymnastics and contents itself with taunting, teasing, and misleading both man, beast, and bird.

On general principles the Chat is a mischief-maker, who starts petty deceits and fosters them, is quick to grasp a situation, knowing at once the most provoking thing to say, and is, in fact, a wood-imp. Near the garden wall there is

PLATE 19.

1. YELLOW-BREASTED CHAT.

Length, 7.50 inches.

2. BANK SWALLOW.

Length, 5 inches.

a tangle of cedars, before which are the kennels where the dogs are chained at night. Early one morning they set up a chorus of grieved and disappointed howls, and, on going to find the cause, I found them tugging at their chains and casting longing glances toward the cedars. I listened a moment, and there came a succession of whistles, like their master's call, and I found that a Chat was working off his spirits in this way. A few days later, in going up the lane road with a very slow horse, I heard the same whistle from the bushes, and it was not imagination alone that gave these syllables to the chattering: "Whew! whew! whew! Hi! get a whip. Chuc-a-chuck, chuck. Whew! Hi!" Then the Chat flashed into the open, just to show that it was really he himself, and was gone.

Hooded Warbler: *Sylvania mitrata.*

Length: 5–5.25 inches.

Male: *Black hood, chin, and upper breast.* Yellow face, lower breast, and under parts. Above rich olive; white spots on outer tail feathers. Bill black, feet light.

Female: Similar, but with the cowl restricted or lacking.

Song: "Che-we-eo-tsip, tsip, che-we-eo!"

Season: May to September. A rare summer resident here, according to Mr. Averill.

Breeds: Through its United States range.

Nest: In bushes in damp woods, of bark strips, skeleton leaves, catkins, and grasses, woven with spider webs.

Eggs: 4, white, with reddish brown speckles.

Range: Eastern United States, west to the Plains, north and east to Michigan, southern New York, and southern New England; in winter, West Indies, eastern Mexico, and Central America.

In general appearance like the Yellow-throat, save that the black on the head forms a complete hood (except for the yellow face) meeting under the chin like a cape. This jaunty little bird looks as if he had assumed his black cowl for masquerading purposes only, and might be expected to throw it off at any moment. Quite plentiful in some parts of this state; it has been known to nest near Bridgeport, and also in the vicinity of Saybrook. It has a particular fondness for our Connecticut swamps, where the pink azaleas and laurels crown the intersecting banks, and it usually nests at the time when the azalea fades, and the laurel comes into bloom.

Wilson's Warbler: *Sylvania pusilla.*

Black-capped Warbler.

Length: 4.75 inches.

Male and Female: Black cap. Above olive-yellow, olive-yellow edgings to wings and tail. Under parts rich yellow, shades to olive on sides. Line over eye and forehead deep yellow. Bill dark above lower mandible and feet light. Female without the black cap.

Song: An indistinct warble.

Season: An uncommon migrant, seen here in May.

Breeds: Chiefly north of the United States.

Nest: On the ground.

Eggs: 4–5, white, heavily spotted and sprinkled with mauve and lilac.

Range: Eastern North America, west to and including the Rocky Mountains, north to Hudson's Bay Territory and Alaska, migrating south to Eastern Mexico and Central America.

This striking bird ranges quite freely through the state as a migrant, but little is known of its New England breeding possibilities. Mr. H. D. Minot found its nest on Pike's Peak at an altitude of 11,000 feet, almost at the timber line.

Canadian Warbler: *Sylvania canadensis.*

Length: 5.25–5.50 inches.

Male: Above ash-blue, crown spotted with arrow-shaped, black marks blending on the brow. *Below pure yellow, with a showy necklace of black longitudinal bars across the breast.* Yellow line over eye, black patch under it. Bill dark, feet flesh-coloured.

Female: Paler all through, and the black obscured.

Song: "A fine sibilant chirp, reminding one of a canary's song, but broken and incomplete." (Nehrling.)

Season: Common migrant in the latter half of May.

Breeds: Casually in New England, and north to the tree limit.

Nest: Of dry grass and leaves on the ground.

PLATE 20.

AMERICAN REDSTART.

1. Male. 2. Female.

Length, 5–5.50 inches.

Eggs: 4–5, white, with irregular small blotches of reddish brown.
Range: Eastern North America, westward to the Plains, and north to the Arctic regions; south, in winter, to Central America and northern South America.

The Canadian Warbler may be identified by the beautifully wrought jet necklace which he wears across his yellow throat, the black crown streaks, and the peculiar bluish ash back. He has charming manners, and a dainty way of giving a little old-fashioned bob courtesy whenever he sees a passer-by. His song is quite pretty, but not by any means a certain mark of identification; in fact, I do not think that there are more than eight or ten of the whole Warbler tribe whose notes will serve as a guide to any one but an ornithologist well up in field practice.

American Redstart: *Setophaga ruticilla.*

PLATE 20.

Length: 5–5.50 inches.
Male: Above brilliant blue-black, white belly, *sides of body and wing linings salmon-orange*, which colour sometimes flushes the breast. Some orange on base of wings; tail feathers half orange and half black. Bill and feet black.
Female: Brownish olive above and the orange of the male replaced by yellow.
Song: Resembling that of the Yellow Warbler, "Sweet, Sweet, Sweeter!" but the word is only used three times, while it is repeated seven times by the Warbler.
Season: May to September; a common summer resident.
Breeds: From middle United States northward.
Nest: A carefully made structure of moss fibres and sometimes horse-hair, set in a forked branch usually about twenty feet from the ground; I have seen one at the top of a small spruce.
Eggs: Indistinguishable from other Warblers.
Range: North America, north to Fort Simpson, west regularly to the Great Basin, casually to the Pacific Coast; in winter the West Indies, and from southern Mexico through Central America to northern South America.

Again the colour title of a bird is a misnomer. Redstart, a corruption of the German *roth stert*, red tail, being very misleading in this day of accurate colour distinctions. Mrs.

Olive Thorne Miller is on the right path when she describes it as wearing the Oriole's colour combination, — except that the Redstart has a more salmonish cast.

This Warbler, when it flutters through the spruces, seems the veriest mite of creation, appearing much smaller than its measurements indicate. The female is equally charming in her brown and yellow habit, and together they are one of the most interesting couples of the bird world, as well as being capital illustrations of perpetual motion.

Though the Redstart is a summer resident here, it is more visibly abundant during the May migration, as those that breed retire from the vicinity of dwellings to nest. I once found a nest in process of construction in a spruce in a remote part of the garden, and had the satisfaction of seeing it completed and occupied. Its composition was very similar to that of the Yellow Warbler, but smaller, and with the addition of some green moss which decorated the outside. One of their most characteristic motions while searching for food, is to raise the wings slightly and alight on a higher branch or else one a little in the rear of the spot where they were before, as if a breeze had lifted them.

In brilliancy of flame-like colouring the Redstart only yields precedence to the Scarlet Tanager, Baltimore Oriole, and the Blackburnian Warbler, and, in contrast to the dark evergreens, it seems a wind-blown firebrand, half glowing, half charred.

FAMILY VIREONIDÆ: VIREOS.

Red-eyed Vireo: *Vireo olivaceus.*

PLATE 17. FIG. 2.

Length: 5.75–6.25 inches.

Male and Female: Olive-green above, crown ash with a dark marginal line. White line over eye and a brownish stripe through it. Below whitish, shaded with greenish yellow on sides and on under tail and wing coverts. *The iris ruby-red.* Bill dusky above and light below, feet lead-coloured.

Song: Emphatic staccato and oratorical, — "You see it — you know it, — do you hear me? Do you believe it?"

Season: Common summer resident; late April through September.

Breeds: Through its United States range and northward.
Nest: Cup-like, pensile in slender forked branch of maple, birch, or apple tree; made of bark fibres, cobwebs, bits of paper, scraps of hornets' nests, etc.
Eggs: 3–5, usually 4, white, with brown spots on the larger end.
Range: Eastern North America to the Rocky Mountains, north to the Arctic regions.

The Vireos are a very interesting family, which, though it may be somewhat overlooked in the general spring chorus, comes to the front in the latter part of May. Of the six Vireos that inhabit New England, five are reasonably plentiful, and of these the Red-eyed is the most familiar. You cannot fail to name this Vireo, for he is omnipresent; if you do not see him, you hear him; if he chances to be silent, which seldom happens, he peers at you with his sparkling, ruby eyes that look out between a white line and a brown stripe. Wilson Flagg has forever identified him with the name of the *Preacher*, in reference to his elocutionary powers. "You see it — you know it, — do you hear me? Do you believe it?" he hears the Vireo say, and if you keep these words in your mind you will recognize the bird the first time that you hear his song.

May, June, July, and August, and still this Vireo sings on; in mid-August he does not articulate as nicely perhaps, but as the month ends he has recovered his speech and delivers a farewell exhortation in September.

Four pairs nested in the garden this season, and after the young had flown the parents stayed about the same trees, singing from five in the morning on through the scorching noontime — when the locust strove in vain to drone them down — until sunset sometimes, never leaving the particular tree where they began. Not that they sit and prate in a state of idleness; — far from it, they are constantly gleaning their daily bread. This is very well for Matins and Vespers, but the noon song becomes monotonous, it is in one key, and there is such a thing even as too much good conversation. At noon in summer, silence softened by the whispering leaves is best. At such times the Vireo seems to me like an over-active housewife, who accompanies every motion of her broom or flash of her needle with random advice, maxims, etc., having all active gifts, but lacking the grace of judicious silence.

Though the Vireo's pensile nests are usually built upon one plan, — a cup or little pocket in a branch fork, — you will never find two alike. Of half a dozen collected in the garden, one is of cobwebs, soft cedar bark, and white worsted; one of paper, fibres, and bits of hornets' nest; and a third is a perfect collection of scraps of all sorts.

The Red-eyed is the largest of the Vireos, and may be distinguished from the Warblers, with whom you will be apt to confuse them, by its heavier build and a slight Shrike-like hook at the point of the upper mandible.

Warbling Vireo: *Vireo gilvus.*

Length: 5.50–6 inches.

Male and Female: Above pale olive-green; head and neck ash; dusky line over eye. *No bars on wings.* Below dull yellowish; whiter on throat and belly; deeper on sides.

Song: A liquid and expressive voice, but not so powerful as the Red-eyed. Wilson Flagg gives it these words: "Brig-a-dier—Brig-a-dier—Brigate!" The song lacks the jerky, colloquial style.

Season: May to September and early October.

Breeds: Through its United States range.

Nest: Similar in construction and shape to the Red-eyed, with generally a free use of moss; in trees, usually at some height from the ground.

Eggs: Slightly smaller; otherwise not to be distinguished from the last-named species.

Range: North America in general, from the Fur Countries to Mexico.

The Warbling Vireo is a common summer resident, and a constant and delightful songster, having much more music in its voice than any other member of the family. It *warbles,* as its name implies, the notes rippling easily; and an air of pleasant mystery is given to the performance by the shyness that keeps the singer in the leafiest tree-tops. Plainness is the chief characteristic of the plumage of this Vireo; it has no sharply contrasting colours, no wing bars, and a dusky line through the eye. It frequents the garden in spring and at midsummer, but prefers greater seclusion for its nest-building. When in the garden, it invariably sings either in the elms or in a particular birch, locations that the Purple Finch also chooses. Samuels thinks the song of these two birds so identical that he has frequently mistaken one for the other. I partly agree with him; but the Vireo lacks the power and richness of tone that the Finch possesses. I have heard this Vireo warbling with all his might while brooding on the nest.

There is a lane, a mile away, that separates a birch wood from a clearing, and the Warbling Vireo is housed, to his complete satisfaction, in the trees of this border-land. So plentiful are they in the birches, that it is perfectly safe in late May and June to take people to see and hear the birds in this haunt, for you are sure that they will make good your promise, at least in part, and give a private concert morning or afternoon; they decidedly disapprove of evening performances.

* * * * * * * *

The Philadelphia Vireo (*Vireo philadelphicus*) closely resembles this species, but is very rare in New England.

Yellow-throated Vireo: *Vireo flavifrons.*

Length: 5.75–6 inches.

Male and Female: Splendid *yellow throat* and *upper breast;* cheeks yellow, shading to olive-green on head, back, and shoulders. Yellow line over and around the eye. Wings and tail dark brown. Two white bands on wings; tail edged with white. Bill and feet lead-coloured.

Song: Rather sad — "Preeò-preeà-preeò-preeà."

Season: Common summer resident; May to September.

Breeds: Through its United States range.

Nest and Eggs: Pensile as usual, but more beautifully finished than that of any other species; usually at some height from the ground. Eggs normal.

Range: Eastern United States, south, in winter, to Costa Rica.

The Yellow-throated Vireo is of a stout, vigorous build, and has all the brilliancy of colouring of the Chat. Though in northern New England it is counted rare, it is quite abundant in southern Connecticut, New York, and Pennsylvania. Its somewhat melancholy song is varied by cheerful outbursts; and Mr. Bicknell says that it is the only Vireo that he has noticed singing while on the wing.

All authorities agree as to the great beauty of the nest of this species, even though they differ as to its exact location. It is considered to be wholly a woodland bird, loving tall trees and running water, haunting the same places as the Solitary Vireo. Dr. Warren says that during the migrations he has seen the Yellow-throat in orchards and in the trees along sidewalks and lawns, but that in Pennsylvania it breeds in the woods, nesting twenty-five to thirty or forty feet from the ground.

On the other hand, Mr. Minot describes the nest as,—"altogether one of the prettiest nests to be found. It is placed in the fork of a horizontal branch, from *three* to *fifteen* feet above the ground, as often in the orchard as in the wood; though I have found it in pines."

Blue-headed Vireo: *Vireo solitarius.*

Solitary Vireo.

Length: 5.26–5.75 inches.

Male and Female: Above dark olive, *head bluish gray.* White line from beak to and around eye. Below white, with yellow wash on sides and dusky tail and wings. Some tail feathers white-edged. Female, *head dusky olive.*

Song: "Pitched in a higher key than the other species." (Stearns and Coues.)

Season: Sometimes a summer resident, but common from middle New England south in the migrations only.

Breeds: From New England northward, and also in the Middle States.

Nest and Eggs: Resembling those of the last species, but the nest being sometimes placed in bushes.

Range: Eastern United States to the Plains, north to southern British Provinces; in winter, south to Mexico and Guatemala.

This Vireo, whose mark of identification is an ash-blue crown, is by no means as much of a recluse as the name *Solitary* would indicate. It does, indeed, prefer remote and swampy woods, but, though much rarer than the preceding species, is often seen about orchards, and in the migrations exhibits many of the cheerful, sociable family qualities, peering at you in the woods, and often coming quite near in its rather anxious curiosity.

Its song is of the unmistakable Vireo type, but is rather shrill, and is continued for a long period; according to Mr. Bicknell, as late as October 9 on its return migration. To learn to judge accurately and quickly between the songs of the five Vireos is an accomplishment that you must not expect to acquire until your ear is thoroughly seasoned; but three of the five — the Red-eyed, the Warbling, and the White-eyed — will give you but little trouble.

White-eyed Vireo: *Vireo noveboracensis.*

Length: 5 inches.

Male and Female: Above olive-green, rump obscurely yellow. Below white, sides of breast and belly clear yellow. Yellow line from beak to and round eye. *Two yellow wing bars. Iris white.* Tail feathers yellow-edged. Bill and feet dark lead-coloured.

Song: Colloquial. "Delivered with strong expression and very variable in intonation."

Season: May to September. Common summer resident.

Breeds: Through its United States range, but more sparingly in the Northern States.

Nest and Eggs: Similar to the Red-eyed, but in a low bush or vine; eggs decidedly smaller than the other species.

Range: Eastern United States, west to the Rocky Mountains, north to southern New England and Minnesota; south in winter to Guatemala. Resident in the Bermudas.

This small, nervous Vireo, with a Wren's vehement scolding powers, is a common garden and wood-lot bird, taking refuge in bushy places like the Chat, Catbird, and Maryland Yellow-throat. In other parts of New England it is rare in varying degrees. Dr. J. A. Allen, writing of it from Springfield, Mass., says that out of a thousand of the smaller land-birds taken during three years by different collectors not a single White-eyed Vireo was found among them. It is at times noisily talkative, and prefers the tangle to the tree-tops, managing, however, to give great expression to its simple song; sometimes scolding and arguing, and then dropping voice, as if talking to itself.

Without having the imitative and ventriloquistic powers of the Chat, you cannot fail to be reminded of that exasperating gamin when the White-eyed Vireo, ambushed in some blackberry tangle and trembling for the safety of his nest, undertakes to give you a piece of his mind.

FAMILY LANIIDÆ: SHRIKES.

Northern Shrike: *Lanius borealis.*

Butcher-bird.

PLATE 21.

Length: 9–10.50 inches.

Male and Female: Powerful head, neck, and blackish beak with hooked point. Above bluish ash, lighter on the rump and shoulders. Wide black bar on each side of head from the eye backward. Below light gray with a brownish cast, broken on breast and sides by waved lines of darker gray. Wings and tail black, edged and tipped with white. Large white spot on wings, white tips and edges to outer quills of tail. Legs bluish black.

Song: A call note, and in its breeding-haunts a sweet, warbling song.

Season: A roving winter resident; seen from November to April.

Breeds: North of the United States.

Nest: In a low bush; a basis of sticks, upon which is matted and felted a thick, warm superstructure of bark-strip, grass, and soft vegetable substance. (Coues.)

Eggs: 4–6; marblings of reddish brown and purple covering the gray-green ground.

Range: Northern North America, south in winter to the middle portions of the United States (Washington, D.C., Kentucky, Kansas, Colorado, Arizona, northern California).

The Northern Shrike, though somewhat irregular in its comings and goings, is always present in varying numbers as a winter resident. In common with all winter birds, its

NORTHERN SHRIKE.

Length, 9–10.50 inches.

movements are guided by the food supply, and if severe cold and heavy snows drive away the small birds and bury the mice upon which it feeds, the Shrike must necessarily rove.

Grasshoppers, beetles, other large insects, and field mice are staple articles of its food in seasons when they are obtainable; in fact, next to insects, mice constitute the staple article of its diet, and protection should be accorded it on this account, even though we know the Shrike chiefly as the killer of small birds. The victims are caught by two methods: sneaking,—after the fashion of Crows,—and dropping upon them suddenly from a height like the small Hawks. In the former case the Shrikes frequent clumps of bushes, either in open meadows or gardens, lure the little birds by imitating their call notes, and then seize them as soon as they come within range. They often kill many more birds than they can possibly eat at a meal, and hang them on the spikes of a thorn or on the hooks of a cat-briar in some convenient spot, until they are needed, in the same manner as a butcher hangs his meat, and from this trait the name *Butcher-bird* was given them.

Their depredations are by no means confined to lonely fields and gardens. I was told by a friend living in Chicago, that last winter a Shrike visited her back yard regularly in search of English Sparrows. He would hide in the bushes, and, after killing half a dozen Sparrows, impaled them on the frozen twigs of a lilac bush. After they had hung a few days, he eat portions of them, and then proceeded to kill more, a proceeding for which he should receive unlimited applause.

In the Hawk-like method of killing, the Shrike sits motionless upon the bare branch of a high tree, and, as the little birds pass unconsciously underneath, he drops upon one with unerring aim. He will also try to seize cage birds that are hung out of doors or even inside the window. Last spring I was startled by a violent blow, struck upon a window near which a Canary's cage stood upon a chair. The Canary was trembling with fright, and on going outside

I found some Shrike's feathers, with their wavy markings, adhering to the glass. He had evidently swooped without taking the heavy glass into his calculations, and had bruised his breast.

Twice only, in middle April, I have heard the Shrike's real song; the notes are soft and very musical, and our bird-loving Danish gardener tells me that in his country the native species is prized as a cage bird and often shows great cleverness as a "mocker."

FAMILY AMPELIDÆ: WAXWINGS.

Cedar Waxwing: *Ampelis cedrorum.*

Cedar-bird.

PLATE 22.

Length: 6.50–7.25 inches.

Male and Female: Above grayish cinnamon. Crest, breast, throat, wings, and tail, purplish cinnamon. Black line from back of crest, extending through eye, and forming black frontlets. *Secondary wing quills tipped with waxy points.* Tail feathers banded with yellow, and sometimes red tips. Bill and feet black.

Song: A buzzing call,—"Tweé, tweé-zeé." "A dreary whisper," Minot calls it.

Season: A resident, breeding here, and wandering about in flocks the remainder of the year, feeding upon various fruits, and in winter upon cedar berries.

Breeds: Irregularly through its North American range.

Nest: A deep bowl made of twigs, lined with grass and feathers, and much miscellaneous material, either in a crotch, or saddled on the limb of a stout cedar bush or a tree, preferably the apple tree.

Eggs: 3–5, blue-white, with brown and lilac spots.

Range: North America at large, from the Fur Countries southward; in winter, south to Guatemala and the West Indies.

You will at once recognize the Cedar Waxwing by its crest, yellow tail tips, red wing appendages, and straight black bill. Its feathers are more exquisitely shaded than those of our more brilliantly coloured birds. The specimen I have

PLATE 22.

CEDAR WAXWING.

Length, 6.50–7.25 inches.

before me is a male in full plumage, who came to an untimely end by flying against a treacherous wire trellis. Nowhere except in the black frontlet, the tail, and wing tips does he show a distinct colour demarcation; all the rest of the feathers are tinted like a skilful blending of water-colours. The Cedar Waxwings only remain in pairs during the breeding-season (from late May until August), and at other times travel in flocks. It is only when in these flocks that they are conspicuous about the garden and old pastures; for when they are nesting they are very shy and stealthy in their movements.

Last May a flock of fifty or more lodged for a whole morning in a half-dead ash tree, near the house, so that seated at ease, I could focus my glass carefully, and watch them at leisure. They were as solemn as so many demure Quakers sitting stiffly in rows; once in a while they shifted about, and then seemed to do a great deal of apologizing for fancied jostlings. Their movements interested me greatly, until finally, to my surprise, I saw an illustration of the old story of their extreme politeness in passing food to one another, which I had always regarded as a pretty bit of fiction. A stout green worm (for they eat animal as well as vegetable food) was passed up and down a row of eight birds; once, twice it went the rounds, until half way on its third trip it became a wreck and dropped to the ground, so that no one enjoyed it,—a commentary, in general, upon useless ceremony. I could not help wondering, however, whether it was all disinterested politeness, or whether the worm was of a variety repugnant to Cedar-birds; as Hamlet put it, "Caviare to the general."

FAMILY HIRUNDINIDÆ: SWALLOWS.

Purple Martin: *Progne subis.*

PLATE 23.

Length: 7.50 inches.

Male and Female: Deep, glossy, bluish purple, turning to black on wings and tail, which is forked. Bill dark; feet black. Female more brownish and mottled, below grayish white.

Song: Very soft and musical, beginning "peuo-peuo-peuo."
Season: Late April to early September.
Breeds: Through range, rearing two broods a season.
Nest: A little heap of leaves; in the East in boxes, but in the West in hollow trees.
Eggs: 4–6, glossy white.
Range: Temperate North America, south to Mexico.

Without being precisely a common bird, the Purple Martin is with us every summer, and its iridescent coat is a familiar sight. Its size and colour easily separate it from the rest of the family, and the sweet song completes the identification.

A little after dawn, in early May, you may see pairs of these Martins hovering in mid-air, half caressing, half quarrelling, while from time to time you will hear the liquid "peuo-peuo-peuo" merging into a more throaty ripple, like laughter.

The Martin is a favourite, and always seems to have been regarded as such. Houses are provided for his shelter, children are cautioned not to molest him, and the farmer, usually so callous toward bird attractions, has no word for him but of praise; as he consumes a vast quantity of evil insects, and these, too, of a larger size and different class from those captured by other Swallows, and he does not claim a single bud or berry to discount his utility.

Even among the wild men he was always a protected guest. Wilson relates that the Choctaw and Chickasaw Indians used to strip the leaves from small trees near their encampments, and hang upon the prongs, hollowed-out gourds that the Martins might nest in them, and the Mississippi negroes also hung similar contrivances on long canes to coax the Martin to stay.

The Purple Martin is as courageous as the Kingbird in attacking Crows and Hawks, but for all this he seems unable to cope with the English Sparrow, who is steadily and persistently appropriating his houses. The Sparrow has the advantage of being more prolific, as well as more gross and brutal in its methods, and represents in the bird

PLATE 23.

PURPLE MARTIN.

1. Male. 2. Female.

Length, 7.50 inches.

world a class of emigrants whose human prototypes the native American can barely withstand.

Cliff Swallow; Eaves Swallow: ***Petrochelidon lunifrons.***

Length: 5–5.50 inches.

Male and Female: Above brilliant steel-blue; beneath dusky white. Sides of head, throat and chin rufous. Wings and tail glossed with black. Bill dark; feet brown. *White, crescent-like frontlet,* hence its specific name *lunifrons*, from *luna*, the moon, and *frons*, front.

Song: A squeak, more than a twitter.

Season: Early April to late August.

Breeds: In colonies, raising two broods a year.

Nest: Either a bracket, or gourd-shaped, with the opening at the neck; of mud, with straws and feather-lined; placed under eaves or rocky cliffs.

Eggs: 4–6, white with brown and purple markings.

Range: North America at large, south in winter to Brazil and Paraguay.

This familiar Swallow, which we in the East know as the bird who builds its much-modified, gourd-shaped nest under the eaves of old houses, is in the West wholly a cliff-dweller. With us the shape of the nest depends greatly upon the site chosen, many nests being merely elongated brackets. When it builds under the protection of shelving cliffs, the nests are of the typical bottle shape, and are often squeezed as closely together as the cells of a wasp nest.

This species is almost as brilliantly coloured as the Barn Swallow, but lacks the grace in flying which the sharply forked tail gives to the latter. Like all its tribe, it feeds upon insects, which it takes on the wing.

Barn Swallow: ***Chelidon erythrogaster.***

Plate 24. Fig. 2.

Length: Variable, 6–7 inches.

Male and Female: Glistening steel-blue back, *tail deeply forked.* Brow and under parts rich buff, which warms almost to brick-red on throat. A partial steel-blue collar. Tail shows white band from beneath. Female smaller and paler.

Song: A musical twitter like a rippling, merry laugh, — "Tittle-ittle-ittle-eè."

Season: April to September.

Breeds: Everywhere.

Nest: A shallow bracket, made of pellets of mud and straw, placed on or against rafters, etc.

Eggs: 4-6, white, curiously spotted with all shades of brown and lilac.

Range: North America in general, from the Fur Countries southward to the West Indies, Central America, and South America.

The Swallows belong to the air, as the Warblers do to the trees and the Thrushes to the ground. Swallows, unless when gathering before the fall migration, are seldom seen perching, except upon telegraph wires, and they leave these with such sudden and forking flight that they seem spurred by the electric current. If, in the daylight hours, you see a bird in rapid but nonchalant pursuit of insects, you may safely assume that it is either a Swallow or the Chimney Swift, for the Flycatchers have a different flight, the Nighthawk is more ponderous, and Whip-poor-wills seldom take to the air between dawn and dusk.

The distinguishing mark of the Barn Swallow is his sharply forked tail, brick-red throat, and buff breast. It is the commonest species and the most familiar, owing to the fact that it builds so freely about barns and dwellings. Its nest is one of the earliest that country children learn to know; and the first eggs that many a boy has stolen and concealed, while his conscience was still keen enough to prick him, have been those of the Barn Swallow.

Several broods are sometimes raised in a season, the hatching continuing to late July. In fact, the last brood has entered the world, through our hayloft window, the first week in August. These Swallows have very sympathetic natures; for when danger threatens or disaster destroys a brood, the friends quickly gather about and seem to offer advice or condolence.

PLATE 24.

1. TREE SWALLOW.

Length, 6 inches.

2. BARN SWALLOW.

Length, variable, 6–7 inches.

Tree Swallow: *Tachycineta bicolor.*

White-bellied Swallow.

PLATE 24. FIG. 1.

Length: 6 inches.

Male and Female: Entire upper parts iridescent green, inclined to black on wings and tail. Under parts soft white. Bill black; feet dark. Female dull.

Song: A warbling twitter.

Season: April to the middle of September. A few stragglers remain later.

Breeds: Irregularly through range.

Nest: In dead trees, often in great colonies; here I have seen two or three pairs occupying old Woodpecker holes in telegraph poles.

Eggs: 4–9, usually 6, pure white.

Range: North America at large, from the Fur Countries southward, in winter, to the West Indies and Central America.

She is here, she is here, the Swallow!
Fair seasons bringing, fair years to follow!
Her belly is white,
Her back black as night.
— *Greek Swallow Song*, J. A. SYMONDS, Trans.

The Tree, or White-bellied Swallow seems nearly to correspond with the bird which was the herald of spring in Greece; for though our Swallow is a beautiful green above, except when at close range or when the light glances across its feathers, it appears black. The Tree Swallow, in times before the country was inhabited by white men, like many of its family, lived in hollow trees, but it now nests in Martin boxes and other convenient nooks, though it may be still found colonizing in old sycamores and willows.

If you live near the sand dunes or by a strip of beach edged with scrub bushes, go out and watch the gyrations of these lovely Swallows before the fall migration, the first part of September; you may also see the Bank Swallows or Sand Martins gather at the same time.

The Tree Swallow always seeks the vicinity of water at the time of the migration, probably because insects are more plentiful in such places. This has led people to form the theory that it passed the winter under the mud bottom of large ponds and rivers in a state of hibernation. The matter has even been treated seriously, in spite of its manifest absurdity, the construction of the bird's breathing-apparatus precluding such a possibility.

Bank Swallow: *Clivicola riparia.*

Sand Martin.

PLATE 19. FIG. 2.

Length: 5 inches. The smallest of our Swallows.
Male and Female: Above dull mouse colour, wings and tail brownish, below white, with a brownish breast band. Bill and feet dark.
Song: A giggling twitter.
Season: Common summer resident, arriving in May.
Breeds: All through its North American range.
Nest: In tunnelled holes in clayey banks; made of grass and lined with a few feathers.
Eggs: 4–6, pure white.
Range: Northern Hemisphere; in America, south to the West Indies, Central America, and northern South America.

The Bank Swallow is the plainest, as well as the smallest, of the family. His back is the colour of the damp mottled gray sand with which he is closely associated, and he shows no glints of purple, steel-blue, and buff, like his brethren, but wears a dusky cloak fastened about his throat with a band of the same colour.

There is always a large colony of these Swallows near Southport, where Sasco Hill is cut off abruptly by the Sound. The bank is high, and shows a face of various grades of loam and some strata of gravel; below there is a bit of stony beach, bare at low tides, but in storms the water breaks half-way up the bank. A few feet above high-water mark you can see the holes in the bank which are the entrances to the Swallows' nests. They are not arranged with any sort of regularity, but the birds have chosen invariably the stiff loam, which was the least likely to crumble away in the boring-process. None of the tunnels are within

PLATE 25.

SCARLET TANAGER.

three feet of the top, and they are almost all wider than they are high, as is frequently the case with mouse-holes. These tunnels vary from a foot to eighteen inches in length, and at the end are the wisps of grass and feathers that hold the fragile white eggs. The feathers of many different birds are found in the nests of this colony, — the breast-feathers of Ducks, Gulls, and various Shore-birds, which are not in this vicinity at the Swallow's nesting-time. In the autumn and winter many Water-birds are wounded by gunners, but escape notice, and, drifting ashore, become wedged between rocks and stones, and I think that it is mainly from the scraps of down adhering to such carcasses that this colony lines its nests.

The Swallows, as a family, show great inventive qualities in the way in which they have adapted their habits to the encroachments of civilization. Now, almost wholly domesticated, they seem to prefer man's company, and each one has appropriated a separate location for nesting. The Bank Swallow adheres the most closely to his original haunts; but even he may be found occasionally building under a bridge.

* * * * * * * *

The Rough-winged Swallow is another species, which closely resembles the Bank Swallow, being slightly larger; but, as you would scarcely distinguish it when on the wing, it does not need a separate description.

FAMILY TANAGRIDÆ: TANAGERS.

Scarlet Tanager: *Piranga erythromelas.*

PLATE 25.

Length: 6.75–7 inches.

Male: A rich scarlet. Wings and tail black. Feet deep horn colour.

Female: Olive-green above; dull olive-yellow below. Wings and tail dusky.

Song: Mellow and cheerful, — "Pshaw! wait — wait — wait for me, wait!" Call note "chip-chur!"

Season: Arrives the middle of May, and leaves in late August. No longer common.

Breeds: Through its United States range.
Nest: Rather flat and ragged; made of sticks, root fibres, etc.; placed on the high horizontal branch, preferably of an oak or pine.
Eggs: 3–5, dull green, thickly spotted with brown and mauve.
Range: Eastern United States, west to the Plains, and north to southern Canada; in winter the West Indies, Central America, and northern South America.

A few years ago the Scarlet Tanager was as familiar hereabout as the Yellow Warbler, or the Wood Thrush; but now it has, in a great measure, left the gardens and frequented woodlands, and become the resident of lonely woods. Together with all of our brilliantly plumed birds, it has been persecuted almost out of existence. Now that this bird slaughter is against the law in all communities that pretend to be civilized, the killing is at least abated, but the Tanager's confidence in humanity has not yet returned.

It is impossible to mistake this bird in full spring dress, for any other. His fall coat, however, is olivaceous like the female, and, as for the unmoulted young, they are a motley lot, mainly olive-green, but with little tufts of scarlet, yellow, and bright green, appearing at random, as if they were examples of feather patchwork. It is easy to see the wisdom that clothes the female and young of this flaming Tanager in sober colours. If a brooding female wore a scarlet covering, it would surely betray the nest to all enemies; and if the young were likewise conspicuous, they would be gobbled by Hawks before they understood that Hawks are hardly friendly.

The Tanager, though of a brilliant scarlet, lacks the luminous quality that reveals the Baltimore Oriole and Blackburnian Warbler, when partly concealed in dark green foliage; you will be most likely to find it in a grove of oaks, hickories, or swamp-maples, where there is an undergrowth of ferns, — not briars, — near by a stream or flag-edged pond. It is a fruit and berry eater, as well as the consumer of beetles, and other large winged insects, together with many larvæ.

PLATE 26.

1. PINE GROSBEAK. 2. WHITE-THROATED SPARROW.

Length, 9 inches. Length, 6.50–7 inches.

FAMILY FRINGILLIDÆ: FINCHES, SPARROWS, GROSBEAKS, ETC.

Pine Grosbeak: *Pinicola enucleator.*

PLATE 26. FIG. 1.

Length: 9.10 inches.

Male: Heavy bill, giving it almost the appearance of a Parrot. Above *general colour strawberry-red*, with some gray fleckings, *deepest* on *head* and *rump*. Wings and tail brown; some feathers edged with lighter brown and some with white. Below paler red, turning to grayish green on belly. Bill and feet blackish.

Female: Ash-brown, with yellowish bronze wash on rump, head, and breast.

Song: "A subdued, rattling warble broken by whistling notes."

Season: A winter visitor whose appearance is as irregular as the length of its stay.

Breeds: Far north in evergreen woods; also casually in Maine, New Hampshire, and Vermont, but mainly north of the United States.

Nest: Saddled on a branch or in a crotch. Twigs, roots, and fibres below, with a soft upper section.

Eggs: 4, a greenish blue ground with dark brown spots.

This finely coloured Grosbeak comes to us only in winter, and can be easily identified at a season when such brilliant birds are rare. It is a resident of northern New England, and, however much it may wander about in the more southern states, it can only be regarded as an irregular and capricious migrant.

The song of this species is said to be very attractive, but is of course seldom heard so far away from the breeding-haunts. Mr. Bicknell calls it a subdued, rattling warble, which is sometimes heard as early as February and March, and Dr. Coues calls the birds fine musicians. They come in pairs or in flocks, and as the young males do not attain their strawberry-coloured feathers until the second year, and the females are a brownish yellow, the proportion of red birds in these flocks is quite small.

Severely cold winters and strong gales seem to blow them down to us; a number appeared here in the snowy season of 1892–93, while in the open winter of 1893–94 I did not see or hear of one. Twice I have noticed pairs keeping together and apart from the flock. In January, 1893, when the snow had been on the ground since November, two pairs roosted nightly in a very thick honeysuckle. In the day the birds spent their time between an arbor-vitæ hedge and a group of pines. After an unusually severe snow they became very hungry and descended to the ground for food, and, while they refused to eat crumbs, relished some cracked corn which had been soaked in boiling water until it was partly softened.

Aside from their striking size and colour, and the fact that they come in winter, a season at which any bird is a welcome excitement, these Grosbeaks are not very interesting. They have no playful ways, and here, at least, are silent to the verge of stupidity. They feed upon various small seeds and also upon tree buds, particularly those of the maple and hickory. Berries are also eaten, if other food fails.

Purple Finch: *Carpodacus purpureus.*

Length: 5.75–6.25 inches.

Male: Until two years old resembles a dull-coloured, heavy-billed sparrow; when *mature*, the head, shoulders, and upper breast have a wash of *raspberry-red*, lower parts grayish white, wings and tail dusky with some reddish brown tips. Bill and feet brown.

Female: Olive-brown, clearer on rump, and streaked above and below with dusky brown. Whitish beneath, and streaked on sides of breast with arrow-shaped marks.

Song: Joyful and sudden, — "O, list to me, list to me, hear me, and I'll tell you,—you, you!"

Season: March to November; a common summer resident, individuals remaining sometimes all winter.

Breeds: From Middle States northward.

Nest: In a bush or tree, of grass and fibre, and lined with horsehair; a flat nest.

Eggs: 4–5, greenish white, scratched and spotted with black and lilac.

Range: Eastern North America, from the Atlantic coast to the Plains.

This is the most melodious of the Finches, who, perching high in the elms on the lawn or in the birches by the river-bank, pours out his gushing, liquid warble, while at the same time he is completely hidden from sight. Long ago, being told that a song which had delighted me belonged to the Purple Finch, I tried to obtain a good view of him, expecting to see a bird whose purple coat should match his regal voice, — but not at all. The first specimen that I caught (with my field-glass), when in the act of singing, was dull and Sparrow-like. Then followed the explanation that the males take two seasons to perfect their plumage, and that even then they are not *purple*, but merely washed locally with a peculiar shade of red.

I think many early ornithologists who were responsible for the naming of our birds must have been either colour-blind or possessed of very limited vocabularies, for a modern reading of many of their colour terms means dismay and total collapse to the unfortunate novice. Burroughs, with his fine sense of perception and language combined, at once locates this Finch. "His colour is peculiar," he says, "and looks as if it might have been imparted by dipping a brown bird in diluted poke-berry juice. Two or three more dippings would have made the purple complete."

In looking for this Finch, then, you must rely greatly upon his song, remembering that he may or may not be red coloured on the head and back, and that whether he is or not, you will find it difficult to discover.

The suddenness with which the Purple Finch bursts into song renders him one of our most conspicuous songsters, and recalls the notes of the English Chaffinch. May and June are the months of his most perfect music, but the birds who have wintered here begin to warble early in March, and occasional subdued songs may be heard in October, so that the season of melody is almost as long as that of the Song Sparrow.

English Sparrow: *Passer domesticus.*

House Sparrow; Gamin, Tramp, Hoodlum. (Coues.)

Length: 5 inches.

Male and Female: Ashy above, shoulders and back striped with black and chestnut. Dark chestnut mark over eye and on sides of neck. Chestnut and white bar on wings, bordered by a black line; tail gray. Bill blue-black; feet brown. Female paler; wing bars indistinct.

Song: A harsh chirp.

Season: A persistent resident.

Breeds: Everywhere in towns and in villages.

Nest: Rough, and loosely made of straws, sticks, or any material which circumstances offer.

Eggs: 4–8, greenish white, speckled with chocolate and lavender.

Range: Eastern United States. Introduced about twenty years ago into the United States, where it has become naturalized in nearly all inhabited districts.

This unfortunate Sparrow, bearing a load of opprobrium which he deserves, though largely through no fault of his own, has for some time been furnishing an avi-social problem to both England and America. In the first-named country, even the investigation of a special committee of the House of Commons has failed to ascertain, with anything approaching certainty, whether this Sparrow's services as an insect-destroyer equal his own destructive qualities.

In Australia, it is said that the fifty birds originally imported now flock by millions, and make the third of the triad of emigrants with which unthinking people have scourged the country, the other two being rabbits and the Scotch thistle.

Here in America, the Sparrow is an absolute and unmitigated nuisance, but for this, the unwise and superficial theory that brought him over is chiefly to blame. No thought was given to the change of habits that the change of climate might effect in the bird's whole nature. A partial insect-eater, at home, though of a seed-eating family, brought here to free the trees from canker-worms, he, instead, relapsed soon after, and became a rigid seed-eater.

PLATE 27.

AMERICAN CROSSBILL.

Length, 6 inches.

Theodore Wood, in his instructive little book, — "Our Bird Allies,"[1] — devotes two chapters to an unprejudiced review of the Sparrow question, which are well worth reading, in which he quotes Prévost-Paradol and many other authorities. "What wonder," he says, "if the Sparrow, both in America and New Zealand, should turn from a diet of insect to one of grain and fruit? Does not even man himself alter his food in accordance with the climate? Does he not, leaving England for a warmer country, depend more upon vegetable food and less upon animal?"

It is not the grain that he consumes that makes us at war with the Sparrow, but because he steadily puts to rout our most familiar birds, destroys their young, and gives us only his ugly chirp in the place of their songs, and his useless presence instead of their insect-consuming powers. The destruction of the Sparrows, eggs and nests, is now almost universally approved in the United States. Dr. C. Hart Merriam of the Department of Agriculture, Washington, has prepared a consensus of reports from many sources, containing evidence for and against the Sparrow, — 168 being for, 837 against, and 43 neutral. The report also contains a list of native birds that have been more or less molested by the Sparrow, among which are not only the Wrens, Bluebirds, and Martins of our garden bird-boxes, but the valiant Kingbird, the Horned Lark, Hermit and Wood Thrushes, the Mockingbird, Purple Grackle, Meadowlark, and many Woodpeckers.

American Crossbill: *Loxia curvirostra minor.*

PLATE 27.

Length: 6 inches.

Male: General colour Indian red. Head shaded with olive. Back and shoulders brown with red edgings to the feathers; wings and tail brown. *Beak crossed at the tip.*

Female: General colour greenish yellow. Dull yellowish tints on the head, throat, breast, and rump. Wings and tail brown with lighter edges to some feathers.

[1] New York, E. & J. B. Young & Co.

Song: Winter note; a snapping chirp.
Season: An irregular winter visitor.
Breeds: Northward in late winter and early spring.
Nest: Among the twigs or in the fork of a tree, having a base of bark and sticks, and being lined with finer materials.
Eggs: 3–4, greenish, marked with brown and lilac at larger end.
Range: Northern North America; resident sparingly south in the Eastern States to Maryland and Tennessee, and in the Alleghanies; irregularly abundant in winter; resident south in the Rocky Mountains to Colorado.

This bird of evergreens and cold weather, the Red Crossbill, is chiefly a winter visitor here, varying greatly in abundance. It is impossible to confuse it with any other bird, as the colour is of a different shade from the red of the Pine Finch and Cardinal, and its warped bill is a distinctive mark. The beak seems especially constructed for snapping the scales from the cones, whose seeds furnish its food.

A very strange effect is produced when a flock of Crossbills settle in the pines north of the garden, and mingle their snapping chirp with the dry crackling of the cones that they are dissecting. There is a suppressed bustle about the whole proceeding; and if you close your eyes you may imagine that the sounds proceed from the rending of the corn from the stalk at an old time husking-bee. As with all weird looking birds and animals, the Crossbill is the subject of many tales, one of which Longfellow translated from the German of Julius Mosen, under the title of "The Legend of the Crossbill."

Redpoll: ***Acanthis linaria.***

Redpoll Linnet.

Length: 5.50 inches.
Male: *Head, neck, breast, and rump* washed with rich *crimson*, over a ground of gray and brown. Back, wings, and tail dusky; dusky white beneath. Tail short and forked; wings long and pointed. Bill very sharp, and either yellow, tipped with dusky, or black; feet dark.
Female: Dingy, having the crimson only on the crown.
Song: A Canary-like call note and a lisping song; sometimes given when flocking as well as in the breeding-season.

Season: A winter visitor from the north.
Breeds: In boreal regions.
Range: Northern portions of Northern Hemisphere; south, irregularly, in winter; in North America, to the middle United States (Washington, D.C., Kansas, southeastern Oregon).

The Redpoll, Redpoll Linnet, or Little Snowbird, as it is locally called, comes out of the north on the snow clouds, with the Buntings and Crossbills, and returns to its breeding-grounds usually before its spring song is heard. It is most frequently to be seen in weedy pastures, where it feeds upon the seeds of small herbs, and after heavy snows have covered the lowlands it retreats to the many-seeded compositæ that swarm along the sides of grass-grown roads, and in an extremity, feeds upon tree buds, especially those of the black birch. It never becomes as friendly as its cousin, the American Goldfinch, but you can easily identify it and watch its movements when it is feeding upon some conspicuous spray that protrudes from the fresh snow. At such times a flock of Redpolls, with their little ruddy crowns, are the prettiest things imaginable. Thoreau's soliloquy upon these winter birds, as he stood looking over the late November landscape, is too beautiful to quote merely in part. He says: "Standing there, though in this bare November landscape, I am reminded of the incredible phenomenon of small birds in winter, that erelong, amid the cold, powdery snow, as it were a fruit of the season, will come twittering a flock of delicate, crimson-tinged birds, Lesser Redpolls, to sport and feed on the seeds and buds just ripe for them on the sunny side of a wood, shaking down the powdery snow there in their cheerful feeding, as if it were high midsummer to them. . . . They greet the hunter and the chopper in their furs. Their Maker gave them the last touch, and launched them forth the day of the Great Snow. He made this bitter, imprisoning cold, before which man quails, but He made at the same time these warm and glowing creatures to twitter and be at home in it. He said not only let there be Linnets in winter, but Linnets of rich plumage and pleasing twitter, bearing summer in their natures. . . . I am struck by the perfect confidence and success of Nature."

American Goldfinch: *Spinus tristis.*

Wild Canary, Thistle-bird, Yellowbird.

PLATE 28. FIG. 2.

Length: 4.80–5.20 inches.

Male: Body, all but wings, tail, and frontlet, a *clear gamboge-yellow.* Frontlet black. Wings black, varied with white. Tail blackish with spots of white on interior of quills. Bill and feet flesh-coloured. In September the black frontlet of the male disappears, his colours pale, and he resembles the female and young. In April the spring moult begins, and often is not completed until middle May.

Female: Above brownish olive, below yellowish.

Song: A wild, sweet, Canary-like warbling. Call note, "Ker-chee-chee-chee, whew-é, whew-é!"

Season: Resident in this section, but the numbers increase in May and diminish in October.

Breeds: Southward to the middle districts of the United States (to about the Potomac and Ohio rivers, Kansas, and California).

Nest: Round, very neat, and compact; of grass and moss, lined with seed and plant down, usually in a branch crotch.

Eggs: 4–6, blue-white, generally unmarked.

Range: North America generally, wintering mostly south of the northern boundary of the United States.

The American Goldfinch, known under many titles, is as familiar as the Robin, Catbird, and Wren, but its beauty and winning ways always seem new and interesting. In southern Connecticut, as well as in locations further north and east, it is resident, and is revealed through its various disguises of plumage by its typical dipping flight.

Its spring song begins early in April, though its plumage does not resume the perfect yellow until late May; the song remains at its height all through July and well into August, but ceases, almost abruptly, at the end of that month (from the 20, to the 30, according to Mr. Bicknell).

These Goldfinches do not mate until June, and sometimes not until the last half of the month. They always choose

PLATE 28

1. SNOWFLAKE.

Length, 7 inches.

2. AMERICAN GOLDFINCH.

Length, 5 inches.

for their nesting-place some large maples that grow by the southwest wall of the garden, extending their branches over a waste field, where dandelions, thistles, wild asters, and goldenrod hold sway. A little before this time flocks of birds assemble about the garden and every Jack chooses his Jill, or *vice versa.* There is no more cheerful and confiding garden companion than this Goldfinch. Seen even at a distance his markings are distinct, his identity complete; you do not have to puzzle or worry, but simply enjoy his society; he does not wish your berries, but helps you remove the dandelion down from the lawn before the wind sows it broadcast, and all the while you hear Canary-like music, but wilder and more joyous, from behind a twig lattice instead of cage bars.

The black cap gives the male a ferocious look, wholly at variance with his character, while his mate is agreeably feminine and gentle. These birds combine the rich colours, which we associate with the tropics, and the stout-hearted, cold-enduring New England nature, softened by the most agreeably cosmopolitan manners. If you wish them to live with you and honour your trees with their nests, plant sunflowers in your garden, zinnias, and coreopsis; leave a bit of wild grass somewhere about with its mass of compositæ. Coax the wild clematis everywhere that it can gain footing; and in winter, when these joyous birds, gathered in flocks, are roving, hard-pressed for food, scatter some sweepings of bird seed about their haunts, repaying in this their silent season, their summer melody.

Pine Siskin: *Spinus pinus.*

Length: 4.75 inches.

Male and Female: Striped generally; above olive-brown and gray, darkest on head and back. Below lighter, sometimes having a decidedly sulphur-yellow tinge on rump and base of wing and tail feathers. Bill and feet brown.

Song: Resembling that of the American Goldfinch, but in a more fretful key, and seldom heard in this locality.

Season: An erratic winter visitor. Late October to March and early April.

Breeds: Mostly north of the United States, and in the Rocky Mountain region. Casually in northern New England and New York State.

Nest: Rare, high in evergreens, principally.

Eggs: Light green, spotted with brown.

Range: North America generally, in winter south to the Gulf States and Mexico.

The Pine Siskin, as its name implies, is a lover of evergreens, and spends the winter in roving from copse to copse. It is strictly a seed-eater, and consumes alike the kernels of large cones and the seeds of low herbs. It has the dipping flight of the Goldfinch, and many other characteristics of the two birds are similar. You will be most likely to identify the Pine Siskin as it clings to tufts of spruce cones, peering between their scales; the sulphur-yellow tinge of the feathers showing plainly against the deep green.

Dr. Jonathan Dwight, Jr., who heard these Siskins singing between March 15, and May 2, at Rockaway and Cypress Hills Cemetery, says that their song is a "soliloquizing gabble, interspersed with a prolonged wheeze — a prolongation of their usual note while flying." Mr. Bicknell adds: "This hoarse note sometimes sounds like a common note of the English House Sparrow. Before it was familiar to me, it was with no little surprise that I heard at Big Moose Lake, deep in the Adirondack wilderness, a bird note so suggestive of city streets."

Snowflake: *Plectrophanes nivalis.*

Snow Bunting.

Plate 28. Fig. 1.

Length: 7 inches.

Male and Female: *Summer plumage* white, with the exception of black back, white-banded wings, tail, and band across back. *Winter plumage* soft browns and white, — dead-leaf colours and snow. Bill and feet black.

Song: Thoreau says, "a soft, rippling note."

Season: A midwinter visitor, especially in snowy seasons.

Breeds: In the Arctic regions.

Nest: Thickly lined with feathers set in a tussock.

Eggs: 4–6, variable in size and colour, whitish speckled with neutral tints.

Range: Northern parts of the Northern Hemisphere. In North America, south in winter into the northern United States, irregularly to Georgia, southern Illinois, and Kansas.

A bird well named, for the Snowflake, hurried from the north by fierce winds and weather, comes to us out of the snow-clouds. Travelling in great flocks, which are described as numbering sometimes a thousand, they settle down upon the old fields and upland meadows, subsisting upon various seeds. Their winter plumage, by which we alone know them, is exquisitely soft and beautiful, and the birds themselves have a wonderfully mild and spiritual expression as if they had come from an unknown region, and craved a little food and shelter, but conscious that while here they are the veriest birds of passage.

Though a native of Arctic latitudes, Snowflakes, belated on their return migration, have been known to breed in the Northern States. In July, 1831, Audubon found a couple nesting in the White Mountains, and Dr. J. A. Allen notes a pair as breeding near Springfield, Mass. In its home it is said to have a cheerful inspiriting song, but here we only know its Sparrow-like call note.

The Snowflake is very capricious in its visits, as are, in fact, all the winter birds along the Connecticut shore of the Sound. An easterly wind prevailing for several days drives them two or three miles inland behind the Greenfield ridge of hills. During the snowy winter of 1893–94 not a single flock appeared, though the weather was evenly cold and marked by northeasterly storms. On February 15, 1894, — one of the only days of the season when there was sufficient snow for sleighing, a day with heavy, drifting clouds and wind gusts which scattered the loose snow so suddenly that it was driven with the sharpness of sand, — I drove for several miles along the road that separates the shore and marshes from cultivation, and was rewarded by seeing Gulls,

Meadowlarks, Horned Larks, Redpolls, Snowflakes, and, rarest of all, Lapland Longspurs, the first time that I had identified them here.

The Redpolls and Snowflakes were feeding under similar conditions,—the Redpolls keeping under cover of bushes and furrows, while the Snowflakes were in the open, and the flock continually arose with the drifting snow and settled again like a part of it, uttering a soft chirp as they shifted.

Lapland Longspur: *Calcarius lapponicus*

Length: 6.50 inches.

Male: *Winter plumage*, top of head black, edged with rusty, black above, the feathers all tipped with white. A rusty black patch behind and beneath the eye. Below grayish, with faint black markings. Bill yellow, tipped with black; feet and legs black. Long hind claw or spur.

Female: Rusty gray above, whitish below.

Song: A charming song in the breeding-season, uttered while soaring like the Skylark's.

Season: A winter visitor; rare locally, but common on the Massachusetts coast and also noted by Mr. Averill as associating with Shore Larks near Stratford, Conn.

Breeds: In the Arctic regions, where it has a thick, fur-lined, grass nest, set in moss on the ground.

Range: Northern portions of the Northern Hemisphere; in North America, south, in winter, into the northern United States, irregularly to the Middle States, accidentally to South Carolina, and abundantly in the interior to Kansas and Colorado.

When we are fortunate enough to see the Longspur, he is wearing his winter dress, which resembles somewhat the plumage of the Titlark.

I always considered them rare birds hereabout, until I found them near the shore last February. I was first attracted by unusual claw marks in the new snow, where it was soft enough to take distinct impressions, under the south side of a rick of salt hay. The Longspur is a ground feeder like the Larks and Buntings, and the mark of the long hind claw, or spur could be seen plainly; on the opposite side of the rick were the birds themselves, seven

PLATE 29.

2. SLATE-COLOURED JUNCO.

in all. They were climbing up the sloping sides, picking seeds from the coarse grasses and weeds which served as covering for the finer hay. The Longspurs, as well as the Horned Larks that were with them, were so hungry and intent upon feeding that they were not in the least disturbed, even though they must have seen me plainly. This lack of fear produced by hunger often gives the winter birds an air of charming familiarity, and, though both winter residents and visitors are comparatively few, a little food, suited to their various needs, wisely scattered about the door and around the hayricks and sheds, will bring you a troop of grateful guests to whisper cheerfully, even if they do not sing to you.

Vesper Sparrow: *Poocætes gramineus.*

Bay-winged Bunting.

PLATE 29. FIG. 1.

Length: 5.75–6.25 inches.

Male and Female: Above brown, varied with dusky. *Lesser wing coverts bright bay.* Below soiled white, striped everywhere except on the belly with brown. *No yellow anywhere.* Outer tail feathers partly white, appearing conspicuously like two white quills when the bird flies. Upper mandible brown; lower and feet yellowish flesh-coloured.

Song: Sweet and clear, less loud than the Song Sparrow's,—"Chewee-chewee-cheewee, tira-lira-lira-lee!"

Season: Common summer resident; April to October.

Breeds: From Virginia, Kentucky, and Missouri northward.

Nest: Sunk to the rim in the grass or ground, quite deep; of grasses; as carefully made as if it were a tree nest.

Eggs: 4–6, thickly mottled and spotted with brown.

Range: Eastern North America to the Plains; from Nova Scotia and Ontario southward.

This is the Sparrow which is identified by the red-brown shoulders and the two white tail quills, and who, though living near the ground, often soars singing into the air. Its song, though less constantly heard, is as familiar as the Song Sparrow's, and its habit of singing from late afternoon until twilight has given it the name of Vesper Sparrow.

In the garden, from the nook looking toward sunset, I am always certain to hear a half dozen of these little soloists, continuing their music after the evening chorus has ceased, until finally, with the Veery and Rose-breasted Grosbeak, they form a final trio which precedes such silence as Nature allows to the early summer nights.

The Vesper Sparrows are, in the main, seed-eaters, but during the summer they also feed upon insects, earthworms, and berries. They are birds of the roadside and of waste fields, where they are abundant in early autumn, fluttering about in flocks, now perching on a fence rail, and as you approach them, scattering widely, only to collect again a few feet further on. They are dingy-looking birds in the distance, but the white tail quills will always name them.

Ipswich Sparrow: *Ammodramus princeps.*

Length: 6.25 inches.

Male and Female: Above grayish, with a reddish cast to back; dusky streaks on top of head, separated by a broad stripe of pale yellowish white. Below pure white, sides of throat and broad band across breast and sides, streaked with red-brown; bill and feet brown.

Song: Poor and halting, as if the voice weak and tired.

Season: A rare winter resident.

Breeds: In the grass-covered sand-hills of Sable Island, Nova Scotia.

Nest: A few strands of grass in a hollow of the ground.

Eggs: Harlequin, pale green groundwork, jumbled with blotches of brown of every shape and tint.

Range: Nova Scotia, south; in winter, to South Carolina.

The Ipswich Sparrow is a puzzling bird to identify. It was discovered by Mr. Maynard among the Ipswich sand-hills — hence its name. Its plumage is difficult to describe tersely; perhaps it is best to say that it resembles the Vesper Sparrow, but has a yellowish head stripe and two dull white wing bars. Here it is seen either as a winter resident or a migrant, and is decidedly a local species. It is a very hardy Sparrow; Mr. Torrey has found it near Nahant, Mass., in every one of the colder months from October to April.

Savanna Sparrow: *Ammodramus sandwichensis savanna.*

Length: 5.50–6 inches.

Male and Female: Above, back, wings, throat, and sides striped in various shades of brown and bronze. *Yellowish stripe on crown and over eye,* and *yellowish wash around neck.* Cheeks golden bronze. *Below whitish.* Bill dark above, light below; feet light flesh-coloured.

Song: Described by Samuels as sweet and soft. "Chewee-chewitt-chewitt-chewitt-chewé-et-chewee!"

Season: A common resident, on the salt-marshes all the year, whose migrating flocks arrive in April and leave in October.

Breeds: From New England to Labrador and the Hudson's Bay Territory.

Nest: A slight affair, sunken in the ground like the last species.

Eggs: Also motley, like the last.

Range: Eastern North America.

The Savanna Sparrow is a common resident, being found in the thickets bordering the salt-marshes as well as in the marshes themselves, where numbers remain even in severe weather, and, while it is abundant along the coast, it is proportionately rare in the interior. It is essentially a ground Sparrow (which is one of its local names); for, in addition to building on the ground, it limits its flight to low bushes. Its plumage is so streaked and mixed that it blends with the earth,—a great protection to the bird, but a condition which makes identification difficult. Keep in mind that its *under parts* are *whiter than in other Sparrows.*

I associate this Sparrow with early June walks through the marshes and upland meadows, when the wild flowers are calling "Come pick us"; when the beach plum's white plumes are fading with the iris, and the star-grass and yellow thistles are in bloom, and the tall blackberry bushes trace the tumble-down fences with their wands. Then you may see the Savanna Sparrow hurrying through the sand-grass, seeking the cover of bayberries, only to slip through and disappear. He will not indicate by the slightest hint which little circle of grass margins his home, barely separating the young from the earth itself. He will lead you as far away from it as he is able, and, if it is late afternoon, will beguile you with his simple song, from no more ambitious perch than a fence rail. The migrant flocks come to us before or during the spring moult, and are not then in full song; and when they leave, in October, they are quite voiceless.

Grasshopper Sparrow: *Ammodramus savannarum passerinus.*

Yellow-winged Sparrow.

Length: 4.80 inches.

Male and Female: Line over the eye, centre of crown, lesser wing coverts, and shoulders yellow. Above red-brown with an ash-gray wash; upper breast brownish drab; belly whitish; bill stout and short, dark above, pale below; tail feathers edged with white; feet dark.

Song: Note like a grasshopper's chirp; song somewhat resembling the Chipping Sparrow's, but in a different key.

Season: Common summer resident.

Breeds: Throughout its United States range.

Nest: Like the Vesper Sparrow's, on the ground.

Eggs: Sparkling white, with spots and flecks of red and brown.

Range: Eastern United States and southern Canada to the Plains, south to Florida, Cuba, Porto Rico, and coast of Central America.

If you search for a Sparrow with yellow wings, as one of its names suggests, you will altogether miss this species. But if you look for a plain bird, with yellowish stripes on the crown and over the eyes, lesser wing coverts dull yellow, and bend of the wing bright yellow, who runs elusively through the grass, giving a shrill, grasshopper chirp, you will easily locate the Grasshopper Sparrow. The Sparrows and the Warblers will be inevitable stumbling-blocks to you; and when you have positively named half a dozen species, and guessed at as many more, you will feel that you have conquered ornithology. This particular Sparrow keeps so persistently to the ground and to low bushes, in addition having but the ghost of a voice, that it will not be strange if you overlook it.

Sharp-tailed Sparrow: *Ammodramus caudacutus.*

Length: 5–5.50 inches.

Male and Female: Bill extremely sharp for a Sparrow. Above olive-gray with bronze glints, streaked with black on the back, some feathers with light edges; marroon stripes on head; buff stripe through eye; buff or orange cheeks; buff sides to breast, streaked with brown; belly gray; *edge of wings yellow;* tail feathers sharply pointed; feet grayish blue.

Song: Wheezy and choking, which Dr. Dwight describes as "Lĭc-sè-è-è-oop."

Season: Common summer resident.

Breeds: Through its range; two broods a season.

Nest: Of coarse grasses, lined with grass and furze, firmly fastened between tussocks.

Eggs: Grayish white, thickly speckled with brown.

Range: Salt-marshes of the Atlantic coast, from Prince Edward Island and Nova Scotia to the Gulf States.

The Sharp-tailed Sparrow must be identified by the brownish orange or buff colouring of the sides of its head and the *sharp point* which *terminates each separate tail feather.* I specify this because many people mistake the term *sharp*-tailed for *forked*-tailed, and expect the bird to have a tail like the Barn Swallow.

These Sparrows are shy and rather uninteresting, keeping close under cover of sedges and the marsh weeds that edge tide water, and have a feeble flight and a very poor song. They tend to breed in colonies, and choose their haunts here and there without any seeming method, so that they appear to be rare in many eligible places.

Wilson credits them with all the nimbleness of Sandpipers, running about after dusk and roosting on the ground; and says that they are so fond of the vicinity of water that they are only driven from it by strong northeasterly storms. He also says that their diet is chiefly sea-food, scraps of shell-fish, drift, etc., which gives the flesh a sedgy taste.

Seaside Sparrow: *Ammodramus maritimus.*

Length: 5.75–6.25 inches.

Male and Female: Very dull brownish gray bird. Gray wash on shoulders and the edges of some feathers. Breast mottled gray with buff tinge. Throat yellow-white. Wings and tail dusky. *Yellow spot before eye and yellow mark* on edge of wing, the only bright colouring. Bill lead-coloured; dark feet.

Song: Very similar to that of the last species.

Season: Common summer resident, breeding on salt-marshes. Present December 9, 1889. Probably sometimes winters. (Averill.)

Breeds: Through range.

Nest and Eggs: Indistinguishable from last species.

Range: Salt-marshes of the Atlantic coast, from Massachusetts southward, and along the Gulf coast to the Rio Grande.

One of our two common Sparrows that have a maritime turn of mind, breeding freely about Fairfield and Stratford on the marshes. The two species are so closely associated that it is easy to confuse them; the Seaside Sparrow has the least definite colouring, no distinct black stripes on the back, and a blunt tail.

White-crowned Sparrow: *Zonotrichia leucophrys.*

Length: 6.50–7 inches.

Male and Female: *White crown* set between two black stripes; white eye stripes. Cheeks, throat, and back of neck gray. Below light gray; some buff on sides and belly. Wings edged with bay, and having two white cross-bars; tail plain. Female, head rusty, paler all through. Bill and feet reddish brown.

Song: 6 or 7 notes, forming a plaintive cadence.

Season: Rare migrant; October and May.

Breeds: Chiefly in the Rocky Mountain region (including Sierra Nevada), and northeast to Labrador.

Nest and Eggs: Not to be distinguished from those of the White-throated Sparrow.

Range: North America at large.

One of the largest Sparrows, and also conspicuously marked, the White-crown is scarcely the inferior of the White-throat itself. It has a northerly range, and only comes to us as a very restless migrant in middle autumn and late spring, when it is occasionally seen feeding with Juncos and White-throats.

White-throated Sparrow: *Zonotrichia albicollis.*

PLATE 26. FIG. 2.

Length: 6.50–7 inches.

Male and Female: A plump, handsome bird. *White throat and crown stripes.* Back striped with black, bay, and whitish. Rump light olive-brown. Bay edgings to wings, and two white cross-bars; under parts gray. *Yellow spot before eye.* Female crown, brown, markings less distinct.

Song: Sweet and plaintive, — "Pee-a-peabody, peabody, peabody!"

Season: Abundant migrant; also a winter resident from September to May.

Breeds: From New England and the Northern States northward.

Nest: A deep grass nest partly sunken in the ground or in a low bush.

Eggs: Variable, greenish, and thinly speckled with reddish brown to gray, blotched heavily with chocolate.

Range: Eastern North America west to the Plains, north to Labrador and the Fur Countries, and winters from the Middle States southward.

This is unquestionably the most beautiful of all the Sparrows, not excepting the great Fox Sparrow, and its rich velvety markings and sweet voice have made it one of the welcome migrants, and the few that remain through the winter are carefully fed and cherished.

The past season (1894) the upward migration began early in March, the 7, being the first day that I noticed a decided movement, and then no more large flocks appeared until the first week of May. A flock settled on a bit of ground newly sown with grass seed, and devoted themselves to it with such zest that at the end of three days every seed had found its way into their little stomachs; however, as the ground was near the piazza it gave me a fine opportunity to watch them, and four quarts of grass seed was a small price to pay for their society.

The White-throat's song has been expressed in many different syllables. It certainly says, "Pee-a-peabody, peabody, peabody"; words from which it received the name of Peabody Bird.

Wilson Flagg says that the Maine folk interpret the notes as, "All-day, whittling, whittling, whittling." And then there is the evidence of Farmer Peverly, whom Hamilton Gibson interviewed, who, upon being perplexed and undecided as to the crop that he ought to sow in a particular field, understood the Sparrow to say, "Sow *wheat,* Peverly, Peverly."

You may take your choice as to the *words*, but pray notice that all these interpretations have the *same accented* value, and so equally imitate the song. This Sparrow also sometimes sings softly in the night, —

"* * * *
Nestling in his tree
The sleeping Sparrow
Dreams a melody."

Tree Sparrow: *Spizella monticola.*

Winter Chip-bird.

Length: 5.75–6.25 inches.

Male and Female: *Bright bay crown.* Gray stripe over eye, cheeks, throat, and breast. Dark brown back with feathers pheasant-like, edged with orange and brown. Wings dark brown with paler edgings and two white bars. Bill black above, lower mandible yellowish, feet brownish black.

Song: In winter a twittering trill.

Season: Winter resident; October to April.

Breeds: North of the United States, east of the Rocky Mountains.

Nest: Of grass, bark, and feathers; on ground, in a bush, or occasionally in a tree.

Eggs: 4–7, light green, finely sprinkled with reddish brown.

Range: Eastern North America westward to the Plains, and from the Arctic Ocean south, in winter, to the Carolinas, Kentucky, and eastern Kansas.

Like the Junco, the Tree Sparrow is a winter resident, though not so constant and abundant as the former. It is much larger than the Chipping Sparrow, which it so closely

PLATE 30.

1. SONG SPARROW.

Length, 6–6.50 inches.

2. CHIPPING SPARROW.

Length, 5 inches.

resembles as to be called the Winter Chip-bird, coming at a season when the sociable Chippy has gone south. Why it is called Tree Sparrow is not so plain, as it does not build in trees as frequently as the Chippy, and it haunts low bushes. I have seen these Sparrows in December, feeding in flocks on the ground, in company with Snowbirds and a few stray White-throats; dashing about and sometimes singing in a sort of undertone, perfectly careless of cold. Burroughs calls the song "a soft, sweet note, almost running into a warble."

They are very hardy birds, and to them, as with all winter birds, mere cold is secondary in comparison with cutting winds. I have often seen them huddled under stone walls, and once found a flock feeding in the bottom of a dry ditch; and in ploughed fields you will notice that they keep closely to the furrows in windy weather. At night they troop into the evergreen hedge, the piazza vines, and under the rick edges,—anywhere that the wind may not pierce, for that, together with scanty food, reduces their vitality.

Chipping Sparrow: *Spizella socialis.*

Hair-bird, Chippy.

PLATE 30. FIG. 2.

Length: 5–5.25 inches.

Male and Female: Dark chestnut poll, gray stripe over eye, brown stripe through it. Stripes along back, dark orange and brown. Wings and tail dust-brown. Under parts light gray. Young with some black streaks on crown. Bill black; feet light.

Song: An insect-like tremolo, varying a little in tone from a locust. Call note, "Chip-chip!"

Season: Common summer resident; April to October.

Breeds: In the greater part of its range.

Nest: In bushes and also high trees, made of fine grasses and lined with horsehair—hence the name, Hair-bird.

Eggs: 4, greenish blue, with dark brown speckles.

Range: Eastern North America, west to the Rocky Mountains, north to Great Slave Lake, and south to eastern Mexico.

This is the precentor who, in early May dawns, gives the key on his little pitch-pipe and leads the chorus that makes four o'clock the most melodious hour of the day. T-r-r-r-r-r-r-r-r-r-r he trills from the ground, before even a Robin wakes, and then, as the music swells, he is lost in the harmony.

Who can fail to know the Chippy, whose mite of a gray-brown body is set off by a chestnut-coloured velvet cap, whose chirp, as he hops about the door craving crumbs, is as familiar as his pretty air of sociability. He has many little points of identity that separate him from the mazes of the Sparrow tribe. He seldom, if ever, nests upon the ground, and his nest, well built and carefully lined, is distinctive. Here in the garden he shows a preference for high trees; out of eight nests built last season within the garden limits, one was in a Deutzia shrub about three feet from the ground; four were in tufts of needles on the horizontal boughs of spruces, varying from eight to twenty feet high; and three were in white pines at distances of from twenty to forty feet from the ground.

I am inclined to think that the nesting-habits of birds are adapted by circumstances and their desire to locate in certain places. The Chippies like the protection and society of the house and build near it. Low bushes and undergrowth in this vicinity are limited, and the Catbirds usurp the most desirable shrubs. Not finding room below the Chippy ascends, as his fellow-men adapt themselves to the apartment house, so that from being ground-walkers they become "cliff-dwellers."

Field Sparrow: *Spizella pusilla.*

Length: 5.25–5.75 inches.

Male and Female: Pale red beak. Bright bay on the back between wings. Crown dull chestnut, no black or white. Whitish wing bars, tail longer than wings, below grayish white; very light-coloured feet.

Song: Very pleasing and melodious, "Whee-whee-whee-iddle, iddle, iddle, ee!"

Season: Common summer resident.

Breeds: From Virginia northward.

Nest: Of grass, in low shrubs or on ground.
Eggs: 4, cloudy white, spotted and specked with brown.
Range: Eastern United States and southern Canada, west to the Plains.

This is the tuneful Sparrow of fields and meadows that, rising as you approach, goes with a wavering flight to the next rift of grasses, never letting you come near it, and yet not appearing to be shy. At first you will think it a Chippy, but a glance with your field-glass will show you its reddish bill, longer tail, and red-brown upper back, and while you are considering these differences it will perhaps perch on a branch and sing (it seldom sings while flying), and then you will have been formally introduced to the Field Sparrow.

The three whistles which begin the song are very soft and sweet, having nothing sibilant about them, and the final trill dies away gradually, as if the bird was moving away as he sang. The quality of song resembles the Vesper Sparrow's, but has less variety. I have seen Field Sparrows here as late as Thanksgiving, but the records go to prove that the general range is more southerly than the Chippy's, and that it cannot be called common north of Massachusetts.

Slate-coloured Junco: *Junco hyemalis.*

Snowbird.

PLATE 29. FIG. 2.

Length: 6–6.50 inches.
Male and Female: Dark bluish slate all over, except lower breast and belly, which are grayish white and form a vest. Several outer tail feathers white, conspicuous in flying. Female, with a more rusty cast and vest less distinct. Bill flesh-white, dusky at tip.
Song: A crisp call note, a simple trill, and a faint whispering warble, usually much broken, but not without sweetness. (Bicknell.) Song sometimes heard before it leaves in spring.
Season: Common winter resident; late September to April.
Breeds: From the higher parts of the Alleghanies and northern New York and northern New England, northward.
Nest: On ground, Sparrow-like.
Eggs: 4–6, white, peppered with reddish brown.
Range: North America at large, but chiefly east of the Rocky Mountains; south in winter to the Gulf States.

The Juncos, whose habits are Sparrow-like, come to us after the summer moulting, varying their return with the weather. In 1893, they appeared September 25, but they may be expected to increase in number from this date until late October, while in November they go off on excursions in little parties, a habit that they keep up all winter.

You cannot fail to name the Junco, with his sad-coloured coat, light vest and tail feathers; his cheerful habits will allow you to become quite intimate with him before winter is over, for he will come freely to the door for food, and is a frequenter of city parks and even back yards.

Juncos are winter residents upon whom we can always depend, although the numbers vary greatly. A small flock has lodged for many seasons in the evergreen honeysuckles about the house, and one bitterly cold February, when every seed was frozen down, a number came into the barn, feeble and exhausted, and pecked about the grain bin, mutely waiting for food; nor were they disappointed.

Together with the Chickadee they are frequently to be seen around the kennels, where the dogs always treat them with courtesy. They usually leave in early April, but sometimes lingering into May, they let us hear their song before they go northward for their wooing.

Song Sparrow: *Melospiza fasciata.*

PLATE 30. FIG. 1.

Length: 6–6.50 inches.

Male and Female: Brown poll, somewhat striped. Above gray and brown, thickly striped. Gray stripe over eye; brown stripe each side of throat; dark stripes across upper breast, forming *a black spot* in front. Beneath gray, slightly striped. Bill dark brown; feet pale brown.

Song: "Olit, olit, olit, — chip, chip, chip, che-char, — che-wiss, wiss, wiss!" (Thoreau, "Walden.") "Maids, maids, maids, hang on your teakettle-ettle-ettle!" (A local interpretation. Thoreau, "Summer.")

Season: March until November. Individuals remain through the year.

Breeds: From Virginia and the northern portion of the Lake States northward. Sometimes three broods are reared.

Nest: Location variable; on ground or in low bush.
Eggs: Grayish white, spotted, marked, and clouded with browns and lavender.
Range: Eastern United States to the Plains.

The Song Sparrow is the darling among the Song-birds; the Goldfinch's gay coat, the Bluebird's confidential murmur, or the melody of the Thrushes cannot rival him in our affections, even though they may possess superior qualities. Plain as his coat is, he carries his identity in the little black streaks that form two spots on his breast, and all the year we may hope to hear his simple domestic ballad. Thoreau says: "Some birds are poets and sing all summer. They are the true singers. Any man can write verses in the love season. We are most interested in those birds that sing for the love of the music, and not of their mates; who meditate their strains and amuse themselves with singing; the birds whose strains are of deeper sentiment."

This is the Song Sparrow. He is the most constant singer among our northern birds; he has other songs in his repertoire beside love-songs, even though he excels in these, his later efforts lacking their variety. He sings to you from the snow-powdered trees in February, to keep up your spirits. In March he comes out on a bush and tells you that the buds are swelling and that it is really spring. In April, May, and June he is in an ecstasy; he sings to his mate, to the earth, to the sky, and to you, varying his theme until the simple melody of three notes and an *appoggiatura* is lost in endless changes.

In July his song loses quality, and August heat drives him, somewhat discouraged, to moult in bushy seclusion, but does not wholly silence him. With middle September he emerges and begins anew, greeting the migrating birds as they return; and all through October his notes sound clearly above the rustling leaves, and some morning he comes to the dogwood by the arbour and announces the first frost in a song that is more direct than that in which he told of spring. While the chestnuts fall from their velvet nests, he is singing in the hedge; but when the brush heaps burn away to fragrant smoke in November, they veil his song a little, but it still continues.

December daunts him, — so long to spring, he thinks, but even then a warm sunbeam draws out a note or two; and when January's iron hand numbs him, he whispers, "so long since summer," and breathes a note in undertone for memory's sake; so is completed this Sparrow's year of song.

Swamp Song Sparrow: *Melospiza georgiana.*

Length: 4.50–4.80 inches.

Male and Female: Crown bright bay, gray stripe over eye and gray wash over brown around neck. Back striped with various browns. Tail reddish brown. Much bay on wings. Mottled gray below.

Song: A liquid though monotonous trill.

Season: Migrant; March and April, October and November. Breeds here sparingly.

Breeds: From Northern States northward.

Nest and Eggs: In tussock or bush in swamp, otherwise like Song Sparrow's; eggs also similar.

Range: Eastern North America to the Plains, accidentally to Utah, north to the British Provinces, including Newfoundland and Labrador. Winters in the Middle States and southward.

The distinctive marks of the Swamp Song Sparrow are its *bright bay crown, bay wing-edges, and absence of any yellow washes,* or *white tail feathers.* The Chipping Sparrow has the bay crown, but lacks the bay on the wings; the Vesper Sparrow has the bay wings, but lacks the crown, but the Swamp Sparrow has both.

This Sparrow has neither the vocal powers or the sociability of the Song Sparrow. It is a shy bird that loves deep, cool thickets and haunts such impenetrable shrubberies as border sphagnum bogs; and though it is common in such places, when you look for it you will find it as elusive as the Veery and Marsh Wrens.

Its fresh trill can be heard from middle April until it passes on in May; where it breeds it sings almost continu-

TOWHEE.

Length, 7.50–8.75 inches.

ously until August, and after moulting has an intermittent period of song before it leaves in October.

Fox Sparrow: *Passerella iliaca.*

Length: 6.50–7.25 inches.

Male and Female: The largest and reddest of the Sparrows, the size of the Hermit Thrush. Above red-brown, varying from dark to bright chestnut, brightest on rump and tail. Breast light gray, arrowhead markings on throat and breast, sides streaked with reddish brown. Bill dark above, lower mandible yellowish, feet pale.

Song: A sweet, varied warble, sometimes heard during migrations. Call note a feeble zip-zip.

Season: In migrations. Common in March, April, October, and November. Found by Mr. Averill as late as December 29.

Breeds: North of the United States.

Nest: Usual Ground Sparrow nest.

Eggs: Greenish white, speckled with red-brown.

Range: Eastern North America, west to the Plains and Alaska (valley of the Yukon to the Pacific), and from the Arctic coast south to the United States. Winters chiefly south of the Potomac and Ohio rivers.

This bird, whose fox-red feathers, and not a sly disposition, give it the name of Fox Sparrow, is a delightful songster as well as a large and boldly marked species. They come in flocks in very early spring, — when the Bluebird and Song Sparrow are sharing the musical honours, — and, settling on the pastures, send up a wave of gentle music, and when they return in autumn they still give a few soft notes.

Mr. Bicknell has heard them sing as early as February 29 and as late as November 17. He says that this Sparrow seems indisposed to sing unless present in numbers. This probably applies only to the anti-nuptial song; for, as a rule, the *perfect* song of wild birds is not heard before they leave and after they rejoin the flocks, but only at the period when they assert themselves as individuals.

Towhee: *Pipilo erythrophthalmus.*

Chewink, Ground Robin.

PLATE 31.

Length: 7.50–8.75 inches.

Male: Head, neck, chest, back, and all but outer tail feathers black. Belly and spots on outer tail feathers white, sides light bay. Bill black; feet light brown.

Female: Drab or brownish where the male is black.

Song: Clear and ringing, "Tewéek—tewéek—towhee—blure—towhee blure!"

Season: Common summer resident; late April to October.

Breeds: In its range generally.

Nest: On the ground; of grass, fibres, hair, etc.; large but well concealed by underbrush.

Eggs: White, heavily speckled with brown.

Range: Eastern United States and southern Canada, west to the Plains.

In early May when the Thrushes are scratching in the shrubbery, a stranger appears among them, clad in bay, white, and black, who hops with such exaggerated precision that he seems like a messenger bearing important news. But it is only another of the Sparrow tribe, wearing the thick bill of the Buntings. He has probably been in the vicinity a week or two but has kept aloof. He bears the local name of Ground Robin, because he nests upon the ground and has partially reddish under parts.

Although common summer residents they are so shy that they are rarely seen after the breeding-season. If you approach the nest, the male will run through the bushes in an opposite direction, uttering his sharp "tewéek, towhee" (a note which suggested the name Towhee) and in his anxiety exposes himself fully to view. Late in the afternoon he mounts a tree, at some distance from his nest, and rings out his rather defiant song.

He is a very restless bird, prying about continually for seeds and insects, upon which he feeds equally, and in autumn he also eats such berries as he can glean. After the moulting he only gives his call note and, being affected

PLATE 32.

CARDINAL.

Length, 8–9 inches.

by cold, leaves before hard frosts. A pair or two always nest in the garden under a tangle of wild grape-vines.

Cardinal: *Cardinalis cardinalis.*

Cardinal Grosbeak, Virginia Nightingale.

PLATE 32.

Length: 8–9 inches.

Male: Magnificent red, conspicuously crested; black throat and band around beak. Wings at some seasons washed with gray. Bill light red; feet brown.

Female: Brownish yellow; crest, wings, and tail reddish.

Song: A full, rich whistle,—"Cheo-cheo-chehoo-cheo!" Female also sings.

Season: A notable bird of the Southern States, straggling as far north as Massachusetts.

Breeds: Through its range.

Nest: Bulky and loosely made of bark, leaves, and grass placed in a bush.

Eggs: Pale gray, marked with brown, varying from red to chocolate.

Range: Eastern United States, north to New Jersey and the Ohio Valley (casually farther), west to the Plains.

As a cage bird the Cardinal is familiar to nearly every one; although in confinement he soon loses the brilliancy of his plumage, he often keeps his full song. He is regarded as a semi-tropical species, yet in the breeding-season he strays into the New England States; winters plentifully in lower Pennsylvania, while a small colony are resident in Central Park, New York.

The Cardinal owes many of his misfortunes to his "fatal gift of beauty." It is simply impossible that he should escape notice, and to be seen, in spite of laws to the contrary, means that he will either be trapped, shot, or persecuted out of the country. The fact that this bird has not become extinct is a wonderful proof of the endurance and persistency of the species.

In the vicinity of New York, Mr. Bicknell says that its song lasts from April to August, and that he has seen the Cardinal in every month from October to March. Wilson writes that the full song lasts, in the South, from March to

September, and that in January and February this bird's clear notes are the only music. In Europe, where they are highly prized as cage birds, the name of Virginia Nightingale is given them.

The most delicate and pathetic description of this bird, whose beauty is his knell, is to be found in J. L. Allen's "Kentucky Cardinal," — that story in which a knowledge of wild Nature and of the human heart are so perfectly blended: — "Lo! some morning the leaves are on the ground, and the birds have vanished. The species that remain, or that come to us then, wear the hues of the season and melt into the tone of Nature's background, — blues, grays, browns, with touches of white on tail and breast and wing for coming flecks of snow.

"Save only him, — proud, solitary stranger to our unfriendly land, — the fiery Grosbeak. Nature in Kentucky has no wintry harmonies for him. He could find these only among the tufts of the October sumach, or in the gum-tree when it stands a pillar of red twilight fire in the dark November woods, or in the far depths of the crimson sunset skies, where, indeed, he seems to have been nested, and whence to have come as a messenger of beauty, bearing on his wings the light of his diviner home. . . . What wonder if he is so shy, so rare, so secluded, this flame-coloured prisoner in dark green chambers, who has only to be seen or heard and Death adjusts an arrow! . . . He will sit for a long time in the heart of a cedar, as if absorbed in the tragic memories of his race. Then, softly, wearily, he will call out to you and to the whole world: *Peace . . . Peace . . . Peace . . . Peace . . . Peace . . .!* — the most melodious sigh that ever issued from the clefts of a dungeon."

Rose-breasted Grosbeak: *Habia ludoviciana.*

Plate 33.

Length: 7.75–8.50 inches.

Male: Breast rose-carmine, which colour extends under the wings. Above black; belly, rump, three outer tail quills and two spots on wings white; white bill.

ROSE-BREASTED GROSBEAK.

Length, 7.75–8.50 inches.

Female: Brownish, sulphur-yellow under wings; no rosy tint; heavy brown bill.

Song: A delightful, rolling warble, often heard toward evening.

Season: Common summer resident; May 1 to middle September.

Breeds: From the Middle States northward.

Nest: A perfect circle, neatly made of fibres and grass, lined with finer grasses, placed in a low tree, or more frequently a thorn bush in old pastures near the edge of woods.

Eggs: Dirty green, with dark brown spots and speckles.

Range: Eastern United States and southern Canada; west to the eastern border of the Plains; south in winter to Cuba, Central America, and northern South America.

You will always remember the day when you first see this Grosbeak. Its song may be familiar to you, though you are wholly unconscious of it; for in the great spring chorus you may mistake it for a particularly melodious Robin, who has added a few Oriole notes to his repertoire. The Grosbeak's song, however, has a retrospective quality all its own, and shared by neither Robin or Oriole, — a sort of dreaminess, in keeping with its habit of singing into the night. Gibson says that its song is suffused with colour like a luscious tropic fruit rendered into sound.

The songster itself, if seen feeding, as it sometimes does, upon the grass, is a dark, clumsy-looking bird, with an awkward beak; and it is only when you look at it from beneath, as it perches in the trees, that you see the rosy shield and flush under the outspread wings.

I first identified bird and song one June twilight, after a day when the roses had burst into sudden bloom; and it seemed as if their glorious colour was reflected on this novel bird and mingled with his song. I have never found the nest near here, but Mr. Averill says that they breed freely in the vicinity, and that this spring he saw a male covering the nest, an unusual occurrence with birds of such conspicuous colouring.

In some parts of Pennsylvania, according to Dr. Warren, the farmers protect this Grosbeak, owing to its services in killing potato-bugs, and have christened it the Potato-bug Bird. Its diet is varied, comprising beetles, flies, larvæ, seeds, the buds of hickory, beech, and birch, and fruit blossoms.

The distribution of the Grosbeak is somewhat irregular; it will be common on one side of a river and rare on the other, or plentiful on both sides of a range of hills and unknown among the hills themselves. The song is continued well into August, but the bird is quite silent before leaving in September. Two or three years are required to bring the rose-coloured markings to perfection; but Mr. Bicknell once shot a young male on the 23, of September, whose breast was crimsoning, and who was in full song. This last fact adds proof to a pet theory of my own, that the best autumn music is made by the birds of the season.

Indigo Bunting: *Passerina cyanea.*

PLATE 34.

Length: 5.50 inches.

Male: Deep blue (in some lights, having a greenish cast), deepest on head; rump, wings, and tail washed thinly with brownish. Bill dark above, lighter below.

Female: Above, warm brown, whitening on breast.

Song: Sweet but weak,—"Tshe—tshe—tshe—tshay!"

Season: Middle of May to third week in September.

Breeds: Through its United States range.

Nest: In bushes, bulky and rude, of leaves and grass.

Eggs: Bluish or pure white, with brown spots.

Range: Eastern United States, south, in winter, to Veragua.

Beautiful plumage and a very small voice is the sum of the Indigo Bunting's attractions. It comes about the middle of May with the Scarlet Tanager, and if you should chance to find these birds in company, as sometimes happens, resting on the same rough fence rail, while a Goldfinch swings near them among the wayside grasses, you will have seen the primary colours as illustrated in bird life.

When the Bunting feeds upon the ground, as is his usual habit, his food consisting mainly of the seed of small grasses and herbs, his plumage is brought out wonderfully by the play of light upon it, varying from deep blue to a tint of *verde antique*, unlike the Bluebird's sky colour.

PLATE 34.

INDIGO BUNTING.

1. Male. 2. Female.

Length, 5.50 inches.

The most likely place to find him is in old, bush-grown pastures, and along the lane hedges; like all the bright-hued birds he is beset by enemies both of earth and sky, but his Sparrow instinct, which has a love for mother-earth, bids him build near the ground. The dangers of the nesting-time fall mostly to his share, for his dull brown mate is easily overlooked as an insignificant Sparrow. Nature almost always gives a plain coat to the wives of these gayly dressed cavaliers, for her primal thought is the safety of the home and its young life.

FAMILY ICTERIDÆ: BLACKBIRDS, ORIOLES, ETC.

Bobolink: *Dolichonyx oryzivorus.*

After moult Reed-bird.

PLATE 35.

Length: 6.50-7 inches.

Male: Black head, chin, tail, wings, and under parts. Buff patch on back of neck; also buff edges to some tail and wing feathers. Rump and upper wing coverts white. Bill brown. *In autumn similar to female.*

Female: Below yellowish brown. Above striped brown, except on rump, with yellow and white tips to some feathers. Two dark stripes on crown.

Song: A delightful, incoherent melody; sung oftentimes as the bird soars upward.

Season: Early May to October.

Breeds: From the middle United States northward, and winters south of the United States.

Nest: A loose heap of twigs and grass on the ground in low meadows and hay-fields; common, but very difficult to discover.

Eggs: 4-6, clear gray, with clouds and markings of dark brown.

Range: Eastern North America to the Great Plains, north to southern Canada; south, in winter, to the West Indies and South America.

The Bobolink, the bird of two lives in one! The wild, ecstatic black and buff singer, who soars above the May meadows, leaving a trail of rippling music, and in autumn the brown striped bird who, voiceless but for a metallic "chink," is hunted through the marshes by the gunners, making his last appearance as an article of food, heralded on the restaurant bill of fare thus: "Reed-birds, four on a skewer, 50 cents."

Strange to say that two-thirds of the gunners who do the shooting deny that the birds are identical and that they are killing so much latent music. "The brown birds are all females," they say, "which, being greatly in excess of the males, remain after the latter have disappeared." I would advise all such incredulous ones to buy *The Auk* (an intelligible ornithological quarterly) for October, 1893, where they will find a paper on this subject by Mr. Frank M. Chapman, and a coloured plate showing the Bobolink life-sized, in the spring transition, when he is again moulting the stripes for the breeding-coat.

Of all our songsters none enter into the literature of fact and fancy more fully than the Bobolink, and none so exhilarates us by his song. Sit upon the fence of an upland meadow any time from early May until the last of June, watch and listen. Up from the grass the Bobolinks fly, some singing and dropping again, others rising Lark-like until the distant notes sound like the tinkling of an ancient clavichord. Then, while you are gazing skyward, from the choke-cherry tree above your head will come the hurried syllables in which Mr. Burroughs interprets the song: "Ha! Ha! Ha! I must have my fun, Miss Silver-thimble, if I break every heart in the meadow, see, see, see!" Meanwhile, the grass is full of nests and brown mothers, neither of which you see, for you are wholly entranced by the song.

Bryant's poem on Robert of Lincoln contains a good description of the bird's plumage, but is too precise and measured to express the rapture of the song. It may describe a stuffed Bobolink, but never a wild, living one. Wilson Flagg's verses on The O'Lincon Family, one of which I quote, are in truer key: —

"Every one's a funny fellow; every one's a little mellow;
Follow, follow, follow, follow, o'er the hill and in the hollow.
Merrily, merrily, there they hie; now they rise and now they fly;

PLATE 35.

BOBOLINK.

1. Male. 2. Female.

Length, 6.50–7 inches.

They cross and turn, and in and out, and down the middle and wheel
about,
With a 'Phew, shew, Wadolincon; listen to me, Bobolincon!
Happy's the wooing that's speedily doing, that's speedily doing,
That's merry and over with the bloom of the clover;
Bobolincon, Wadolincon, Winterseeble, follow, follow me!'"

The prose writers vie with the poets in singing the Bobolink's praises, their own words turning to music under his spell. Listen to what Thoreau says of the song: "It is as if he [the bird] touched his harp with a vase of liquid melody, and when he lifted it out the notes fell like bubbles from the strings." . . . "away he launches, and the meadow is all bespattered with melody."

What matters it to us who hear his song in the north if the singer, in his migrations, is at war with the rice-growers of warmer regions? Here he is the peerless musician, whom no one should wittingly destroy; and yet we buy "Reedbirds, four on a skewer, for 50 cents."

Cowbird: *Molothrus ater.*

PLATE 39. FIG. 1.

Length: 7.50–8 inches.

Male: Head, throat, and shoulders glistening dark brown; all other parts iridescent black. Bill dark brown; feet rusty black. A walker.

Female: Dull, brownish gray.

Song: A whistle and a few short, rasping notes. Call note, "Cluck-see!"

Season: March to November; occasionally winters.

Breeds: Through range.

Nest: Builds none, but lays its eggs at random in the nests of other birds, *usually choosing those of species smaller than itself.*

Eggs: Almost an inch long, white, speckled with brown and various shades of gray.

Range: United States from the Atlantic to the Pacific; north into southern British America; south, in winter, into Mexico.

The Cowbird is the pariah of bird-dom, the exception that proves the rule of marital fidelity and good housekeeping. It is the bird that you see so frequently in pastures, walking after the grazing cattle and feeding upon the insects dislodged from the grass by their cropping. Other birds build a home and seek a mate, often remaining with the same one a lifetime. The Cowbirds are polygamous, living in roving flocks, building no nests, and providing in no way for their offspring. When the laying impulse seizes them, they slyly deposit the egg in the nest of some smaller bird. This shows forethought, however; for there is less likelihood of the eggs being thrust out, and it also obtains a greater share of warmth than the other eggs in the nest and hatches more rapidly.

Many birds do not allow themselves to be so imposed upon, and either eject the strange egg, build a new nest over it, or abandon their nest entirely; others seemingly less intelligent will rear the ungainly stranger, even though from its greater size and appetite it crowds and starves the legitimate tenants of the nest. I have many and many a time seen a young Cowbird, after leaving the nest, being fed by a bird so much smaller than itself that the poor foster parent had to stand on tiptoe.

Cowbirds' eggs have been found in the nests of the Chat, Baltimore Oriole, Wood Thrush, Mourning Dove, Kingbird, Towhee, Vireos, Warblers, and all the Sparrows, and even in the secluded hut of the Ovenbird, while many nests are so unfortunate as to contain more than one of these eggs.

Vagrants as the Cowbirds are in the breeding-season, after the nesting the young do not continue with their foster parents, but return to the flocks of their progenitors, and remain with them. Thus these Cowbirds are the socialists among birds, and are like their human prototypes, who send their young to free kindergartens and mission schools that they may be fed and clothed at the expense of others; *then* drawing them surely back, with their inherited principles unchanged. Some evils are inextricably mixed up with the foundations of things.

PLATE 36.

RED-WINGED BLACKBIRD.

Length, about 9 inches.

Red-winged Blackbird: *Agelaius phœniceus.*

PLATE 36.

Length: Very variable; 8.25–9.85 inches.

Male: Rich blue-black; scarlet shoulders, edged with yellow.

Female: Finely speckled with rusty black, brown, and orange. Shoulders obscurely orange-red.

Song: A rich, juicy note, — "Oucher-la-ree-ê!"

Season: Late March to October. Sometimes winters.

Breeds: Through summer range.

Nest: A bulky pocket hung between reeds or stems of alders, etc.; made of rush blades and grass, and lined with finer grasses.

Eggs: 4–6, light blue, fancifully marked with lines, dots, and patches of black and lilac.

Range: North America in general, from Great Slave Lake south to Costa Rica.

As a summer resident the Red-winged Blackbird is a familiar sight in low meadows and along roadsides. At a little distance he appears to be only a plain, black bird, but as he extends his wings his brilliant epaulets come into prominence. The plumage of the female, though inconspicuous, is singularly beautiful when seen at close range. It looks like a fabric of which the warp is black and the woof a twisted thread of brown and yellow. The Redwings are essentially early birds, often returning in spring when their marshy haunts are still frozen over. Their vocalization is suggestive of cool, moist ground and hidden springs; it continues until late July, and is briefly renewed in October. The deep nest is half hung, half twined between the stems of marsh-growing plants, and often holds two broods of a season; the boggy location chosen serves to protect it quite thoroughly from human invaders.

This Blackbird's clear notes are associated with those of the Meadowlark, as they are both early singers and are found in similar places. They are useful birds to the agriculturist, as they are great destroyers of cutworms. They are sometimes polygamous, though as frequently seen in pairs; being very gregarious birds, many nests are usually found in the same locality.

Meadowlark: *Sturnella magna.*

PLATE 1.

Length: 10.75 inches.

Male and Female: Much variegated above, general colour brown. Bill stout and straight. Crown with brown and black streaks, black line behind eye. Tail black with white outer quills; wings edged with yellow. *Under parts yellow, black crescent on throat.* Strong legs, a walker. Female paler.

Song: Clear and piercing, — "Spring o' the Y-e-a-r!"

Season: A resident, the migrants remaining from April until late October.

Breeds: Abundantly throughout its range.

Nest: Of dried grass; placed on the ground; usually concealed by a tuft of grass, which makes a partial roof.

Eggs: 4-6, brilliant white, speckled with purple and reddish brown.

Range: Eastern United States and southern Canada, to the Plains.

This abundant bird, common in the migrations, and present with us all winter in considerable numbers, is not a Lark at all; it has superb plumage, and its song, though consisting of but a few syllables, is sweet and thrilling. Almost before a tinge of green has come upon the meadows, these birds are searching for worms and larvæ, which form a large part of their diet, and it is at this time that they show their yellow breasts, with the striking black crescent, to the best advantage. While they are feeding, they constantly give their calling song, varying the intonation and accent in a way which is very expressive — "Spring o' the *Y-e-a-r*, *Spring* o' the Year!" It has a breezy sound, as fresh and wild as if the wind were blowing through a flute. They sing from March until July, and then again after the moulting, though at this time they never equal their spring song, and I have heard a few notes in January, when they were lingering about the stubble fields. In winter they often come about the barns for food, and will stand quite still, and watch me while I scatter seeds to them and other such way farers.

The Meadowlark is one of the most constant of the winter colony, associating with the Horned Lark on the shore

PLATE 37.

ORCHARD ORIOLE.

1. Male. 2. Female.

Length, 7 inches.

meadows, and with the Snowflakes in the inland fields, from which he announces "Spring o' the Year" with his penetrating voice, almost before that coy season has awaked and warmed her fingers in the sun's grudging rays.

Orchard Oriole: *Icterus spurius.*

PLATE 37.

Length: 7 inches.

Male: Black head, chin, neck, throat, tail, and part of wings. Breast, belly, rump, and shoulders chestnut-brown. White wing bar, and some feathers edged with black and chestnut. Round black tail edged with lighter. Bill and feet bluish black.

Female: Upper parts brown, wings with pale buff edges and shoulder bars. Throat black, rump and edges of some tail feathers olive-green. Under parts olive-yellow.

Song: Resembling that of the Baltimore Oriole, but less shrill.

Season: Summer resident; May to September.

Breeds: Throughout United States range.

Nest: A round basket-like structure, notable for its even weaving. It may be pensile or only partly so, and is usually placed in a fruit tree at a moderate height.

Eggs: 4, cloudy white, spotted with blackish brown.

Range: United States, west to the Plains; south, in winter, to Panama.

The Orchard Oriole is less known in New England than the Baltimore Oriole, not only because of its duller colouring but because its range is more southerly, and though it goes all through the Eastern States it is not plentiful north of Massachusetts.

I can always rely upon seeing a few pairs about the garden in May, when the early apples are in bloom; for though these Orioles are chiefly insect-eaters, they will sometimes help themselves to the fruit blossoms, and later on to an occasional meal from the raspberry vines or the strawberry bed. These depredations, however, are trifling in comparison to the good they do in destroying plant-lice, beetles, rose-slugs, and cabbage-worms.

As singers their notes are more harsh and rapidly uttered than those of the other species, and are not particularly distinguishable in the bird chorus; but as nest-builders they excel, and there is no nest that more closely resembles man's primitive efforts at basket-weaving. It is usually suspended between branches or twigs, and is woven of dried grasses of nearly equal size, so that the nest is very neat and even. Old orchards are favourite haunts of this bird, for it is very shy and seldom builds near dwellings. Its song season is brief, being over in July, and even immediately after the nesting, when the young birds mingle their immature plumage and attempted song, the identification of either song or bird is difficult for the novice.

Baltimore Oriole: *Icterus galbula.*

Golden Oriole, Hang-nest, Golden Robin.

PLATE 38.

Length: 8 inches.

Male: Black head, throat, and upper half of back. Wings black, with white spots and edges; tail quills spotted with yellow. *Everywhere else orange-flame.* Bill and feet slatish black.

Female: Paler, the black washed with olive. Below dull orange.

Song: Somewhat shrill and interrogative, but withal martial. In the breeding-season they have an anxious call, — "Will you? Will you really, really, truly?" Female's note a plaintive "I w-i-ll."

Season: 1st of May to the middle of September.

Breeds: Through range.

Nest: A pensile pocket, woven of milkweed, flax, fine string, or frayings of cotton, rope, etc.; suspended at the end of a swaying branch at considerable distance from the ground.

Eggs: 4–6, whitish ground, scrawled with black-brown.

Range: Eastern United States, west nearly to the Rocky Mountains.

There is a bit of history as well as tradition connected with the naming of this splendid bird. George Calvert, the first Baron Baltimore, who penned the charter of settlement in 1632 of the country which now comprises the states of Delaware and Maryland (a grant which fructified later for the benefit of his son), is the subject of the tradition which still lingers in Maryland, and has sufficient facts for a foundation to be credible. The story says that Calvert, worn out and discouraged by the various trials and rigours of temperature in his Newfoundland colony, in 1628 visited the Virginia settlement. He explored the waters of the Chesapeake, with its noble tributaries and delicious climate, and found the shores and woods teeming with birds, and among them great flocks of Orioles, who so cheered him by their song and colour that he took them as good omens and adopted their colours for his own. Be this as it may, it is a likely story; for the Oriole has gone on cheering and charming mankind to this day.

The Oriole comes in full plumage and song in time to sing the praises of the blooming orchards, but if the season is cold and late and the cherries do not yield their mimic snow-storm, — my Lord Baltimore also delays his coming. When these Orioles first arrive the males are in the majority, and they sit in the spruces calling by the hour, with a lonely querulous note.

In a few days the females appear in force, and then the martial music begins, and the birds' golden trumpeting often turns to a desperate clashing of cymbals when two males engage in combat; for the Oriole has a temper to match his flaming plumage and fights with a will.

The next step is the selection of a nesting-tree. It must be tall with swinging branches to yield when the wind blows, and near enough to civilization to intimidate the Hawks.

Hush! 'tis he!
My Oriole, my glance of summer fire,
Is come at last, and ever on the watch,
Twitches the pack-thread I had lightly wound
About the bough to help his housekeeping, —
Twitches and scouts by turns, blessing his luck,
Yet fearing me who laid it in his way,
Nor, more than wiser we in our affairs,
Divines the providence that hides and helps.
Heave, ho! Heave, ho! he whistles as the twine
Slackens its hold; *once more, now!* and a flash
Lightens across the sunlight to the elm
Where his mate dangles at her cup of felt. — LOWELL.

If the situation is protected from birds of prey, the nest is made quite open at the top; but if it is in a wild and remote region, the structure is more bottle-shaped, with a small opening, which completely hides the sitting bird. This accounts for the great variation in the form of nests found in different localities.

The Oriole is a beneficent garden guest; his food is largely insectivorous, and he not only eats worms and grubs, but also strips cocoons of their latent mischief; so we will not begrudge him a few cherries for dessert.

He is a quick-witted bird, and a good neighbour to his fellows. Many instances of his power of thinking have come under my eyes, but none more forcible than an episode of last season. In June I was sitting under the trees, watching the evolutions of a pair of Redstarts, when a violent commotion in the shrubbery attracted me. Catbirds were screaming lustily, and Robins, Wrens, and Sparrows collected at the call in a body, while a gorgeous Oriole shot through the trees, close above my head. The cause of the rumpus was a chipmunk, who had dragged a young Catbird from the nest by the leg (for this little pest steals birds as well as eggs, though I have never seen them *eat* a bird). The troop of birds succeeded in frightening away the intruder, and I returned to my hammock, thinking no more of it. Not so with the Oriole. He silently watched the chipmunk, who sat chattering in a pine. Several minutes passed, and then the chipmunk ran out in full view on a long bough. Quick as a flash the Oriole darted at him, and pierced the poppy eyes with his slender beak, in rapid succession. The unfortunate chipmunk fell to the ground, and was put out of misery, while the Oriole flew off as if nothing unusual had happened, and was soon swinging and singing in the elm again, the type of summer fervour. Unlike many highly coloured birds, he retains his brilliancy after moulting, and also has a second period of song, which lasts from August until early September, when he leaves us.

BALTIMORE ORIOLE.

Length, 8 inches.

1. COWBIRD.

Length, 7.50–8 inches.

2. PURPLE GRACKLE.

Length, 12–13.50 inches.

Rusty Blackbird: *Scolecophagus carolinus.*

Thrush Blackbird.

Length: 9–9.50 inches.

Male: In breeding-plumage. Glossy black with metallic glints and a rusty wash. In autumn more decidedly rust-coloured. Bill and feet black.

Female: Deep rusty brown above, grayish below.

Song: Only a clucking call note.

Season: Common migrant; April, October, and November; may winter.

Breeds: From northern New England northward.

Nest: Bulky, of dried grasses, lined with mud and slung among reeds or bushes over water like that of the Red-wing.

Eggs: 4, colouring very variable, greenish blue to grayish white, mottled with brown.

Range: Eastern North America, west to Alaska and the Plains.

You may identify these inconspicuous Blackbirds by their pale, straw-coloured eyes, and the rusty wash that dims their feathers, also from the fact that in spring they arrive in single pairs and not in flocks like the Grackles, while in fall they travel in *small* flocks and mingle with the Cowbirds in the pastures.

Purple Grackle: *Quiscalus quiscula.*

Crow Blackbird.

PLATE 39. FIG. 2.

Length: 12–13.50 inches.

Male and Female: Glossy metallic black, iridescent tints on head, tail, and wings. Iris bright yellow, tail longer than wings, feet black. Female more dull and smaller.

Song: A crackling, wheezy squeaking; call note a rasping chirp.

Season: Common summer resident. I have also seen them in every month but January and February.

Breeds: Through range, most freely in the northern part of it.

Nest: A carefully built nest of rather miscellaneous materials, mud-lined, usually in trees, sometimes in a hollow tree. In evergreens in many localities but never here, orchards being their favourite spot.

Eggs: Indescribable, different sets wholly unlike; the average groundwork soiled blue or green, waved, streaked, and clouded with brown.

Range: Atlantic States from Florida to Long Island.

The most familiar of the Blackbirds as well as the most persecuted. Hated by the farmer for the alleged destruction of corn-fields while even at the harvest season, they rid the soil of noxious insects and grubs and all the rest of the year are either harmless gleaners or beneficial scavengers, their gravest fault being that they sometimes destroy and eat the eggs of other birds.

The Grackles begin their upward migration early in March, and some gray morning an immense flock will appear festooning the bare tree, in which they settle with scintillating black, uttering at the same time a series of unique and discordant cries which would put the wildest *banshee* to shame. Hereabout they always choose an old stumpy orchard as their nesting-place though many authorities consider that they nest preferably in conifers, — Dr. Abbot among others, giving a detailed account of their preference, during a particular season, for pines, ignoring the great beeches where they had previously colonized.

In May of last year I had the pleasure of watching a fine male Grackle sing his ludicrous love-song. Ludicrous from my point of view, though doubtless from a Grackle's standpoint it was exceedingly thrilling, and the lady to whom it was addressed so considered it.

It was the 15th of May, and the Grackle perched in my blighted old ash tree, displaying his glistening coat to the best advantage in the afternoon sun. The female was coyly hidden in the dogwood below him. Suddenly he spread his wings and tail, ruffed his breast, at the same time rising on tiptoe, like a melodramatic tenor, and uttered a high squeak expressive of his deep emotion. I expected that the female would fly away in disgust, but no, at each outburst she crept nearer and nearer and finally ventured upon the same branch that held the frantic singer.

The flocking of the Grackles in early September is one

PLATE 40.

BLUE JAY.

Length, 11–12 inches.

of the first signs of autumn, and they drop and settle in the lane and by the pool as if to warn the leaves that they must soon follow.

FAMILY CORVIDÆ: CROWS, JAYS, MAGPIES.

SUB-FAMILY GARRULINÆ: JAYS.

Blue Jay: *Cyanocitta cristata.*

PLATE 40.

Length: 11–12 inches.

Male and Female: Lead-blue above, head finely crested, a black collar uniting with some black feathers on the back. Below grayish white. Wing coverts and tail a bright blue barred transversely with black.

Song: A whistling bell note in the breeding season, the usual cry a screaming "Jay, jay, jay!"

Season: Resident.

Breeds: Through range.

Nest: Bulky, in appearance like that of the Crow, but only one-quarter the size.

Eggs: 5–6, about an inch long and broad for the length, brownish gray, with brown spots.

Range: Eastern North America to the Plains, and from the Fur Countries south to Florida and eastern Texas.

When you see Jays in small flocks circling the trees in early spring and gathering their crop of chestnuts in the fall and acorns in early winter, you admire their brilliant colouring, jaunty crest and bold flight, merely wishing perhaps that their cry was less harsh.

But how do these birds amuse themselves in the period between April and September, in their breeding and moulting season, when they are comparatively inconspicuous, for they go into the woods to breed and become almost silent, — it is a case of still waters running deeply? Day by day they sally out of their nesting-places to market for themselves and for their young, and nothing will do for them but fresh eggs and tender squabs from the nests of the Song-birds; to be followed later by berries, small fruit, and grain. There are birds that have all the domestic virtues coupled with personal beauty and interesting habits; birds who are of benefit to general agriculture, but still make themselves very unwelcome in the home woods or about the gardens of the lovers of Song-birds. Of this class the Jay and the Crow, fellow members of one family, are conspicuous examples, the Crow of course lacking the attribute of beauty.

It is interesting to be assured by Mr. Beal's report[1] that "19 per cent of the Blue Jay's food consists of harmful insects . . . and that the habit of robbing the nests of other birds is much less common than has been asserted." Nevertheless, that these birds raised sad havoc in my garden while they lived in a neighbouring thicket, I know by sad experience, and I personally prefer administering poisonous beverages to the various insects that enjoy garden rambles, than to be assisted in their destruction by this azure-plumed, jeering bandit.

Nor does the fact that Jays make devoted parents, excuse their audacity. The Robber Barons were doubtless liberal enough inside their own castles, where the tribute from other homes gave the baby barons the wherewithal to wax fat and ferocious. I speak from the view point of the homekeeper and gardener whose first thought is for the Thrush, the Robin, the Catbird, and all other friendly tenants of bush and hedge.

Sub-family Corvinæ: Crows.

American Crow: *Corvus Americanus.*

Length: 18–20 inches.

Male and Female: Glossy black, with a purplish tinge. Wings which appear saw-toothed when flying. Bill and feet black. Female a less brilliant black.

Song: A quavering "Kar-r-r-er-r!" in spring. Call note, "Caw-w!"

Season: Resident.

Breeds: All through North America.

Nest: Consisting of a platform of coarse sticks, upon which rests the nest proper, made of smaller twigs and deeply lined with cedar bark. Tall trees are chosen; preferably evergreens.

1 "Some Common Birds in their Relation to Agriculture," Washington, 1897.

Eggs: 4–7, greenish ground, stained and spotted with brown; variable both in size and colour.

Range: North America, from the Fur Countries to Mexico.

With none of the beauty and daring of the Blue Jay to recommend him, the Crow, at least as a bird of the garden, home fields and woodlands, has not a single good mark to his name. A price has been set upon his head; he sees a gun a mile away, while his only picturesque quality is a negative one — when he completes the dreariness of a November landscape by flapping dolefully over the stacked cornstalks in the brown fields.

From the standpoint of the agricultural economist, however, the Crow seems to be pronounced not guilty, or at least not wholly as black as he usually appears to the naked eye of the casual observer. The white feathers claimed for him are the May beetles, June bugs, grasshoppers, cutworms, caterpillars, mice, etc., that he consumes in off seasons, when corn is too hard to suit him and nests are empty.

Be this as it may, we must be allowed to regard birds somewhat in an æsthetic light, we are not all interested in cataloguing the contents of birds' stomachs, and no one will deny that the average Crow (of course there may be abnormal and angelic exceptions) is a coward, with a hoarse voice and disagreeable manners added to a most offensive, crouching personality hiding a world of cheap craft. In fact, a sort of feathered Uriah Heap, whom we do not desire for a near neighbour, though there may be people and communities where he is appreciated.

Fish Crow: *Corvus ossifragus.*

Length: 14–16 inches.

Male and Female: Glossy, purplish black.

Song: Resembling the last species, but with a different intonation.

Season: Summer resident.

Breeds: Through range.

Nest and Eggs: Hardly to be distinguished from those of the last species.

Range: Atlantic coast, from Long Island to Florida.

It is easy to confuse this Crow with the ordinary species, the only marks of identification being its inferior size and different call. It frequents the shore chiefly, and may be seen here on its arrival in early spring, before the Gulls have left, clamming on the mud flats and sand-bars of the creeks that run into Long Island Sound. These Crows seem to tread for the long-necked clams as people do, and then dislodge them with a blow from their strong beaks, breaking the shell in the same manner, and tearing out the contents with the aid of their claws. In winter I have seen the common Crows flock to the beach and procure shell-fish in the same way. The Fish Crow is said, by Audubon, to catch fish like the Osprey, and flocks were seen by him sailing through the air, above the St. John's River, Florida, the aerial excursion lasting for hours, after which the Crows would turn their attention to fishing for half an hour, and then alight in the trees to plume themselves.

FAMILY STURDIDÆ: STARLINGS.

English Starling: *Sturnus vulgaris.*

Length: 8.50 inches.

Male and Female: Bill yellow in summer; dark brown in winter. Upper parts with metallic lustre, feathers tipped with buff, lower parts and tail dusky gray edged and spotted with buff. Spotting more distinct in winter and nearly white on underparts. *Walkers.*

Song: A clear, melodious whistle.

Season: All the year.

Breeds: In all parts of its American range.

Nest: Of small sticks, twigs and grass, in tree hollows, church towers, or behind blinds of unused buildings.

Eggs: Pale bluish, 4–6.

Range: Europe and Asia; introduced into Central Park, New York, in 1890, now spreading in a radius of seventy-five miles or more from that city. (See page xxv.)

FAMILY ALAUDIDÆ: LARKS.

Horned Lark: *Octocoris alpestris.*

Shore Lark.

Length: 7–7.50 inches.

Male: Upper parts brown with a pinkish cast, most marked on neck and rump. Black crescent on breast; black bar in front of head, extending to side of head, forming two tufts or horns; frontlet, throat, and neck pale yellowish; below whitish, streaked with black; bill dark; feet black.

Female: Paler and somewhat smaller.

Song: Only a call note here, but a charming song in the breeding-haunts.

Season: Winter resident along shore; October to April.

Breeds: In March and April in boreal regions, and raises two broods a season.

Nest: Of grass, in ground hollow.

Eggs: Variable, greenish white or gray, heavily marked with dark gray.

Range: Northeastern North America, Greenland, and northern part of the Old World; in winter south in the eastern United States to the Carolinas, Illinois, etc.

The pinkish gray colouring of the Horned Lark is very beautiful, but in the Middle and Eastern States he is rarely seen in his spring garb, and his winter plumage lacks the vivid contrasts and pure colour.

These Larks, if the snow is not too deep, settle in the marsh-meadows, where they pick up a living from various seeds; or, if the snow has covered the fields, they take refuge in sheltered spots by hayricks and even near houses. I have seen them quite close to the village, picking up oats under a shed where straw had been thrashed recently. According to Audubon, they have, in the breeding-range, the habit of singing as they soar in the air, after the manner of the European Skylark.

For Prairie Horned Lark now breeding in the Eastern States see page xxiii.

PERCHING SONGLESS BIRDS.

ORDER PASSERES: PERCHING BIRDS.

SUB-ORDER CLAMATORES: SONGLESS PERCHING BIRDS.

FAMILY TYRANNIDÆ: TYRANT FLYCATCHERS.

Kingbird: *Tyrannus Tyrannus.*

Bee Martin.

PLATE 41.

Length: 8 inches.

Male and Female: Above black, orange-red streak on poll. Beneath grayish white, darkest on breast. Tail terminating in a white band.

Bill and feet black.

Note: A piercing call note, — " Kyrie-K-y-rie ! "

Season: Common summer resident; May to September.

Breeds: Through its United States range.

Nest: Bulky and deeply cupped, made of sticks and grass, lined with matted fibres, usually in a conspicuous position on a horizontal branch in orchards or thin woods.

Eggs: Nearly an inch long and almost round, cream or bluish white, boldly scratched and spotted with brown and lilac. Very handsome and richly coloured.

Range: Eastern North America, from the British Provinces south to Central and South America. Rare west of the Rocky Mountains.

That the Kingbird — the second largest of our Flycatchers — is a tyrant, as his Latin name indicates, no one will doubt who has watched his tactics for a single day. He is born a fighter; he fights for his mate, he fights to protect his nest, and when he cannot find an opponent he emulates Don Quixote. His greatest tyranny is over the ravenous insects that he holds so well in check; and the clumsy Crows and Hawks he drives at will.

PLATE 41.

KINGBIRD.

Length, 8 inches.

Look at him as he sits motionless on the top wire of the fence, resting from an aerial excursion. He is easy to identify, for his grays and blacks are so distinct and the clear white tail band is decisive. Suddenly he dashes into the air or sweeps above the ground and secures an insect with a sharp snap of the beak, — a drone bee, perhaps, although the bees that he captures are comparatively few, — and returns to the precise spot from which he started. This is a habit peculiar to the Flycatchers. I once watched a Kingbird for nearly two hours, his point of vantage being a rail and wire fence between low meadows, and, though he would sail many hundred yards away, he always returned to his original perch. If a Crow or Hawk appears ever so far in the distance, he gives his shrill alarm note and goes in instant pursuit; and lucky is the chicken yard that has a pair of these gallant knights at hand and the garden that shelters them.

He does not seem, however, to care to cross swords with the Catbird, not, perhaps, that he is absolutely afraid, but he becomes suddenly near-sighted when that cunning musician crosses his path. Dr. Abbott once tested the valour of a particularly saucy Kingbird, by sending up a red and yellow bird kite in the vicinity of its nest, pulling the kite backward as the bird advanced and then when he was close upon it slackening the string so that the Kingbird, unable to check itself, plunged through the paper and bolted off, not returning for many hours, doubtless because his enemy was intangible, and not from fear.

Kingbirds make most devoted parents, and the young birds are delightful little things to watch as they develop if you are as fortunate in finding a nestful as was Mrs. Olive Thorne Miller, who has recorded their ways for all bird-lovers present and future in her "Chronicle of Three Little Kings."[1]

Opinions differ as to the Kingbird's bee-destroying proclivities, for which he received the name of Bee Martin; neighbouring farmers even tell different stories, — one having assured me that last year his hives were impoverished,

[1] "Little Brothers of the Air," p. 19.

while the other, an equally successful apiarist, says that he has never suffered any appreciable loss from this bird. They are said to take only drones.

Crested Flycatcher: *Myiarchus crinitus.*

Length: 8–9 inches.

Male and Female: Head feathers forming a pointed crest. Above grayish olive, browner on wings and tail, feathers of former with light edges. Throat gray, *below sulphur-yellow*, which extends beneath wings. Bill dark, thick, and rather short.

Note: Harsh call, somewhat like the Kingbird's.

Season: Summer resident; May to September.

Breeds: Through its United States range.

Nest: In hollow trees and posts, sometimes in abandoned Woodpeckers' holes; made of varied materials, in which snake skins are often found.

Eggs: Uniquely marked, ground buff or clay-coloured, marked in various ways with purple, chestnut, and chocolate brown.

Range: Eastern United States and southern Canada, west to the Plains, south, in winter, through eastern Mexico to Costa Rica.

This is the great sulphur-bellied Flycatcher, who lines his nest hollow with cast away snake skins. How many little boys, as well as people of larger growth, have worked their hands into the hole of a supposed Woodpecker, only to feel the drying skin of a snake twisted up inside, and have fairly tumbled to the ground, lest the former inhabitant of the skin should be in the vicinity. These birds do not nest as freely in the neighbourhood as the Kingbird, and, though sufficiently pugnacious with their bird kin, keep rather aloof from human society, so that their habits are less familiar. In early May when they arrive, they feed upon ground-beetles, etc., but later in the season frequent the wooded edges of lanes and old pastures, and very little insect life that passes by escapes their snapping gape.

Burroughs, in speaking of the Flycatchers in general, says that "The wild Irishman of them all is the Great-crested Flycatcher, a large leather-coloured or sandy complexioned bird, that prowls through the woods, uttering its harsh, uncanny note, and waging fierce warfare upon its fellows."

PLATE 42.

1. PHŒBE.

Length, 6.75–7.25 inches.

2. WOOD PEWEE.

Length, 6.50 inches.

Phœbe: *Sayornis phœbe.*

Water Pewee.

PLATE 42. FIG. 1.

Length: 6.75–7.25 inches.

Male and Female: Above deep olive-brown; straight black bill. Outer edges of some tail feathers whitish; an erectile crest. Beneath dingy yellowish white; feet black.

Note: "Phœbee, phœbee, pewit, phœbée!"

Season: April to October. Common summer resident.

Breeds: From the Carolinas northward.

Nest: In its native woods the nest is of moss, mud, and grass bracketed on a rock, near or over running water; but in the vicinity of settlements and villages, it is placed on a horizontal bridge beam, timber supporting porch or shed.

Eggs: Pure white, somewhat spotted.

Range: Eastern North America, from the British Provinces south to eastern Mexico and Cuba, wintering from the South Atlantic and Gulf States southward.

The cheerful Phœbe, the first to come and the last to leave of its tribe, can be distinguished by its sociability as well as its musical cry. To those who are familiar with the domestic Phœbe, who builds his bulky moss nest at their very door, and who associate him with the Wren in his love of nooks in the outbuildings, it will seem strange to know that in his primitive state he haunts dim woods and running water. The domesticated Phœbe is a great bather, and may be seen in the half-light dashing in and out of the water as he makes trips to and from his nest.

Here in the garden this bird frequently exhibits its love of water, and after the young are hatched in the various nests, both old and young repair to a maple near the pool, and disport themselves about the water until moulting-time. It is very amusing to watch them as they flash down, one by one, for a dip or an insect, taking both on the wing without a pause.

Do not let the Phœbes build under the hoods of your windows, for their spongy nests harbour innumerable bird-lice, and under such circumstances your fly-screens will become infested and the house invaded.

Olive-sided Flycatcher: *Contopus borealis.*

Length: 7.50 inches.

Male and Female: Dark brown, deepest on head, olive-gray sides. Wings brown, with some white tips. Chin, throat, and centre of breast yellowish white. Bill, black above, yellowish below. Feet black.

Note: "O—wheo, O—wheo, O—wheo!"

Season: In migrations; May and September.

Breeds: From higher and mountainous parts of the United States northward.

Nest: Made of small twigs, grass, and fibres; very crude and shapeless; saddled on a high horizontal branch.

Eggs: 4–5, buff-white, spotted thickly with reddish brown.

Range: North America; in winter, south to Central America and Colombia.

The Olive-sided Flycatcher is an irregular migrant, which is sometimes rarest in spring and sometimes in autumn. I think, however, that it is rather plentiful in this neighbourhood in early September, for I have seen it repeatedly with miscellaneous flocks of Flycatchers in the ranks of the early returning migrants.

Wood Pewee: *Contopus virens.*

PLATE 42. FIG. 2.

Length: 6–6.50 inches.

Male and Female: Dusky olive-brown above, darkest on head, throat paler, middle of belly yellowish, growing lighter below. White eye ring and two whitish wing bars. Feet and bill dusky or black.

Note: "Pewee-a,—peweeà, peer!"—as much a song as that of many birds classified as Song-birds.

Season: May to October.

Breeds: Throughout its range.

Nest: Flat; its evenly rounded edge stuccoed with lichens like that of the Hummingbird; hardly to be distinguished from the bough on which it is saddled.

Eggs: Creamy-white, with a wreath of brown and lilac spots on the larger end.

Range: Eastern North America to the Plains, and from southern Canada southward.

In early May the Wood Pewee comes to the garden lane and whispers of his presence with his plaintive little ditty, and in the autumn the same lonely call is virtually the only wood note left. In spite of his name, he is not exclusively a wood-bird, but comes through the garden, following shyly in the Phœbe's wake. But he only trusts his precious nest to some mossy woodland limb, a trifle softened by decay, where he blends his house with its foundations by the skilful use of moss and lichens.

Alert and swift of motion, he still wears an air of mystery, and his pathetic note seems like the expression of a hidden sorrow. Trowbridge's poem telling of his woodland search for the Pewee is one of the most charming bird epics we have, and the verse describing its plumage and song is the bird's life history told in a few lines,—

"I quit the search, and sat me down
Beside the brook, irresolute,
And watch a little bird in suit
Of sombre olive, soft and brown,
Perched in the maple branches, mute;
With greenish gold its vest was fringed,
Its tiny cap was ebon-tinged,
With ivory pale its wings were barred,
And its dark eyes were tender starred.
'Dear bird,' I said, 'what is thy name?'
And thrice the mournful answer came,
So faint and far, and yet so near,—
'Pewee! pe-wee! peer!'"

Yellow-bellied Flycatcher: *Empidonax flaviventris.*

Length: 5.50 inches.

Male and Female: Above a decided olive-green, which colour extends to the breast. Under parts pale yellow, including wing linings. Yellowish eye ring and two yellowish bars on wings. Lower mandible yellow; feet black.

Note: "Kil-lic, kil-lic!" Love note, "Pea-pe, we-yea!"

Season: In migrations; May and early September.

Breeds: From Massachusetts northward.

Nest: Close to the earth in swampy ground, set in a stump or upturned root; constructed of mosses and thick-walled and bulky, like the Phœbe's.

Eggs: White, spotted.

Range: Eastern North America to the Plains, and from southern Labrador south through eastern Mexico to Panama.

The Yellow-bellied Flycatcher is noted as a rare migrant in this vicinity; the only one that I have identified with certainty in the spring migration was killed by flying against a wire trellis in the garden, but, like the last species, they are more locally abundant in autumn. They sometimes breed in northern Pennsylvania, in tangled thickets near streams.

They are late birds in the spring, and do not arrive in southern New England, en route for their breeding-haunts, until the middle of May.

Acadian Flycatcher: *Empidonax acadicus.*

Length: 5.75-6.25 inches.

Male and Female: Above dull olive-green. Below yellowish, turning to light gray on throat and belly. White eye ring. Bill brown above, pale below; feet brown.

Note: "Hick up! Hick up!"

Season: Summer resident, May to September.

Breeds: From Florida to southern Connecticut and Manitoba.

Nest: Shallow and loosely built, near the end of a slim horizontal branch; made of grass, blossoms, and bark.

Eggs: Cream white, wreathed at the larger end.

Range: Eastern United States, chiefly southward; west to the Plains, south to Cuba and Costa Rica.

This little Flycatcher has a southerly range, only coming over the New England border in summer; there are but two breeding-records of it in Connecticut, one being Greenwich, Conn., where a nest and young were found in June, 1893. It is a common resident along the Hudson as far north as Sing Sing, and Dr. Warren found it breeding freely about West Chester, Penn., where he says the majority

WHIP-POOR-WILL.

Length, 9–10 inches.

of nests were made entirely of blossoms, being rarely more than eight or ten feet from the ground, and so open at the bottom that the eggs could be seen from underneath. He also says that it is a common resident of Pennsylvania from May until late September, at which season it ekes out its insect diet with berries.

Its nest is variously described as "a light hammock swung between forks," and "a tuft of hay caught by the limb from a load driven under it."

Least Flycatcher: *Empidonax minimus.*

Length: 5–5.50 inches.

Male and Female: Olive-gray, brightest on the head, paler on wings and rump. Whitish eye ring, and wing-bars. Breast whitish, growing more yellow toward vent. Bill dusky. Feet black.

Note: "Che-bec! Chebec!" (Coues.)

Season: Common summer resident; May to late September.

Breeds: From Pennsylvania northward.

Nest: In *upright* crotch of tree or bush, substantial and well cupped. Materials varying with the location, plant fibres and weeds, lined with down and sometimes horsehair.

Eggs: Usually unmarked, occasionally faintly spotted.

Range: Eastern North America, south in winter to Central America.

The least of his tribe, the mite, whose olive poll is seen in great numbers darting about the orchard in May and again in late September when the decaying fruit attracts numerous insects. He is abundant, useful, and sociable, though neither possessing gay feathers nor a single musical note, yet he fills his own corner, doing his part in helping man to keep the upper hand over the insect world. These Flycatchers are solicitous parents and, as a rule, show great affection for their young, becoming almost frantic if the nest is approached.

ORDER MACROCHIRES: SWIFTS, WHIP-POOR-WILLS, ETC.

FAMILY CAPRIMULGIDÆ: GOATSUCKERS.

Whip-poor-will: *Antrostomus vociferus.*

PLATE 43.

Length: 9–10 inches.

Male and Female: A long-winged bird of the twilight and night. Large mouth fringed with bristles. Plumage dusky and Owl-like, much spotted with black and gray. Wings beautifully mottled with shades of brown; lower half of the outer tail quills white in the male, but rusty in female.

Note: "Whip-poor-will, whip-poor-will;" repeated usually five times in succession, followed by a jarring noise during flight.

Season: Late April to September. Common summer resident, except near the shore.

Breeds: In all parts of its range, but most freely toward the northern portions.

Nest: Builds none, but substitutes a mossy hollow in rock or ground.

Eggs: 2, creamy-white, freely marked, and spotted with brown.

Range: Eastern United States to the Plains, south to Guatemala.

This weird bird, with its bristling, fly-trap mouth, who sleeps all day and prowls by night, comes to us late in April, if the season is warm, clamouring and waking strange echoes in the bare woods, and in early September, mute and mysterious, he gathers his flocks and moves silently on, for the Whip-poor-will has not at any time even a transient home to abandon; like the pilgrims of old, the earth is his only bed.

This bird is somewhat erratic in its local distribution. It is noted here as a common summer resident, yet is seldom heard within two miles of the beach, except in the spring migration, and I have never but once found it in the garden. After crossing the Greenfield Hill Ridge, the numbers increase, and in the wooded hollow below Redding Ridge they are so numerous as to make the early night noisy.

PLATE 44.

NIGHTHAWK.

Length, 9–10 inches.

Many people are familiar with the cry who have never seen the bird itself; for Nature has taken great pains to blend the colours of its plumage with the browns and grays of the bark and rocks of the forest, and has given it the unusual habit of sitting lengthwise on the branch when it perches, so that it is invisible from below, and so closely resembles the branch against which it is so flattened as to escape notice.

The Whip-poor-will prefers the forest solitude, but in his nocturnal flights he often comes near houses, and sometimes calls close to a window with startling vehemence.

The breeding-habits of this strange bird are not the least of its peculiarities; when the ground-laid eggs are hatched, they are beset by many dangers from weasels, snakes, etc., but the young birds are almost invisible to the human eye, even if their location is known. The female is very adroit, and if she thinks her family has been discovered she will move them to another place, carrying them in her mouth as a cat does kittens. In fact, the Whip-poor-will is well protected both by nature and superstition; the farmer knows its value as an insect-destroyer, and the idle mischief-loving class, who kill birds from pure wantonness, give it a wide berth, as being the possessor of some occult power, akin to the "evil eye," and associate its sudden cry with death or calamity.

Nighthawk: *Chordeiles virginianus.*

Night-jar.

PLATE 44.

Length: 9–10 inches.

Male: Mottled black and rusty above, the breast finely barred, with a V-shaped white spot on throat. Wings brown and large, *white spot extending entirely through them, being conspicuous in flight;* white bar on tail. In the female, the white markings are either veiled with rusty or absent.

Note: A skirling sound while on the wing, — "Skirk — S-k-i-rk!"

Season: May to October; common summer resident.

Breeds: Gulf States to Labrador.

Nest: A ground hollow like the last species.
Eggs: 2, of variable shades of gray latticed with olive.
Range: Northern and eastern North America, east of the Great Plains.

Another bird of the twilight, feeding bat-like upon the insects obtained in the air. It is most conspicuous in the late afternoon, though it flies also by day, and may be distinguished from the Whip-poor-will, which it closely resembles, by the *large white wing spots.* After dark its cry will easily identify the Nighthawk, for, instead of the distinct syllables of the Whip-poor-will, it gives a peculiar harsh whistling note, while on the wing, which is followed every few minutes by a vibrating sound, as if a fully charged telegraph wire was struck with a bit of metal; or, as Nuttall describes it, "a hollow whirr, like the rapid turning of a spinning wheel, or a strong blowing into the bung-hole of an empty hogshead, which is supposed to be produced by the action of air in the open mouth of the bird." In the latter conjecture he was wrong, as the jarring sound, which gave the bird the name of Night-jar, is now conceded to come from its habit of dropping suddenly through the air, thus making a sort of stringed instrument of its pinions.

The Nighthawk has the Whip-poor-will's habit of laying its eggs on a bare surface, only it chooses open fields and waste pastures, or even flat roofs of city houses, instead of the woods. The term *Hawk*, as applied to it, is an entire misnomer; it is in no sense a bird of prey, and subsists entirely on insects, and the stories told of its chicken-killing propensities are wholly unfounded. In early autumn, prior to the migration, the Nighthawks gather in enormous flocks and fly about the entire afternoon, when they may be distinctly seen.

PLATE 45.

CHIMNEY SWIFT.

Length, 5.25 inches.

FAMILY MICROPODIDÆ: SWIFTS.

Chimney Swift: *Chætura pelagica.*

Chimney Swallow.

PLATE 45.

Length: 5.25 inches.

Male and Female: A deep, sooty brown. Wings longer than the tail, which is nearly even, the shafts of the quills ending in sharp spines.

Note: A loud, Swallow-like twitter.

Season: Late April to September and October; a common summer resident.

Breeds: From Florida to Labrador.

Nest: A loose, twig lattice glued by the bird's saliva, or sometimes tree-gum, to the inside of chimneys; or in wild regions to the inner walls of hollow trees.

Eggs: 4–5, pure white, and long for their width.

Range: Eastern North America, north to Labrador and the Fur Countries, west to the Plains, and passing south of the United States in winter.

This bird, popularly known as the Chimney Swallow, but which is more closely related to the Nighthawk, may be easily distinguished from the Swallows when flying, by its short, blunt tail. You will never see it perching as Swallows do; for, except when it is at rest in its chimney home, it is constantly on the wing, either darting through the air, dropping surely to its nest, or speeding from it like a rocket. The Chimney Swift secures its food wholly when flying, and is more active at night than in the day. In the breeding-season its busiest time is that preceding dawn, and it then works without cessation for many hours. The whirling of the wings as the bird leaves the chimney makes a noise like distant thunder, and if there is quite a colony the inhabitants of the house may be seriously disturbed, and the presence of the nests often introduces bedbugs, as they are to a certain extent parasites of these birds. This makes him an undesirable tenant, and in modern houses, where the flues are narrow and easily clogged, wire is stretched over the chimney mouth to keep him out.

Nothing, however, is more picturesque than these Swifts as they circle above the wide stone chimney of some half-ruined house, where the garden is overgrown by old lilacs, and great banks of the fragrant bushes hide the crumbling walls. I know of such a place, only a few miles away, where the Swifts curve and eddy above the huge chimney, bent with the weight of years, in such perfect accord and rhythm, now wholly disappearing within, now curling forth in a cloud, that it is easy to imagine the fire burns again upon the hearth and that the birds are but the columns of hospitable smoke.

In wild districts the Swift retains the habit of nesting in hollow trees, the custom it must have followed until comparatively recent times in this country, as the Indians never possessed even the ghost of a chimney. These trees are used after the breeding-season as roosts, and there is evidence that the birds may sometimes winter in them in a state of hibernation. In building its nest the Swift snaps little twigs from the trees, and in fixing them in place braces itself in the chimney by means of its claws and the sharp spines in which its tail feathers terminate. Its size is nearly the same as the Bank Swallow and the two flock prior to the autumn migration at about the same time, the Chimney Swift being the last to leave.

FAMILY TROCHILIDÆ: HUMMINGBIRDS.

Ruby-throated Hummingbird: *Trochilus colubris.*

PLATE 2.

Length: 3.75 inches.

Male: Above metallic green; belly white. Wings and tail ruddy black, the latter deeply forked. *Glistening ruby-red gorget.*

Female: Colours less iridescent; gorget lacking, tail with rounded points.

Note: A shrill, mouse-like squeak.

Season: Common summer resident; May to October.

Breeds: From Florida to Labrador.

Nest: A dainty circle an inch and a half in diameter, made of fern-wool, plant-down, etc., shingled with lichens to match the colour of the branch on which it is saddled.

PLATE 46.

DOWNY WOODPECKER.

Length, 6–7 inches.

Eggs: 2, pure white, the size of soup-beans.
Range: Eastern North America to the Plains, north to the Fur Countries, and south, in winter, to Cuba and Veragua.

This is the only native Hummingbird of eastern North America, and it is impossible to confuse it with any other bird in its range.

When the late tulips and narcissi are blooming in the garden, and you hear a tense humming near them, varied by an occasional squeak, you know, without looking, that the Hummingbirds have come. All through late May they dart here and there, now among the flowers, and then disappearing high up in the trees, searching for both honey and aphides with their proboscis-like tongues, while their movements exceed in dash and rapidity even the Swallows and Swifts. They seem merely to will to be in a certain spot, and they are there without effort.

With June they settle in or near the garden, where the roses and honeysuckle supply them with nectar and ambrosia, and this is the season to study them. Late afternoon, between six and seven o'clock, is the best hour, for they are taking their supper, and the sun being low behind the trellis its rays shoot sidewise and bring out all the metallic splendour of their plumage. The adult birds seldom perch, but, drawing up their tiny claws, pause in front of the chosen flower, apparently motionless. But the hum of the wings tells the secret of the poise.

The parents jam their bills far down into the little gaping mouths, placing the food in the throat itself,—an effective but barbarous looking operation.

The nest is worthy of the bird, but is rare in comparison with the number of birds that are seen every year. There are two reasons for this; it blends so perfectly with the supporting branch as to be invisible when the leaves are on the trees, and owing to its spongy composition, it seldom retains its shape for any length of time.

Various nesting-sites are chosen, and in the garden I have found them, in different seasons, on a horizontal cedar bough, a slanting beech branch, a sweeping elm branch over the road, and one, which I discovered from a tower window, on the topmost branch of a spruce some sixty feet from the ground. In this last case the nest was covered with small flakes of spruce bark, instead of the usual lichens.

After the nesting the males make themselves exceedingly scarce, while the females and young haunt the garden, feeding in flocks, the young being distinguishable by their dulness of plumage and the fact that they perch frequently. All through August and early September, before cooling nights warn them away, they dart through the mellow haze claiming the last Jacque roses and the blossoms that continue to wreathe the honeysuckle, only leaving them when the twilight chill stiffens their feathered mechanism.

> When the mild gold stars flower out,
> As the summer gloaming goes,
> A dim shape quivers about
> Some sweet rich heart of a rose.
> * * * * * * *
> Then you, by thoughts of it stirred,
> Still dreamily question them:
> "Is it a gem, half bird,
> Or is it a bird, half gem?" — EDGAR FAWCETT.

ORDER PICI: WOODPECKERS, ETC.

FAMILY PICIDÆ: WOODPECKERS.

Hairy Woodpecker: *Dryobates villosus.*

Length: 9–10 inches.

Male and Female: Above black and white, white stripe on middle of back, *red stripe on head.* Wings spotted and striped with black and white, four outer tail feathers white. Under parts grayish white. Bill blunt, stout, and straight, nearly as long as head. Female lacks red spot on head.

Note: A short, tapping sound.

Season: Resident; shifting about in light woods.

Breeds: Through range.

Nest: In holes in trees at moderate height.

PLATE 47.

YELLOW-BELLIED SAPSUCKER

Length, 8.25–8.75 inches.

Eggs: 5, clear white, but, according to Samuels, owing to their transparency, they have a pink tint before they are blown.

Range: Middle portion of the eastern United States from the Atlantic coast to the Great Plains.

The Hairy Woodpecker is a common bird in wooded regions, especially where partly decayed trees have been left standing. Its creeping motion when scanning tree trunks for insects resembles that of the Black-and-white Warbler. Though it is abundant, it is shy in the breeding-season and keeps to secluded woodlands, but in the fall and winter comes freely to orchards and about houses. It has an affection for particular trees and often uses the same tree, if not perhaps the same hole, for several successive seasons.

Eight years ago I noticed this species in May in Samp-Mortar woods, a wild, rocky place, covered with laurel and abounding in the rarer ferns. From the crest of Mortar Rock I could look into the top of a tall hickory, in which a Hairy Woodpecker was boring. A few years later, at the same season, I found a similar bird nesting in the same tree and there were three holes visible in the trunk. This year I went to the place early in June. The tree was entirely dead and branchless from winter storms, the top had crumbled away so that light came through the upper holes, there were five apertures in all, and from the lowest of these flew a Hairy Woodpecker, and when I beat on the tree with a stick the clamouring inside told that the young were hatched.

On seeing me the bird went into one of the empty holes and then flew to a little distance and, joined by the male, refused to go near the nest while I remained. The tree was so shaky that it swayed with every breeze, and it is the last year that it will shelter its black-and-white tenants. The red head band is not very conspicuous in this Woodpecker unless you look at it from above or catch a glimpse of it when the bird is going up the tree trunk.

Downy Woodpecker: *Picus pubescens.*

PLATE 46.

Length: 6–7 inches, the smallest of our Woodpeckers.

Male and Female: Closely resembling the last species. Wings and tail *barred* with white; the narrow, red head band of the male is replaced by a white stripe in the female.

Note: A short, sharp note and a rattling cry, which starts and ends in an abrupt precision, suggestive of a mechanical contrivance set off with a spring. This it uses in lieu of a song. (Bicknell.)

Season: An abundant resident.

Breeds: Through range.

Nest: In tree hole, varying from low apple to high forest trees.

Eggs: Similar to those of last species, but smaller.

Range: Northern and eastern North America, from British Columbia and the eastern edge of the Plains northward and eastward.

The Downy Woodpecker, the persistent apple-tree borer, is a miniature reproduction of the Hairy Woodpecker, except that its tail is *barred* with black and white. This is the little bird that ornaments the fruit trees with symmetrical rows of holes, such as would be made by small shot. He does not, however, drain the vitality of the tree, as many suppose, by taking the sap, but merely bores for insects that lie between the bark and the tissue. In fact, the operation seems to be beneficial, perhaps acts as a system of ventilation, for I have seen some very fine old trees where the holes were so numerous as to form strange hieroglyphics upon every limb. This Woodpecker is much more sociable than his big brother, and is present, about the orchards and gardens, the entire year.

Yellow-bellied Sapsucker: *Sphyrapicus varius.*

PLATE 47.

Length: 8.25–8.75 inches.

Male: Above black, white, and yellowish; below greenish yellow. Tail black, white on middle feathers, white edge to wing coverts. *Crown, chin, and throat bright red.* Bill about as long as head, more pointed and slender than in last species.

Female: Throat and head whitish.

PLATE 48.

RED-HEADED WOODPECKER.

Length, 8.50–9.50 inches.

Note: A rapid drumming with the bill on the tree branch or trunk serves for a love-song, and it has a screaming call note.
Season: In migrations; more abundant in fall than in spring.
Breeds: North from Massachusetts.
Nest: In an unlined hole, which is often 18 or 20 inches deep.
Eggs: 5, pure white.

The Sapsucker is a superbly marked Woodpecker, but its beauty is neutralized by its pernicious habit of boring holes in the tree bark through which it siphons the sap or eats the soft, inner bark.

In some localities they will destroy large tracts of fruit trees by stripping off the entire outer bark. Here, in the garden, they attacked a large spruce one autumn, and the next spring the trunk was white with the sap that leaked from the hundreds of "taps," and the tree has never since recovered its vitality.

Where these birds are plentiful, many orchard owners cover the tree trunks with fine wire netting, and it would almost seem that the destruction of this species is justifiable, but care should be taken not to confuse the other innocent Woodpeckers with this red-crowned, red-throated evil-doer. Only having seen the bird in its migrations, I have never heard the wonderfully rapid drumming to which Mr. Bicknell refers, and which he says does not occur until the birds mate and is never heard in the autumn. This tattoo, beat upon a tree with the beak, is, in fact, the love note of the majority of Woodpeckers.

Red-headed Woodpecker: *Melanerpes erthrocephalus.*

Tricolour.

PLATE 48.

Length: 8.50–9.50 inches.
Male and Female: Head, throat, and neck crimson. Back, wings, and tail blue-black. White below. White band on wings, and white rump. Bill horn-coloured, and about as long as head.
Note: A guttural rattle, similar to the cry of the tree-toad. In April a hoarse, hollow-sounding cry. (Bicknell.)

Season: A casual resident, and an abundant but irregular migrant, especially in the fall.

Breeds: From Florida to northern New York and Manitoba.

Nest: Usually a hole near the top of a blasted tree in mixed woods.

Eggs: Glassy white.

Range: United States west to the Rocky Mountains, straggling westward to Salt Lake Valley; rare or local east of the Hudson River.

This Woodpecker was once a regular summer resident here, but has decreased greatly in numbers and has almost come to be considered as a migrant only, and even then it will be fairly abundant in one season and absent the next. He is an unmistakable bird, when you are lucky enough to see him, for he boldly wears the German flag in his red, white, and black feathers, and you will recognize him at a glance. His increasing rarity is the usual penalty paid by highly coloured birds to thoughtless gunners, and he is a very easy mark when he is feeding flat against a tree trunk.

Flicker: *Colaptes auratus.*

Golden-winged Woodpecker; Yellowhammer, Highhole, Clape.

PLATE 49.

Length: 12–13 inches.

Male: Above golden brown, barred with black. *Black crescent* on breast, red band on back of head. Round black spots on the belly, black cheek patch. Wing linings and shafts of wing and tail quills gamboge-yellow. *Rump white.* Bill slender, curving, and pointed, and dark lead-colour; feet lead-colour.

Female: Lacks black cheek patches.

Note: "Wick-wick-wick-wick!" Also a few guttural notes. "A prolonged, jovial laugh." (Audubon.)

Season: Resident, but most plentiful from April to October.

Breeds: Through its range.

Nest: In partly decayed trees in orchard, garden, or wood.

Eggs: Usually 6, white.

Range: Northern and eastern North America, west to the eastern slope of the Rocky Mountains and Alaska. Occasional on the Pacific slope from California northward. Accidental in Europe.

PLATE 49.

FLICKER.

Length, 12–13 inches.

This, the largest as well as most abundant of our common Woodpeckers, can be easily identified, when at rest, by the black throat crescent and red head patch, and when flying by the white rump and golden wing linings. The Golden-winged is a Woodpecker of many *aliases*, among which Pigeon-woodpecker, Yucker, and Yellowhammer are locally familiar. Individuals remain all the year, and frequent orchards and wooded gardens more than deep woodlands; they walk about on the ground in search of food in the manner of Pigeons, and are in this respect quite independent of trees.

The Flicker is a genial, sociable bird, and its hammering is one of the first bird sounds of early spring that comes from the orchard. In April or May it looks for a suitable tree to bore, or else clears out a last year's hole. The birds are very wary when the excavation is under way, and, instead of dropping the chips by the tree where they are working, carry them to some distance. There is a singular physiological fact connected with the laying powers of this Woodpecker. Six is the usual setting of eggs, but if the eggs are removed from the nest as soon as laid the *female continues laying* uninterruptedly, and according to Dr. Coues eighteen to twenty-three eggs have been taken from one nest.

When the young are hatched the parents redouble their attention, and resent any approach to the hole. They feed their young by the process known as *regurgitation*, conveying the partly softened food from their own crops to those of the young by *un*-swallowing it and placing their slender beaks in the mouths of the nestlings. A tap on the tree at this time will set the youngsters clamouring and the old birds fly out in alarm. On leaving the hole the young are at first very awkward and are unable to fly but a few feet from the ground, and are easily caught in the hand; nor do they seem to develop strength of wing for several days.

In autumn both old and young gather in considerable numbers in the pastures and feed upon the ground, looking in the distance like Meadowlarks.

ORDER COCCYGES: CUCKOOS, KINGFISHERS, ETC.

FAMILY CUCULIDÆ: CUCKOOS.

Yellow-billed Cuckoo: *Coccyzus americanus.*

PLATE 50.

Length: 11–12 inches.

Male and Female: Powerful beak, about as long as head; lower mandible yellow; above olive with gray and metallic tints; two middle tail feathers olive; outer quills black, with white spots; wings washed with bright cinnamon; under parts grayish white.

Note: "Kuk-kuk-kuk!" a harsh, grating sound.

Season: Late April to September.

Breeds: From Florida to New Brunswick.

Nest: Rudimentary; only a few sticks laid in a bush or on a forked bough.

Eggs: 4–8, pale green, sometimes little more than a greenish white.

Range: Temperate North America, from New Brunswick, Canada, Minnesota, Nevada, and Oregon south to Costa Rica and the West Indies. Less common from the eastern border of the Plains westward.

Of similar general appearance to the next species, this Cuckoo may be identified by the following marks: *yellow bill, bright cinnamon wings,* and *white spots* on the *long tail feathers* which are very conspicuous in flight. A few years ago the Yellow-billed Cuckoo was not a common bird here; but it seemed to follow the recent epidemic of tent-worms into Connecticut, and for the past two seasons has been abundant in orchards and gardens containing fruit trees, forgetting its shyness, and coming close to dwellings. Its hatred of the tent-worm is intense, for it destroys many more than it can eat, by tearing the webs apart, and squeezing the worms in its beak. So thoroughly has it done its work, that orchards, which three years ago were almost leafless, the trunks even being covered by slippery webbing, are again yielding a good crop.

PLATE 50.

YELLOW-BILLED CUCKOO.

Length, 11-12 inches.

Audubon gives this bird a bad character, saying: "It robs smaller birds of their eggs, which it sucks upon all occasions, and is cowardly without being vigilant. On this account, it falls a prey to several species of Hawks, of which the Pigeon-hawk may be considered its most dangerous enemy."

Be this as it may, both of our Cuckoos are respectable examples to their romantic but misguided European relative, for, like it, they lay their eggs at long intervals; but they still manage to scramble a nest together and rear their own young, though they have to face the responsibility of feeding nestlings, incubating, and laying more eggs, all at the same time. So let us forgive the Cuckoo its faults, and declare it the patron bird of the orchards and of overcrowded nurseries.

Black-billed Cuckoo: *Coccyzus erythrophthalmus.*

Rain Crow.

Length: 11–12 inches.
Male and Female: Black bill; eyelids red. Above, general colouring same as last species. White spots on tail, small and inconspicuous.
Note: "Kow-kow-kow! kuk-kuk!"
Season: May to late September.
Breeds: Through North American range.
Nest: In a bush; a few sticks, with no edge to confine the eggs.
Eggs: Hardly distinguishable from the last species.
Range: Eastern North America, from Labrador and Manitoba south to the West Indies and the valley of the Amazon; west to the Rocky Mountains. Accidental in the British Islands and Italy.

It seems a slur upon literary tradition to call our birds, which bear the name, Cuckoos. We are so used to associate the word with the merry wanderer that "sings as it flies" of Chaucer and Shakespeare and all the lesser singers since their day. And every child, in thinking of a Cuckoo, expects to find the twin of the irrepressible little foreigner who bobs out of the clock, and will insist upon calling mother's attention to the fact that it is bedtime.

The Black-billed Cuckoo is locally less common than the Yellow-billed, though both species are well represented. It is often called the Rain Crow, because of its habit of calling loudly in damp or cloudy weather. It haunts streams with lightly wooded banks, and sets its rickety nest in a briary tangle or thick shrubbery. In spring it associates in the orchards with the Yellow-billed, but at other seasons its food is quite different, and it lives upon fresh-water mollusks and the larvæ always to be found in numbers near ponds.

FAMILY ALCEDINIDÆ: KINGFISHERS.

Belted Kingfisher: *Ceryle alcyon.*

PLATE 51.

Length: 12–13 inches.

Male and Female: Long crest. Straight bill, longer than head; head appearing large for size of body. Above lead-blue, somewhat variegated with black. Below whitish. Two dull blue bands across breast. White transverse bands and spots on the short tail. Female has rusty bands across breast.

Note: A harsh, rattling cry, as familiar along river banks as the Jay's scream in the woods.

Season: A common summer resident, which might almost be classed as a resident, as it comes in March, and in mild seasons often winters.

Breeds: From Florida to Labrador.

Nest: In hollow trees and in earth burrows; 6–8 feet deep.

Eggs: 6–8, crystal white.

Range: North America, south to Panama and the West Indies.

The Kingfisher may be easily named, as he sits on his usual perch, a dead stump or limb jutting over the water, by his large, long-crested head, which gives his body a bob-tailed appearance. Living entirely upon fish, he is driven from small streams to the larger rivers by the closing in of the ice, but in open winters I have seen this bird in every month from November to March.

PLATE 51.

BELTED KINGFISHER.

Length, 12–13 inches.

The Kingfisher seizes his prey by diving, and if it is small and pliable swallows it at once, but if it consists of the larger and more spiney fish they are beaten to pulp against a branch before they are swallowed, and even then the struggles and contortions the bird goes through before finally mastering the fish, would be very ludicrous were they not so evidently distressing.

The term *halcyon days* (days of fair weather) is derived from this bird's Latin name. The Kingfisher was once supposed to build his nest on a little raft and float out to sea with it, having the power of averting storms during the period of incubation. The modern Kingfisher is too wise to try any such experiment; he well knows that no one can fathom our climate or restrain Apollos from watering at unseemly times, so he digs deep into a bank, road cut, or quarry and the precious eggs are laid many feet from the outer air.

What a racket the old birds make in the breeding-season! There may be loving, harmonious Kingfisher households, but if so these sounds belie them. But who can say however; the seemingly angry shrieks of both parents may be "Rock-a-Bye, Baby," arranged by a Kingfisher Wagner as a duet!

BIRDS OF PREY.

ORDER RAPTORES: BIRDS OF PREY.

FAMILY STRIGIDÆ: BARN OWLS.

American Barn Owl: *Strix pratincola.*

Length: 15–17 inches. Female the largest, as is usual with Owls.

Male and Female: Above tawny yellow, ash, and white, with black and white spots; below whitish specked with dark. Dark bars on tail and wing. Legs long and feathered. *Face disks heart-shaped*, eyes small and bluish black, bill light; *no horns.*

Note: A quavering cry,—"Kr-r-r-r-r-ik!"

Season: Rare resident; has been taken at Stratford, Hartford, Madison, and Sachem's Head, Conn.

Breeds: Through its range, in late February and March.

Nest: In wild regions in tree trunks, but when near villages in barns, towers, and belfries.

Eggs: 3–6, dirty white.

Range: Warmer parts of North America, from the Middle States, Ohio Valley, and California southward through Mexico.

The Barn Owl, having a rather southerly range, is one of the rarest Owls to be found in New England, its records are limited to Connecticut and Massachusetts and there is a recent one for Vermont. In New York State and Pennsylvania it is more common, and breeds in the southern portion of these states. Its appearance is so unique that it is sure to attract attention, and it is not amiss to mention it in connection with our common resident Owls. The face looks like that of a toothless, hooked-nosed old woman, shrouded in a closely fitting hood, and has a half-simple,

PLATE 52.

AMERICAN LONG-EARED OWL.

Length, 14–16 inches.

half-sly expression, that gives a mysterious air. This species has the same characteristics as the European Barn Owl, which is pointed out as a bird of ill omen, having the uncanny voice that calls from ivied turrets and a grinning, witch-like face.

In *fact*, it is a harmless bird, feeding on mice, moles, large beetles, etc.; it is the Monkey-faced Owl of newspaper natural history.

FAMILY BUBONIDÆ: HORNED OWLS.

American Long-eared Owl: *Asio wilsonianus.*

Cat Owl.

PLATE 52.

Length: 14–16 inches.

Male and Female: Above finely mottled with brown, ash, and dark orange. Long, erect ear tufts. Complete facial disk, reddish brown with darker inner circle; dark brown broken bands on wings and tail. Legs and feet completely feathered. Breast pale orange with long brown stripes. Bill and claws blackish.

Note: A variety of hoot, also a moaning mew.

Season: Resident.

Breeds: In early spring, throughout range.

Nest: A rude structure which may be built either on the abandoned nests of Hawks, Crows, or Herons, on the ground, or in hollow stumps.

Eggs: 4–6, the usual soiled white.

Range: Temperate North America.

The Long-eared Owl, or Cat Owl (so called from its mewing cry and round face), has conspicuous ear tufts, as long, for the size of the bird, as those of the Great Horned Owl. These Owls frequent the same lowlands as the Short-eared species; they are very abundant in early winter, both along the marsh borders and in the woods by the river. During December, 1889, they were so common that several were killed by boys with stones, and I have frequently seen them among the evergreens in the garden. This species has a very bright, saucy expression and looks at you as if it was meditating a practical joke of a particularly aggravating nature. From an agricultural standpoint it is a beneficial Owl, feeding chiefly upon mice and other small mammals, beetles, etc., only occasionally eating small birds.

Short-eared Owl: *Asio accipitrinus.*

Length: 13.75–17 inches.

Male and Female: Inconspicuous ear tufts, facial disk with a dark ring enclosed in a lighter one. Plumage varied from bright orange to buffy white, with bold stripes of dark brown, darker above and more mottled below, growing whiter toward vent. Legs feathered with plain buff. Bill and claws dusky blue-black.

Note: A quaver.

Season: Summer resident remaining until late fall.

Breeds: Through its range.

Nest: Of hay and sticks; commonly on the ground in a little hollow or clump of bushes.

Eggs: 4–7, dirty white.

Range: Throughout North America, nearly cosmopolitan.

A very useful Owl, feeding on small mammals, reptiles, etc.; seen here in considerable numbers in the marsh meadows in the fall and early winter, possibly being resident. It is a *day owl*, and can be seen even in sunny weather, prowling about in the long, withered marsh-grass.

Mr. L. M. Turner, the Arctic explorer, says that among the natives of the Yukon district (Alaska) the dried liver of this owl, ground to a powder and administered in food, is used as a love philter.

Nuttall describes the Short-eared Owl as being so fierce that it will sometimes attack men seated by midnight camp-fires. This seems very dubious, as even the powerful Great Horned Owl rarely attacks man, unless he is cornered or attacked first. It is more probable that at some time the Owl, bewildered by smoke and flames, unwittingly flopped into an encampment, and, when seized, fought for liberty.

Barred Owl: ***Syrnium nebulosum.***

Length: 18–20 inches.

Male and Female: Eyes blue-black, instead of the usual yellow iris. *No ear tufts.* Plumage mottled dark brown, rusty, and grayish. Striped on breast with dark brown. Face feathers white tipped. *Wings and tail barred with brown.* Legs and dark feet fully feathered and faintly barred. Bill ivory-coloured.

Note: A loud, guttural call. "Koh! Koh! Ko, Ko, hó!" or "Whah, whah, whah, whah-aa!" (Nuttall.)

Season: Resident.

Breeds: Through range.

Nest: In hollow tree or in crotch at some height from the ground.

Eggs: 4–6, laid in February, March, and April.

Range: Eastern United States west to Minnesota and Texas, north to Nova Scotia and Quebec.

The smooth-faced, twilight Owl of open woods, sheltered farms, and waysides. Its hooting cry is hardly to be distinguished from that of the Great Horned Owl, but it has several mocking and quavering notes peculiar to itself.

Its eyes are unlike those of any of the other Owls of its family and will always identify it; their deep blue colour gives it a very mild expression which is at variance with its ferocity in pouncing upon game-birds and smaller Owls, being in this respect, according to a recent government report,[1] quite a cannibal. The same report says that, though it does make inroads into poultry yards, the result of careful inquiry proves that the greater portion of its food consists of small mammals that are the bane of agriculture.

It frequently lodges in barns and haylofts during the day, and all about this region it is called the Barn Owl. And it really is the Barn Owl of this locality, for the true Barn Owl is practically unknown to the farming population; and when stuffed specimens are occasionally seen, having been

[1] "The Hawks and Owls of the United States in their Relation to Agriculture," prepared under the direction of Dr. C. Hart Merriam, Ornithologist, by A. K. Fisher, M.D., Washington, 1893.

sent as curiosities from some other place, they are invariably known as Witch Owls.

The Barred Owl is a noisy species and announces his presence in no gentle way. It is supposed to be shy and to love deep woods, but last fall a pair lived for a month or more in the garden evergreens, appearing towards evening and being especially active in the late dawns. I have a very perfect specimen of a female shot in the winter of 1893, near the barn where it was perching in an elm, at four o'clock in the afternoon, after having artfully harried a flock of tame Juncos; but now that their usefulness has been made plain, we no longer shoot Owls indiscriminately.

Saw-whet Owl: *Nyctala acadica.*

Acadian Owl.

Length: 7.50–8 inches. Smallest Owl of eastern United States.

Male and Female: No ear tufts. Above brown, spotted more or less with lighter brown and white. Striped beneath with rusty brown. Legs feathered, buffy white. Bill black, claws dark.

Note: A rasping cry resembling the filing of a saw (hence the name Saw-whet) and a clicking noise like "Tlee-Klee, Tlee-Klee!"

Season: A winter resident, locally common in the Eastern and Middle States. Rare here.

Breeds: From Massachusetts and New York northward.

Nest: In old stumps.

Eggs: 3–6, white and nearly round.

Range: North America at large, breeding from the Northern States northward.

The Saw-whet is a night Owl and spends most of the daylight hours in sleepy seclusion. This, together with its small size, makes it pass as *rare* in places where it is really a winter resident.

There are many stories told of the soundness with which it sleeps, Mr. Ridgway citing a case where one was caught by putting a hat over it as it slept, perched on the edge of a Robin's nest in a dense willow thicket. It is a sociable little Owl, of a cheerful disposition, and is easily tamed, and though it cannot, owing to small size, prey upon many

PLATE 53.

SCREECH OWL.

(Gray phase.)

Length, 8–10 inches.

of the stronger mammals, it does good service in killing field-mice, beetles, etc., and only seems to eat birds in times of famine.

I have never seen but one Saw-whet in this neighbourhood, though I have heard their cry many times. This one was found dead after a severe autumn storm in a beech wood; its wings were broken, and it had evidently died from starvation. This poor little Owl is destroyed in great numbers for decorative purposes, and is thus familiar to many people who have never seen it alive. It is the bird that sits in a pensive attitude on a gilt crescent moon, in the taxidermist's window, or yields its pretty head to do duty as a rosette on my lady's hat.

Screech Owl: *Megascops asio.*

Little Horned Owl.

PLATE 53.

Length: 8–10 inches.

Male and Female: Conspicuous ear tufts. Bill light horn colour. Two distinct phases of plumage belong to this species, having, as Dr. Fisher says, "no relation to sex, age, or season." In one state the Owl is mottled grayish and black, and the other rust-red. Feet covered with short feathers; claws dark.

Note: A hissing alarm note,—"Shay-shay-shay!" and a moaning, quavering wail, which is not loud, but penetrating.

Season: Common resident.

Breeds: Through range; in April and early May.

Nest: In hollow trees; sometimes in orchards, near dwellings, and on wood borders.

Eggs: 4–6, almost spherical.

Range: Temperate eastern North America, south to Georgia, and west to the Plains. Accidental in England.

It would be difficult to identify the Screech Owl by a description of its colour alone, for it goes through many different colour changes without regular rotation, passing from shades of wood-brown, hazel, tawny, rust-red, to gray and almost black, and *vice versa.* Plate IX., Figs. 7 and 8 show its most conspicuous conditions, and all the novice can do is to remember its length, and that, of our two small Owls, the one having *horns* is the Screech Owl.

They are bright, handsome birds, no matter what plumage they wear, and inveterate mousers, who should receive every encouragement and protection. They eat a few Song-birds, but have also a fondness for English Sparrows, which wipes out their small sins. Mr. George C. Jones, writing from Brookfield Centre, Fairfield County, Conn., says: "I think the smaller species of Owls feed upon the cutworm to some extent. I have found cutworms in the stomach of the common Screech Owl and in the Long-eared Owl. The fact that both the cutworms and the Owls are nocturnal leads me to believe that the Owls, of all the birds, are the most efficient exterminators of this formidable pest and should on this account receive protection." Let flower lovers protect the Owls by all means then, if in return they will keep the sly cutworm from the young carnations and heliotropes.

Great Horned Owl: *Bubo virginianus.*

Hoot Owl.

PLATE 54.

Length: 19–23 inches; female, 21–24 inches.

Male and Female: Large ponderous birds. Long ear tufts, feathers mottled irregularly, buff, tawny brown, and whitish. Iris yellow, pupil round and large, with great power of contraction. Feet and legs feathered. Bill and claws black.

Note: A wild startling "Hoo-hoo-oooo! Waugh-hoo!"

Season: Resident.

Breeds: In February or March, but the young grow slowly, remaining ten to twelve weeks in the nest.

Nest: Seldom in holes at the north, usually a bulky nest on a horizontal branch, in deep woods. Preferably in evergreens and near the top.

Eggs: Usually 2, dirty white.

Range: Eastern North America, west to the Mississippi Valley, and from Labrador south to Costa Rica.

This vigorous and untamable Owl is easily identified because of its great size and long ear feathers. The largest

PLATE 54.

GREAT HORNED OWL.

Length, 19–23 inches; female, 2 inches larger.

of our common Owls (the rare Great Gray Owl alone being larger), it is a bird of the deep woods, swift in flight and ferocious in the extreme, both in seizing large game as well as in fighting when disabled. A nocturnal species, it can see perfectly in bright sunlight, though it prefers to remain secluded. During the nesting-season, if the weather is cloudy, it searches for food both day and night.

It is the most destructive of Owls and of all the birds of prey except perhaps the Goshawk and Cooper's Hawk. Dr. Merriam, in speaking of its mischief in the farmyard, says, "Indeed I have known one to kill and decapitate three turkeys and several hens in a single night, leaving the bodies uninjured and fit for the table." (In common with many other birds of prey, it prefers the brain to any other portion of the victim.) This savage Owl also destroys vast quantities of large game-birds and may be safely considered undesirable from the standpoint of the small farmer, however much it may aid the tiller of vast fields by its destruction of vermin.

I have seen the Great Horned Owl sit in the daytime with its inner eyelids closed, and then suddenly open them, blink once or twice, and fly away, snapping its beak angrily. Its hooting cry, uttered in the bare woods in early spring, is one of the most weird, uncanny sounds in Nature. Icicles often hang from its nest; and ice still locks the streams as it sweeps about, suggesting every form of dark emotion by its voice, — mocking laughter, despair, and a choking rattle, — until you feel that the Wild Huntsman may be galloping through the shadows blowing his fatal horn.

Snowy Owl: *Nyctea nyctea.*

Arctic Owl.

PLATE 4.

Length: 20–24 inches.

Male and Female: Plumage varying from *pure white* to white barred and spotted with brown and black. No *ear tufts.* Legs and toes thickly feathered. Bill and claws black. Female larger; young darker and more spotted.

Note: A growl, a bark, and a hoot.
Season: A winter visitor.
Breeds: From Labrador northward.
Nest: On ground, lined with feathers.
Eggs: 5–10, laid at long intervals, so that when the last one is deposited the first bird is ready to fly.
Range: Northern portions of the Northern Hemisphere; in winter migrating south to the Middle States, straggling to South Carolina and the Bermudas.

The Snowy Owl is one of the dramatic figures of the winter landscape, and appears like a personification of Boreas himself, coming to superintend the arranging of his snow-drapery. This Owl usually precedes or follows a severe northeasterly storm, and when the snow has ceased, and you go down the lane to the marsh meadows, breaking your own path, the Buntings and Shore Larks are already about searching for the few spears of seeded grass that are not beaten down.

The incoming tide in the creek breaks the thin ice into cakes that lie one over another like transparent shingles on the banks; the flats are hidden by plates of burnished silver, and the Gulls hover over the long bar.

> The sunshine seems blown off by the bleak wind,
> As pale as formal candles lit by day:
> Gropes to the sea the river dumb and blind;
> The brown ricks, snow-thatched by the storm in play,
> Show pearly breakers combing o'er their lee
> White crests as of some just enchanted sea,
> Checked in their maddest leap, and hanging poised midway.
>
> —LOWELL.

The oak island is edged with silver birches that stretch marshward like whitened poles for holding some great nets. Low down in one of them sits a motionless white figure. Is it a Barred Owl, frozen and snow covered? No! it swoops rapidly in a circle, and seizes a hapless Bunting, and you expect to see the snow fall in powder from its wings, but it returns to its perch white-flaked as before, and you know that you are face to face with the Snowy Owl,

PLATE 55.

MARSH HAWK.

Length, 17–19 inches.

— the bird whose ghostly shape furnishes material for supernatural tales told by the humble onion-growers whose cabins touch the marshes.

The Snowy Owl is a great mouser and a skilful fisherman, only devouring birds casually.

FAMILY FALCONIDÆ: FALCONS, HAWKS, EAGLES.

Marsh Hawk: *Circus hudsonius.*

Harrier, Blue Hawk.

PLATE 55.

Length: 17–19 inches; female averaging two inches longer.

Male: Above bluish gray; below white mottled with brown. Wings brownish, long, and pointed; tail long; upper tail coverts white.

Female: Dark reddish brown; below rusty with spots. Bill hooked and black, longer than the Owl's; feet black.

Note: All Hawks have a screaming cry, but it is of little aid in identifying species.

Season: A common summer resident; may winter.

Breeds: Through range.

Nest: On the ground, one foot in diameter, of grasses, etc.; in swampy meadows or among rushes in marshes.

Eggs: 4–5, whitish; sometimes with irregular blotches of brown and gray shell marks.

Range: North America in general, south to Panama.

The Marsh Hawk is the most harmless and beneficial of its family; it feeds upon reptiles, locusts, grasshoppers, and small mammals, and never disturbs domestic poultry.

In this locality it is more plentiful in the bogs near fresh ponds, and in the vicinity of rivers, than in the salt-marshes.

It is the summer-day Hawk, and the species most frequently seen in the warmest months. It flies by night as well as day, however, and is often a companion of the Screech Owl in its nocturnal rambles.

When on the wing the females and young may be distinguished by the warm, rusty colour of their under parts, and while at rest by the white upper tail coverts.

I have seen companies of the females and young every

season in a strip of woods near Ciecos Brook, but the old males are very wary, and seem to disappear soon after the breeding-season.

Sharp-shinned Hawk: *Accipiter velox.*

PLATE 56.

Length: 12 inches; female 14 inches.

Male and Female: Wings longer than tail. Eyes reddish. Above bluish gray, deepest on head. Beneath whitish, barred on the sides and breast with rusty and dark brown. Tail even or notched. The young are spotted more or less on the back and streaked below. Head of this and next species smaller than last, while legs and tail are relatively longer. Feet slender.

Season: A common resident; coming about farms and even city parks in the winter.

Breeds: Through its range; in May.

Nest: Occasionally on a rocky ledge, but usually in some thick evergreen at a moderate height from the ground; a bulky platform of sticks with an upper story of bark, leaves, and moss.

Eggs: 4–5, purplish white, spattered heavily with dark brown; sometimes the spots form a wreath at the large end.

Range: North America in general; south to Panama.

This small and very common Hawk is possessed by a spirit of dash and daring altogether out of proportion to its size. Dr. Abbott, in speaking of the rapidity of its movements, says: "It is feathered lightning. He ceases to be before you realize that he is."

The Sharp-shinned is one of the most destructive of our common Hawks and shares, with the next species, the reputation of being an inveterate poultry-killer, and it causes such sad havoc among Song-birds that a black mark may be set against it to denote that it is a worthy target for rifle practice. Its dexterity in flying allows it to capture by surprise game which larger Hawks secure by weight and strength combined. Nuttall tells of a Hawk of this species that came day after day to a farmhouse, until before it was killed it had destroyed between twenty and thirty young chickens.

PLATE 56.

SHARP-SHINNED HAWK.

Lengtl : Male, 12 inches ; female, 14 inches.

Cooper's Hawk: ***Accipiter cooperi.***

Chicken Hawk.

Length: 15–16 inches.

Male and Female: Uniform bluish gray above, top of head blackish; tail crossed by several blackish bands; below white, with breast and sides barred with dusky or rufous. This species resembles the last, but is distinguishable by its greater size and rounded tail. Feet rather stout, greenish yellow.

Season: Common summer resident from March to December; occasionally winters.

Breeds: Through range in April and May.

Nest: In the tops of trees in thick woods, some authors say in evergreens; those I have seen have been in hickories.

Eggs: 3–4, bluish white, either plain or spotted with reddish.

Range: North America in general, south to southern Mexico.

A mischievous harrier of all birds from barnyard fowls to Song-birds, doing by craft what it cannot accomplish by daring alone.

A country woman, who is a very successful chicken-raiser, tells me that she loses annually more chickens by this Hawk than by weasels, rats, or disease, no matter how carefully the broods are cooped. The Hawk takes up his post on an old stump or tree in an adjoining wood lot and gives a peculiar cry, which seems to lead the chickens in its direction, and before the mother can give a warning cluck one will be borne off. They will seize rabbits, squirrels, and Partridges readily, but hesitate to tackle a fully grown fowl, unless it is disabled in some way.

The protective instinct of the mother Hen, when a Hawk is in the vicinity, and the unquestioning obedience of the brood, is one of the prettiest, though most ordinary, spring scenes on the farm. The hen-coops are perhaps barrels, laid on their sides with slatted ends, ranged along the roadside fence opposite the farmhouse, so that an easy watch may be kept upon them. The Hen ventures out, scratching and clucking to the chicks as she goes; they follow, straggling more or less on private investigations. The sky is blue and cloudless; in the distance hovers a bird of some sort, but it is a mere speck. The Hen does not appear to look up, but suddenly she becomes motionless. The speck develops into a Hawk, which nears, flying in circles and descending at the same time, so that it is difficult to predict where it will alight. The Hen crouches, spreads her wings, and gives a short cry, different from her usual cluck; instantly the brood rushes pell-mell to the offered shelter, the wings drop, and when the Hawk makes a final swoop within two feet of the ground he finds nothing but a very broad-backed and resolute Hen flattened in the dust, and he disappears over the meadows without having paused an instant. But his mate — for Hawks often prowl in pairs — is still sailing far off and mother Hen, having had one narrow escape, hustles her family back to their barrel.

Red-tailed Hawk: *Buteo borealis.*

Red Hawk, Hen Hawk.

Length: 19–22 inches; female, 22–24 inches.

Male and Female: Above dark brown, variegated with white, gray, and tawny; below whitish and buff, streaked across belly with brown. *Tail rust-red,* with a black band near end; in young, tail gray with numerous narrow brown bars. Moderate, horn-coloured bill; feet stout and strong.

Season: A common resident.

Breeds: Through range.

Nest: Built in March, in a tall tree in deep woods. A bulky affair of sticks with an upper nest; lined with soft bark like the Crow's.

Eggs: 2–3, dirty white, thickly blotched with purplish brown.

Range: Eastern North America, west to the Great Plains.

Owing to different phases of plumage, it is often difficult to identify the larger Hawks on the wing; but the *red tail* is a distinctive mark of the adults of this species at all seasons.

Farmers regard it as a nuisance, and kill it whenever they can as a punishment for poultry stealing; but Dr.

PLATE 57.

RED-SHOULDERED HAWK.

Length, 18-20 inches.

Fisher thinks it is a mistake to destroy it unless when caught in the act; as, after careful investigation, it has been found that eighty-five per cent of its food is made up of rodents destructive to agriculture. But still farmers make scare-crows, and, when possible, shoot a Hawk and hang it in the barnyard as a warning.

A persevering boy, living on the outskirts of the woods near Aspetuck Mills, secured a male Red-tail and two young, this spring, and I saw them after they had been in confinement for a week. The nest was in a particularly dangerous location, in the top of a tall hickory, and was reached by an arrangement of three ladders; a steel trap was placed over the nest, and the old bird secured in this way. The male was evidently rearing the young single-handed, his mate having probably been shot; for she did not answer his cries, and was never seen about the tree.

The young, at the time I saw them, May 30, must have been about five weeks old. They were downy and poorly feathered with buffy white, barred and flecked with gray and brown. The old bird did not struggle for liberty, but seemed perfectly stoical, only turning occasionally when the young clamoured (making a noise like the sharp peeping of chickens), to ram a scrap of raw meat, of which there was a supply in the cage, into their mouths, as they made no effort to feed themselves.

Red-shouldered Hawk: *Buteo lineatus.*

Also called Hen Hawk.

PLATE 57.

Length: 18–20 inches.
Male and Female: Shoulders rust-red. Above reddish brown, the middle of the feathers darker than the edges. Head, neck, and lower parts rusty, transversely barred with whitish; tail black with white bands. Feet and nostrils bright yellow.
Note: "Kee-o, kee-o!" an agreeable sound.
Season: Common resident.
Breeds: In April and early May all through its range.

Nest and Eggs: Like the Red-tail's; eggs somewhat smaller. Nest often used for several seasons.

Range: Eastern North America, west to Texas and the Plains, south to the Gulf coast and Mexico.

The common Hawk, that we see so frequently in winter, sitting motionless on a bare tree-top or stump, in the vicinity of inundated meadows, or where there are unfrozen springs, for it is particularly fond of frogs, etc. At a distance it resembles the last species, but at short range its red shoulders identify it. The Red-shouldered Hawk is a dignified bird having an Owl-like flight, and when at rest the pose of an Eagle. It is not easily disturbed, and will sit half an hour at a time in one spot, giving you a fine opportunity of observing it with a field-glass or marine telescope, which will bring it so close that every feather is distinct.

In "Upland and Meadow" Dr. Abbott draws a very interesting picture of this species as well as of other Hawks, and says that their soaring and screaming over the winter meadows is one of the few bits of primitive wildness left to us. This species is a hardy and valuable bird; at least sixty-five per cent of its food consists of injurious rodents and the remaining thirty-five per cent is made up of insects, reptiles, etc., with a very small proportion of bird food.

Bald Eagle: *Haliaëtus leucocephalus.*

White-headed Sea Eagle.

PLATE 58.

Length: 3 feet. Female larger.

Male and Female: Neck, head feathers, and tail pure white in adults, brown in young; beak yellow and abruptly hooked; plumage dark brown; *legs feathered only half-way down;* feet yellow.

Season: An uncommon resident, coming more like a visitor.

Breeds: Through range.

Nest: A bulky platform of stalks and litter, some 6 feet across and 3 feet deep; either in large trees or on rocky ledges.

Eggs: 2, white; $2\frac{1}{2}$ to 3 inches in length.

Range: North America at large; south to Mexico.

BALD EAGLE.

Length, male, 3 feet ; female, larger.

PLATE 59.

AMERICAN SPARROW HAWK.

Length, 10–11 inches.

The white head feathers of this Eagle give it the name of "Bald," which in reality, of course, it is not. It is called a resident in Connecticut; but it is by no means common, though a pair may usually be seen sailing over the marshes some time between September and May.

The white head identifies the fully grown bird beyond question; but as it takes the young three years to perfect their plumage, some confusion will arise. The feathers of the first year are uniform dark brown, and the birds are called Black Eagles. The second year they are known as Gray Eagles, not earning the title of *Bald* until the third year. Remember, however, that the Bald Eagle has its *claws and ankles unfeathered* (while the other American Eagle, the Golden, is feathered to the claws), and then you will not confuse the species.

The Bald-headed Eagle is a long-lived bird, of majestic appearance, whose piercing voice can be heard above a wild storm; and for these qualities it was unfortunately chosen as the emblem of our Republic, for its noble qualities are in reality either wholly superficial or else imaginary. It is an inveterate bully, obtaining a great part of its food by robbing the Fish Hawk, while perfectly able to fish for itself; and though it has been known to carry off lambs and young pigs, it has been vanquished in a fair fight by a rooster. Preferring a fish diet, it will, however, eat any kind of animal food, even devouring carrion.

These Eagles are cowardly parents, but devoted as couples, and their union, on the evidence of good authorities, appears to be for life. They travel in pairs, and never in flocks, as is the habit of Vultures. The female is not only the larger, but the braver of the two birds, which fact, perhaps, led an enthusiast in the latest Woman's Suffrage scrimmage to declare that the Eagle on the United States coins is a female. It certainly takes a very bold bird, indeed, to lend its countenance to our silver.

American Sparrow Hawk: *Falco sparverius.*

PLATE 59.

Length: 10–11 inches, sexes the same size.

Male and Female: Above reddish, with or without black bars and spots. Top of head bluish slate with a red patch. Below varying from whitish to dark reddish, with or without black spots. Wings narrow and pointed. Female has dusky bars on back, wings, and tail. Bill dark; feet deep yellow.

Season: Rare resident.

Breeds: From Florida to Hudson's Bay.

Nest: Lays in hollow trees, old Woodpecker holes, and sometimes in Dove cots.

Eggs: Variable; some sets plain buffy brown, others heavily splashed with dark brown or wreathed at the larger end.

Range: Whole of North America, south to northern South America.

This is the smallest, handsomest, and one of the most useful of our Hawks. It is one of the three small species that Dr. Abbott characterizes as belonging to the *impetuous* class, in distinction from the larger Hawks, which he calls *meditative* and *deliberate.*

It is easily recognized from its small size, and it resembles a big Fox Sparrow with a hooked beak and black whiskers.

The Sparrow Hawk has the Shrike's trick of dropping on its prey from a height, instead of approaching in circles. They collect in numbers in the fall and early spring near bird-roosts, and seize their victims when they emerge in the morning, and particularly toward night.

Juncos, Chickadees, and Tree Sparrows lodge in the honeysuckle hedge at the foot of the garden, and late one March afternoon I saw a Hawk in a cedar tree near by. I watched half an hour and thought it had gone. Suddenly a Junco dashed into the hedge, followed by what seemed to be a brown stone, it dropped so quickly, striking at right angles against the heavy wire that supported the vine. The Junco escaped *through* the trellis, and the Sparrow Hawk, in the moment it took to recover itself, gave me a good chance to identify it.

This Hawk is a consumer of beetles and other large insects, mice, etc.; it kills small birds, and sometimes Pigeons, but not preferably.

*   *   *   *   *   *   *   *

In addition to the six Hawks described there are five other species belonging casually, either as migrants or residents, to the same range, but they are rare and not easy for the novice to identify. They are the

Goshawk: A rare winter visitor.
Broad-winged Hawk: An uncommon resident.
Rough-legged Hawk: Rare winter resident.
Duck Hawk: A migrant along the coast. Rare summer resident in Hudson Highlands.
Pigeon Hawk: A common migrant along coast.

American Osprey: *Pandion haliaëtus.*

Fish Hawk.

PLATE 60.

Length: About 24 inches; female larger.
Male and Female: Plain dark brown above, the tail having a white tip and a band of dark brown. Head, neck, and lower parts white; breast plain, or sometimes spotted faintly with brown. Bill bluish black; feet grayish.
Note: "Phew, phew, p-hew!"
Season: April to November.
Breeds: From Florida to Labrador.
Nest: In trees near or over water; a bulky nest on the plan of the Eagle's.
Eggs: 2–3, variable in size and colour; average, $2\frac{1}{2} \times 1\frac{3}{4}$ inches.
Range: North America, from Hudson's Bay and Alaska, south to the West Indies and northern South America.

The familiar, brown, Eagle-like bird, with very large talons, which is seen hovering over Sound, creek, and river, particularly in spring and early fall. The Fish Hawk, as it is popularly called, follows schools of fish, and, dashing from considerable height, seizes its prey with its stout claws. If the fish is small, it is immediately swallowed; if it is large (and it will secure occasionally shad, bass, etc., weighing five or six pounds), it is taken to a convenient bluff or tree and torn to bits. Sometimes the Fish Hawk dives quite deep, and, when he emerges, shakes a shower of spray from his wings and rises slowly. It is at this juncture that the Bald Eagle usually manages to rob him of the fish by either seizing it or startling the Hawk so that he looses his hold. The Osprey when fishing makes one of the most breezy and spirited pictures connected with the feeding-habits of any of our birds, for often there is a splashing and a struggle under water when the fish grasped is either too large or the great talons become entangled. Occasionally the Osprey is carried under and drowned, and large fish have been washed ashore with these birds fastened to them by their claws, though it usually feeds upon fish of little value.

I found an Osprey's nest in a crooked oak on Wakeman's Island in late April, 1893. As I could not get close to the nest (the island is between a network of small creeks and the flood-tides covered the marshes), I at first thought it a monstrous Crow's nest, but on returning the second week in May I saw a pair of Ospreys coming and going to and from the nest, and then obtained a nearer view. I hoped the birds might return another season, as the nest looked as if it might have been used for two or three years and was as lop-sided as a poorly made haystack. The great August storm of the same year broke the tree and the nest fell, making quite a heap on the ground. Among the débris were sticks of various sizes, dried reeds, two bits of a bamboo fishing-rod, seaweeds, some old blue mosquito netting, and some rags of fish net, also about half a bushel of salt hay in various stages of decomposition, and malodorous dirt galore.

The Fish Hawk is said to breed in colonies along the New Jersey coast. Here I have only seen it in pairs, and though a common bird it always attracts attention whenever it appears.

AMERICAN OSPREY.

Length, 24 inches.

ORDER COLUMBÆ: PIGEONS.

FAMILY COLUMBIDÆ: DOVES AND PIGEONS.

Passenger Pigeon : *Ectopistes migratorius.*

Wild Pigeon.

PLATE 61.

Length: Dependent upon the development of tail, 12–16 inches.

Male: Upper parts bluish gray, reddish brown below, fading to whitish toward vent. Wings dark, with a few spots, tail quills dark blue at the base and white at tips. Bill black; feet lake-red.

Female: Dull gray above, breast ashy brown.

Note: A guttural "coo."

Season: A rare summer resident. Last considerable flight some 20 years ago. (Averill.)

Breeds: Locally and irregularly in the more northerly parts of its range.

Nest: Merely a lattice of small twigs, through which the eggs may be seen.

Eggs: 2, white.

Range: Eastern North America, from Hudson's Bay southward, and west to the Great Plains, straggling westward to Nevada and Washington Territory.

The beautifully tinted Wild Pigeon is now almost a thing of the past. Thirty years ago it was one of our most abundant Game-birds, but it has become exterminated in some localities and is a rare summer resident whose appearance is carefully noted. Old housekeepers remember when, in New York and Boston every winter, carts loaded with these birds went from door to door and potted pigeon was a standard New England dish, alternating with roast beef, turkey, and sparerib.

The disappearance of this Pigeon is only a page in the sad history of the destruction of bird life in the United States, and it seems as if the founders of the country, as well as the ever-increasing stream of emigrants, had too much faith in its resources, believing it to be a land not amenable to the laws of Nature. So ruthlessly have these

Pigeons been slaughtered, that one account from the West records instances where they have been shot down by the hundred, and left on the ground as food for the pigs! The result is, that all game is only locally plentiful, and that we have less in general than countries hundreds of years older where a reasonable protection has existed. The only flights of Wild Pigeons heard of now belong to the Northwestern States and the Mississippi Valley at large. Then, too, the destruction of the forests and far-extending blizzards have hastened the extinction that the gun began.

Mourning Dove: *Zenaidura macroura.*

PLATE 62.

Length: 12–13 inches.

Male and Female: General appearance when in the trees, a bluish fawn colour. Above olive-brown, varying to a bluish gray, neck and head washed with metallic tints. Below a dull purplish, changing to reddish brown. Two middle tail feathers as long as the wings. Bill black, feet lake-red. Female duller.

Note: A plaintive mournful "Coo-o, coo-o!"

Season: Common summer resident; March to November.

Breeds: From southern Canada to the Gulf of Mexico.

Nest: A few loose sticks, sometimes laid on an old Robin's nest.

Eggs: 2, white.

Range: North America, from southern Maine, southern Canada and Oregon south to Panama and the West Indies.

This Dove is one of most prettily shiftless housewives among birds. She has softly coloured plumage, a refined, though sad, voice, and many gentle, lady-like ways; but when it comes to nest-building (and the female is always rightly held responsible for the neatness of the home), she is utterly wanting. Even though her mate should decline to furnish her with a more liberal supply of sticks, she could arrange those she has to better advantage; but she evidently lacks that indispensable something, called *faculty*, which must be inborn.

The eggs or bodies of the young show plainly through the rude platform and bid fair either to fall through it or

PLATE 61.

PASSENGER PIGEON.

Length, 12-16 inches.

roll out, but they seldom do. Meanwhile she coos regretfully, but does not see her way to bettering things, saying, "I know that I'm a poor housekeeper, but it runs in our family"; but when the Doves choose a flattened-out Robin's nest for a platform, the nestlings fare very well.

Though inhabitants of woodlands, these birds are coyly sociable and always build a nest or two in the garden. They usually choose the pines and spruces, and put the nest close to the trunk where two adjoining branches start; sometimes the nest will be twenty feet from the ground, but it is usually lower. The monotonous cooing, which gives them their name, is a rather desolate sound except as it blends with the morning chorus.

They seldom feed upon insects; but prefer seeds of various sorts, and glean grain from the fields after harvest, though I have never seen them take it from the ear, and they cannot be said to do any damage. The young are easily tamed, if taken from the nest, and make very gentle and attractive pets, but are of too gross a habit to be kept in the house.

ORDER GALLINÆ: GALLINACEOUS BIRDS.

FAMILY TETRAONIDÆ: GROUSE, PARTRIDGES, ETC.

Bob-white; Quail: *Colinus virginianus.*

PLATE 65. FIG. 1.

Length: 10.50 inches.

Male and Female: Crown feathers slightly crested. White forehead; eye line and throat patch edged with dark. Above variegated reddish brown flecked with black, white, and tawny. Below whitish, warming on the sides to reddish, with dark streaks. In female the forehead, throat, and eye stripes are buffy. Bill rusty black.

Note: "Bob-white! Bob-*white!*" Sometimes also "Poor-Bob-white."

Season: Resident.

Breeds: Throughout range; pairs here in April.

Nest: Small twigs and grass in a ground hollow.

Eggs: 10–15, white and blunt.

Range: Eastern United States and southern Canada; from southern Maine to the South Atlantic and Gulf States; west to Dakota, eastern Kansas, and eastern Texas.

The most abundant and attractive of our Game-birds, whose note is so cheery and melodious as to be as welcome as an elaborate song. In April and May the clear call — "Bob-white! Bob-white! Poor-Bob-white!" — comes from the stubble fields and bushy roadsides, with the staccato ring, at the same time that the Meadowlark sings in the pastures and marshlands. At this time Bob-white may be seen sitting upon an old fence rail, telling of his lonesome plight, and calling with a total disregard of the presence of man. Again, in August, you will see him with his spouse and flock of young running through the underbrush, or in fields where the grain has been reaped. When the first gun is fired in November, they take warning and retire from the neighbourhood of settlements to thickly bushed hillsides, where they remain until absolutely flushed.

In early winter, after light snow, you may often see Quails scratching in the buckwheat fields; for they are particularly fond of this grain, and you cannot do a kinder act than by scattering a little every day on the snow where you see their tracks, as they frequently suffer from hunger. Like the Ruffed Grouse, they sometimes burrow in the snow to hide from intense cold, and an ice crust forming above them they are unable to get out, and die, often in great numbers. They are keenly alive to the benefits of protection; for three successive years broods were raised in a tangle underneath some old quince bushes at the foot of the garden, and old and young continued to range in the vicinity all summer, returning to hide in the shooting-season under a hemlock hedge. The fourth year they were disturbed by rock-blasting in the adjoining land, and have not since nested in the garden. Two and often three families are raised in a season, and the breeding sometimes continues so late in the fall that winter overtakes a half-grown covey. Twenty-five is not an unusual annual family for these vigorous birds.

PLATE 62.

MOURNING DOVE.

Length, 12–13 inches.

Ruffed Grouse: *Bonasa umbellus.*

Partridge (*New England*), *Pheasant* (*Middle and Southern States*).

PLATE 63.

Length: 16–18 inches.

Male and Female: Slightly crested head; yellow eye stripe; neck mottled with reddish and dusky brown. Back variegated chestnut; lower parts lighter, buff or whitish, with dark bars. Long tail, which spreads fan-like, reddish gray, beautifully barred. Neck ruff of dark feathers, with iridescent green and purple tints, which, in the female, is dull. Claws not feathered.

Note: A Hen-like cluck.

Breeds: In woodlands, through range.

Nest: On the ground, among dry leaves; frequently a bunch of leaves between the roots of a chestnut.

Eggs: 10–15, rich buff, usually plain, sometimes specked with brown.

Range: Eastern United States, south to North Carolina, Georgia, Mississippi, and Arkansas.

The Ruffed Grouse, which is called the Partridge in New England, is a case where incorrect *local* nomenclature has created permanent confusion. It is a *true Grouse*, and the *real Partridge is the Bob-white.* The term *Partridge* seems, however, to be a fixture in literature as well as in the markets.

The Ruffed Grouse is familiar to those who have been in the habit of walking in the New England woods or remote lanes in the spring or autumn; it is a resident, but is more apt to be seen at these two seasons. In woods where the underbrush has been thinned out, and not wholly cut away, and where shooting is forbidden, this Grouse shows, in spring, almost the tameness of the domestic fowl; but in autumn it is more shy, for, if protected in some places, it is harried in others and become suspicious.

The Grouse mates in late April; and when the chicks are hatched, they immediately leave the nest and follow their mother. They obey her authority as quickly as chickens do the Hen, except that when they hear the warning note, they dive under leaves and bushes, while she leads the pursuer off in an opposite direction. The female attends to the duties of nest-building and incubation alone; the males seem to feel themselves *de trop* at this time, and keep separate, roosting together, and rejoining their mates when the young are hatched, and then they roam as a family.

The male Ruffed Grouse has the same habit of pluming and strutting as the Turkey-cock, and also makes the drumming noise which has caused so much dispute and which is attributed to at least four different causes. This peculiar sound begins in spring, and, though not belonging to the breeding-season alone, is most frequently indulged in at that time. It seems to be in token of general good health and spirits as well as to call attention to the drummer. Heard at a little distance it is a hollow, vibrating sound, beginning softly and increasing, as if a small rubber ball was dropped slowly and then rapidly bounced on a drumhead.

You may hear the drumming fifty times, without seeing the bird from which it proceeds, and you may even see the bird plainly without having the slightest clue to how the sound is produced.

It is variously stated that the Grouse beats with its wings on a log; that it raises its wings and strikes their edges above its back; that it claps them against its side like a crowing rooster, and, lastly, that it beats the air. You may take your choice of the methods, the result is the same.

Last April, when in the woods near Ciecos Brook, I *saw* a Grouse drum. I was sitting on the ground and the bird flew over my head and lit on a rail that topped an old stone wall; his back was toward me. For a few minutes he remained quiet as if listening, ruffled his feathers, raised his tail, moved his wings slowly, as if to test them. Then beat them more and more rapidly until my eyes blinked hopelessly. When the noise ceased, the wings drooped slightly, and in a moment more the bird flew away.

This almost agrees with Thoreau's positive assertion that he had seen a Partridge drum while standing on a wall, and that it stood upright and struck its wings together behind its back, but striking neither the wall or its body, and he bravely declares that any one who affirms the contrary is

RUFFED GROUSE.

Length, 16–18 inches.

mistaken, even though he were Audubon himself. A snap-shot with a camera might settle the question, but the drummer seldom performs in places where the light would permit of a photograph of whirling feathers.

As a Game-bird the Ruffed Grouse is a favourite, having white meat of a good flavour and less dry than that of the Quail. Sometimes when driven by hunger it feeds upon noxious berries and the leaves of the dwarf laurel or lamb-kill, which may render it unwholesome food; but if the bird is properly cleaned at once no such trouble can ensue, as the leaves and berries when digested cannot injure the flesh, and the only danger comes from the poisonous matter remaining in the crop and intestines and permeating the entire bird.

The eyes of the Grouse are of the most wonderful depth and softness. This autumn, during a violent storm, a young bird with a broken wing and leg was blown against the house door. I took it in, and it lay for some time in my hand, until we found that it could not be cured, and that the kindest act would be to kill it. I shall never forget its eyes, with their deep, expanding pupils and the golden-brown iris. Of all the expressive, speaking eyes that I have seen among animals, the eyes of this bird were the most beautiful and pathetic.

ORDER LIMICOLÆ: SHORE-BIRDS.

FAMILY APHRIZIDÆ: SURF-BIRDS AND TURNSTONES.

Turnstone: *Arenaria interpres.*

Calico Snipe.

PLATE 64. FIG. 1.

Length: 8–9 inches.

Male and Female: Above patched with black, white, red, brown and gray in a calico pattern. Below white, with black throat and breast, divided by a white line. Much white on wings and tail. *Bill black*, shorter than head, and slightly recurved; *feet orange.* Adults, in winter, lack the red on the back and the blacks are less clear.

Season: Common migrant; May, August, and September.
Breeds: In high northern latitudes.
Range: Nearly cosmopolitan; in America, from Greenland and Alaska to the Straits of Magellan; more or less common in the interior of North America, on the shores of the Great Lakes and the larger rivers.

The Turnstone has a bill that looks like two sharply pointed ridge-backed pens placed face to face. He uses this as a pry to displace small stones along the shore to secure the various bits of marine life lodging under them. Hence it is more common about the base of rocky cliffs and coves than on smooth, sandy beaches. It is conspicuous for its size, its boldly marked plumage contrasting with its surroundings, while Sandpipers mingle with the sands and can be hardly seen at a little distance unless revealed by some abrupt movement.

FAMILY CHARADRIIDÆ: PLOVERS.

Black-bellied Plover: *Charadrius squatarola.*

Length: 11–12 inches.
Male and Female: Breeding-plumage black and white, seldom seen in United States. Fall plumage, above mottled with black, gray, and yellowish; beneath whitish. Wings and tail nearly even. Bill long and black; feet black. Axillary feathers black.
Season: Migrant; common in autumn.
Breeds: Far north.
Range: Nearly cosmopolitan, but chiefly in the Northern Hemisphere, migrating south in winter; in America, to the West Indies, Brazil, and New Granada.

The Plovers are wading Shore-birds, feeding on beetles, grasshoppers, worms, larvæ, and fresh-water shell-fish. This species breeds in the Arctic regions and appears here in numbers in the fall migration only. It is then fairly, but irregularly, abundant about the marsh-ponds, and is an extremely handsome bird, having a clear, whistling cry. It arrives about the middle of September, after the general migration of the Golden Plover.

PLATE 64.

1. TURNSTONE. 2. AMERICAN GOLDEN PLOVER.

Length, 8-9 inches. Length, 10-11 inches.

American Golden Plover: ***Charadrius dominicus.***

Field Plover.

PLATE 64. FIG. 2.

Length: 10–11 inches.

Male and Female: Subject to great variations of plumage. Above mottled with black and greenish yellow; whitish below. *Axillary feathers dark ashy.* Bill and feet black.

Season: Common autumn migrant; early September.

Breeds: Arctic regions.

Range: Arctic America, migrating southward throughout North and South America to Patagonia.

This species is the well-known Plover of the markets, and the favourite of sportsmen. They are to be found in the salt-marshes and about sand-bars and tide-pools. Their coming is irregular; sometimes a great flock will alight, and then again only a few stragglers. They usually pass from late August until middle September; heavy storms may delay them, or, if the weather is evenly fine, they often fly over any given locality without pausing. This uncertainty about the arrival of many birds, especially the various Water-birds that visit us only as migrants, is due largely to the chances of weather. If September is a pleasant month and there are few gales, the great body fly out at sea and pass Connecticut altogether. In the spring migration they are but little noticed, the sportsman must not shoot them, and the bird-lover is kept from marshes by the flood-tides; but when a great storm comes during the fall migration, the Golden Plover not only flies close to the land, but flies low, and then he falls an easy prey to the sportsmen who are lying in wait for him.

Killdeer Plover: ***Ægialitis vocifera.***

Length: 9–10 inches.

Male and Female: Gray-brown, washed with olive above; rump variegated with all shades of orange and reddish brown. *White frontlet and red eyelids.* Below white; collar and breastlet of black. Bill black; legs light.

Note: "Killdeér! kill-deér!"
Season: Once a summer resident, now rare, remaining from March to November.
Breeds: Through its range.
Nest: A hollow in the grass or sand in vicinity of *fresh water.*
Eggs: 4, the ground, as with the eggs of many Waders, varying from clay colour to cream, marked with brownish black.
Range: Temperate North America, migrating in winter to the West Indies, and Central and northern South America.

You may hear this Plover cry and yet never see the bird itself, though the black-banded breast, white frontlet, and red eyelids make it easy to identify. It nests in our marsh meadows, arriving in March, with the Bluebirds and Song Sparrows, lingers until ice has formed on the edges of the ponds, and yet we do not think of calling it a common bird. According to Wilson, the Killdeers are somewhat nocturnal in their habits, especially in feeding upon the worms that then rise to the surface of the ground. Their loud cry — "Killdeer! Kill-d-e-e-r!" — has all the shrillness of the Jay's scream, and the Plover uses it frequently to mislead intruders or lure them away from his nest. Coues says that "they abound in the West, are not gregarious or maritime extensively, but somewhat irregularly migratory, and are very noisy birds."

Semipalmated Plover: *Ægialitis semipalmata.*

Ring Plover.

Length: 7 inches.
Male and Female: Bill black, orange at base. An orange ring around eye. Above a dark ash-gray. Below white, with a black ring across breast and above this a white ring across back of neck. Half-webbed yellow feet.
Season: "Abundant migrant, seen on flats at low tide. May and late July to late September."
Breeds: North from Labrador.
Range: Arctic and subarctic America, migrating south throughout tropical America as far as Brazil and Peru.

One of the commonest Plovers, or, in fact, of Shore-birds in general, to be found along the beaches; easily identified by means of the complete neck ring, white upon dark and dark upon light.

Like the Sandpipers, they dance along the shore in rhythm with the ebbing tides, leaving sharp footprints on the wet sand. These footprints will also give you a key to the bird, for they show that its feet are half-webbed or *semipalmated*, from which it takes its specific name.

I have only found these birds along the seashore, but Samuels says that on their arrival in spring, small flocks follow the course of large rivers, like the Connecticut. He also found a single pair breeding on Muskeget, the famous haunt of Gulls, off the shore of Massachusetts. On their return migration, these Plovers are shot down promiscuously with the Sandpipers, with which they associate closely.

Piping Plover: *Ægialitis meloda.*

Pale Ring-neck.

Length: 6.50 inches.

Male and Female: Above light gray. Coloured eye ring; bill yellow with black tip; *partial white collar* on back of neck and a *partial dark* band on throat. A black bar between the eyes. Below white. Legs orange yellow. Female, the eye bar a pale brown, and the neck rings merely spots.

Season: A summer resident, but not common.

Breeds: Northward from Virginia.

Nest and Eggs: No real nest; eggs 2–4, creamy or grayish, with brown scratches or small spots; laid on the sand.

Range: Eastern Province of North America; in winter the West Indies.

This, the second of the Ring-neck Plovers, comes to us in scattering flocks in late April, which a month later separate into pairs. Samuels says that it sometimes strays into the interior, and has been known to breed on the borders of ponds twenty miles from the coast, but that in New England it seldom wanders far from the shore, and prefers sand islands near the mainland for its breeding-haunts. He has found its eggs at Muskeget with those of the last species. The Piping Plover, as well as the Ring-neck, live upon insects, worms, eggs of fish, small crustacea, etc.

FAMILY SCOLOPACIDÆ: SNIPES, SANDPIPERS, ETC.

American Woodcock: *Philohela minor.*

PLATE 65. FIG. 2.

Length: 10–11 inches. Female an inch longer.

Male: Eyes large, set in upper corner of head. Short, thick neck and compact body. Above variegated with brown, black, tawny, and gray. Below brown, ranging from buff to tawny. Legs very short. Bill longer than head, straight and stout.

Note: A peep and a whistle. "P't-ul! P't-ul!" and "peent, peent" (Brewster.)

Season: A summer resident; February to December.

Breeds: Through range in April and May.

Nest: A hollow in the ground, lined with a few leaves.

Eggs: 4 usually, varying from stone-gray to buff, with indefinite brown markings and gray cloudings.

Range: Eastern United States, north to the British Provinces, west to Dakota, Kansas, etc.

The king of our Game-birds, to be distinguished from the Snipe, which it resembles, by its heavier build, shorter legs, and plain red-brown under parts. Though grouped with Shore-birds, it is more frequently to be found in sheltered bogs and in woods bordering swamps than by lakes or rivers.

The Woodcocks obtain the grubs and larvæ on which they feed by probing in the soft mud with the bill, which is so extremely sensitive at the tip as to enable them to select food wholly by the sense of touch. The eyes are set in the head at a very peculiar angle, which gives the birds a rather foolish appearance. This is a protective provision of Nature. The eyes being situated high up and far back in both the Snipe and Woodcock enables them, by increasing the field of vision, to escape from many of their enemies, even though they cannot *see* their food.

2

1

1. BOB-WHITE.
Length, 10.50 inches.

2. AMERICAN WOODCOCK.
Length, 10-11 inches.

Woodcocks are as nocturnal in their feeding-habits as the Nighthawk itself. They may be frequently seen in April and May, an hour before twilight, peeping out from the margin of woodlands, picking their way in a leisurely manner to their feeding-grounds, or you may hear their short song either then or at dawn, and see them make beautiful flights into the air, sweeping in great circles and rising spirally like the Skylark, leaving behind a whistling sound, as if the wind rushed through a sharp-edged reed. At this, the breeding-season, the male does a great deal of strutting and preening, as is the case with many so-called songless birds, who make pose take the place of voice in gaining the attention of the desired mate.

The young are very attractive little chicks, following their mother as soon as hatched. Early in May of last year I happened to see the last of a brood of three emerge from the egg. The callow little bunch had scarcely become accustomed to the light and its down was moist and limp, yet when the mother, on seeing me, gave the warning cry, it disappeared from under my very eyes as promptly as if it had studied wood tactics for a lifetime, and nothing remained but some bits of shell, mingling with the dead leaves, at the roots of a great tuft of evergreen ferns.

Wilson's Snipe: *Gallinago delicata.*

English Snipe.

PLATE 67. FIG. 1.

Length: 10.50–11.50 inches.

Male and Female: Straight greenish gray bill $2\frac{1}{2}$ inches long; eyes set far back, as in last species. Above reddish and dark brown; sides of head and neck buff. Dark, plain wings, margined and tipped with white; tail bay and black, outer feathers dirty white, with brown bars; feet greenish gray.

Note: A peeping cry and several rolling notes.

Season: In the migrations, March, April, October, and November.

Breeds: Northward from the United States; also, casually, farther south.

Nest: A hollow in ground or a bog tussock.

Eggs: 3–4, olive-gray washed with dull brown, marked on the larger end with umber spots and black scratches.

Range: North and middle America; south, in winter, to the West Indies and northern South America.

The true Snipe of sportsmen, which is erroneously called "English Snipe." Wilson's Snipe has many qualities in common with the Woodcock. It is a bird of fresh-water marsh meadows, where it returns in September, and is usually quite plentiful by the middle of October, going south when ice closes its feeding-grounds. It is a nocturnal feeder, and has the habit of soaring into the air at dawn and sunset. Usually, it is only considered from the food standpoint, but it really possesses musical qualities. I only know its peeping cry, that seems to fall from the clouds in the autumn nights when the migrating flocks pass over, but Audubon says that the male and female birds rise into the air,—"now with continued beating of the wings, now in short sailings, until more than a hundred yards high, when they whirl round each other with extreme velocity, and dance as it were to their own music; for at this juncture, and during the space of four or five minutes, you hear rolling notes mingled together, each more or less distinct, perhaps according to the state of the atmosphere. The sounds produced are extremely pleasing, though they fall faintly on the ear."

Dowitcher: *Macrorhamphus griseus.*

Red-breasted Snipe.

Length: Varying from 10.25 to 12 inches.

Male and Female: Bill dark, long and slender like last species, which it generally resembles. "Rump and tail white, the former spotted, the latter banded with black." *In summer* plumage the back is variegated with black, ash, and red, reddish below; tail barred with dark. *In winter* it is ash-gray above and whitish below. Feet greenish black.

Season: A fairly common migrant in August and September.

Breeds: In the far North.

Range: Eastern North America.

A coastwise Snipe, very handsome and richly feathered. It can be distinguished when skimming over the marsh meadows by its erratic and Swallow-like flight, and at shorter range by its conspicuous white rump. It feeds upon marsh snails, water beetles and worms, such as are obtained in large numbers in the mud at the neck of tide bars and in clam beds. Its flesh is delicate, and it is greatly prized by sportsmen.

Knot: *Tringa canutus.*

Robin Snipe.

Length: 10.50 inches.
Male and Female: Straight bill 1½ inches long. Above black, white, ash, and reddish; crown gray streaked with black; nape of neck reddish. Below rich chestnut; legs short and thick. Young, the first two or three years until they put on the full plumage, *gray*, black, and white above, white below, which led to the idea that old males turned gray in winter. Female duller.
Note: "Wah-quoit!" and a honk. (G. H. Mackay.)
Season: Irregular migrant.
Breeds: In high northern latitudes.
Range: Nearly cosmopolitan.

This Sandpiper may be recognized by its large size and very richly coloured feathers. With us it is a bird of the sea-coast and marshes, but in the Interior States it may be found about the larger lakes and rivers.

Mr. Averill has shot it in August on the Housatonic meadows, and it may be occasionally seen pattering about the pools on the beach at low tide, in search of small shell-fish and marine insects, which are its usual articles of food and which impart a marshy flavour to this as well as to many similar Shore-birds.

The Knot is no longer a common Snipe, and any one who reads Mr. George H. Mackay's very interesting monograph upon it, in *The Auk* for January, 1893, will easily see why. He says, not only have they been wantonly killed on the Cape Cod marshes, by the process known as "fire-lighting," but he has every reason to believe that they were formerly shot along the Virginia coast in *spring* on their way to the breeding-grounds; he says, "one such place shipped to New York City in a single spring, from April 1 to June 3, upwards of six thousand Plovers, a large share of which were Knots." This was about thirty years ago, but it nevertheless serves to illustrate what kind of treatment these birds received in those as well as later days, and bears out the current belief of to-day that the Knots have in a "great measure been killed off." The "fire-lighting" method of capturing them was, "for two men to start out after dark at half-tide, one of them to carry a lighted lantern, the other to reach and seize the birds, bite their necks, and put them in a bag slung over the shoulder." It is well to think that this also took place many years ago, and was stopped by law, to the honour of true sportsmen, who, after all that is said against them, have done much to stop the butchery of game.

Pectoral Sandpiper: *Tringa maculata.*

Grass Snipe.

Length: 9–9.50 inches.

Male: Above black and reddish; white stripe over eye; neck short. Below whitish, washed on neck and breast with dusky, broken by brown lines. *Rump black;* wings dusky; some tail feathers tipped with white. Bill straight, half as long as head, flesh-coloured tipped with black. Feet dusky greenish.

Season: Common migrant; August to November.

Breeds: In Arctic regions.

Range: The whole of North America, the West Indies, and the greater part of South America. Of frequent occurrence in Europe.

A fresh-water Sandpiper, found in wet meadows with Wilson's Snipe. It comes in late summer from its northern breeding-grounds in flocks of variable size, and remains as long as the insects upon which it feeds hold out. Its habits are more like those of the Snipes than of Sandpipers, and its flesh has a similar sweetness, lacking the rankness of the true Shore-birds. It has a loud, wiry call: "Tweet-tweet-weet!" which it often repeats when on the wing. In the

PLATE 66.

1. SPOTTED SANDPIPER

Length, 7.50 inches.

2. LEAST SANDPIPER.

Length, 5.50 inches.

breeding-season the male has a curious habit of inflating his throat to a wonderful degree so that it hangs down upon the breast like a great tumour. It is a popular bird with gunners, and is known by them as Grass Snipe.

Least Sandpiper: *Tringa minutilla.*

Peep.

PLATE 66. FIG. 2.

Length: 5.50 inches.

Male and Female: In summer plumage, above dark brown, feathers edged with red. Neck ash-gray, spotted with black. White eye stripe. Wings dusky, *rump* and *tail coverts black.* Below grayish white. In winter becoming gray and white like many other species. Bill black; legs dull green.

Season: Common migrant; April and May, August and September.

Breeds: North of the United States.

Range: The whole of North and South America. Accidental in Europe.

The smallest of all Sandpipers, known everywhere by the familiar name of Peep — the cry they constantly give when congregating on the beaches and flats at low tide. It has a pretty way of dancing up to the shallow, frothy ripples, meeting them, seizing some tiny morsel, and retreating with a sort of courtesy. All the Sandpipers have a half-shy, half-sociable way of flitting afoot about the water's edge that makes them very sociable. Often at low tide I have walked down the beach toward Penfield Bar with three or four of these little birds for companions; they will run on ahead, never letting me quite come up to them, and yet half expecting me to follow. This habit gave motive to one of the best bits of verse that Mrs. Celia Thaxter has left with us: —

"I watch him as he skims along,
  Uttering his sweet and mournful cry;
He starts not at my fitful song,
  Or flash of fluttering drapery;
He has no thought of any wrong;
  He scans me with a fearless eye.
Staunch friends are we, well tried and strong,
  The little sandpiper and I." (3d verse.)

Dr. Coues, in his "Birds of the Northwest," gives a beautiful picture of this bird in its Labrador breeding-haunts, where the fogs hang low and wild waves rage, and the little Sandpipers watch their half-sheltered ground-nest with anxious devotion. "Now, later in the season, when the young birds are grown strong of wing, family joins family, and the gathering goes to the sea beach. Stretches of sand, or pebbly shingle, or weed-loaded rocks, or muddy flats, bestrewn with wrack, invite, and are visited in turn; and each yields abundant sustenance. The unsuspecting birds ramble and play heedlessly, in the very front of man, unmindful of, because unknowing danger; they have a sad lesson to learn the coming winter, when they are tormented without stint, and a part of their number slaughtered in more civilized countries for mere sport, or for the morsel of food their bodies may afford. Blasts fiercer than they ever knew before, come out of the north; autumn is upon them, and they must not wait. Flocks rise on wing, and it is not long before the beaches and the marshes of the states are thronged."

The Semipalmated (half-webbed) Sandpiper—*Ereunetes pusillus*—also shares the name of Peep with the last species, with which it flocks. It can best be distinguished from the Least Sandpiper by it feet, which are *half-webbed*, the Least having no webbing. It is also slightly larger.

Greater Yellow-legs: *Totanus melanoleucus.*

Stone Snipe.

Length: 13–14 inches.

Male and Female: Above dusky, spotted with black and white. Bill green black; over two inches long and slightly recurved. Below white, streaked sparsely with gray on the neck. Rump white, also tail feathers, which are barred with brown. *Long, thin, yellow legs.*

Season: A common migrant; May and August to November.

Breeds: In the cold temperate and sub-arctic portions of North America.

Range: America in general, migrating south to Chili and Buenos Ayres.

A handsome, noisy bird, commonly seen in flocks about sand bars, creeks, and inlets. It has a shrill voice and gives utterance to the most weird and startling cries when disturbed as well as during migration. When half a dozen of these birds converse the sounds are like the ejaculations of a collection of shipwrecked foreigners, each speaking a different tongue and mutually angry at not being understood. It is followed by sportsmen, though as an article of food its desirability is open to dispute.

Solitary Sandpiper: *Totanus solitarius.*

Length: 8–9 inches.

Male and Female: Long, slender, dark bill. In breeding-plumage, dark brown above with an olive wash. Head and neck streaked with white; rest of upper parts spotted with white. Below white, with some dark streaks on the breast. Legs dull greenish. Markings less distinct in the fall.

Season: Common migrant in May and September.

Breeds: From northern United States northward, and believed to breed in more southern localities. Probably a summer resident in New England.

Range: North America, migrating southward as far as Brazil and Peru.

Not a true Shore-bird, but an inhabitant of the neighbourhood of wooded ponds and the margins of out-of-the-way watercourses; which, if startled from its seclusion, penetrates the underbrush rather than expose itself by flight. Wilson states that this Sandpiper lives in watery places in the mountainous region from New York State southwest to Kentucky, but that they are never numerous. Audubon notes the expert way in which they catch insects, saying that they are particularly apt in seizing small dragon-flies in their descent from the trees to the muddy pools where they breed. In this neighbourhood they are generally seen in pairs, and I have never noticed more than six or eight during any one season.

Bartramian Sandpiper: ***Bartramia longicauda.***

Field Plover.

Length: 11.75–12.75 inches.

Male and Female: Bill short, grooved, and tipped with black, but little longer than the head. Above dusky, varied with yellowish and gray, a pale yellow stripe through the eye. Lower wing coverts white, banded with dark gray. Below varying from white to buff, dark lines on breast, and spots on belly. Outer tail quills white, barred with black. Feet dirty yellow.

Season: A summer resident, but becoming rare. Noted by Linsley as breeding at Stratford, Conn.

Breeds: Throughout its North American range.

Nest: A few straws and tendrils to keep the eggs together; in locations similar to those chosen by the Meadowlark.

Eggs: 4, gray or cream ground, with irregular umber spots.

Range: Eastern North America, north to Nova Scotia and Alaska; migrating in winter southward, as far even as southern South America.

This species is classed as a Wading-bird, but is perfectly independent of water, and inhabits meadows and uplands, for which reason sportsmen call it the Upland or Field Plover. It announces itself on its arrival by a long, melodious whistle; it has several other cries in the breeding-season, but they are the reverse of pleasing. After the young are hatched, they flock with the adults, visiting the grass fields and feeding more after the fashion of Meadowlarks than of Sandpipers. As the frost blasts the inland fields they gradually approach the shore. At this season they are very plump, with sweet, well-flavoured flesh.

Spotted Sandpiper: ***Actitis macularia.***

Teeter; Tilt-up.

PLATE 66. FIG. 1.

Length: 7.50 inches.

Male and Female: Slender, flesh-colour bill, black tipped, longer than the head. Above Quaker-gray, with an iridescent lustre, spotted and streaked with black. White eye line. White below, dotted with black: feet flesh-coloured. More dull throughout in winter.

Note: A gentle "peet-weet — peet-weet!"
Season: Common summer resident.
Breeds: Throughout temperate North America.
Nest and Eggs: Resembling last species.
Range: North and South America, south to Brazil. Occasional in Europe.

This is the familiar little bird of roadside brooks and moist meadows, where the marsh marigold of spring is followed by the cardinal flower and gentian of autumn. To me it is indelibly associated with gentian meadows, for the first time that I ever throughly identified it I was balancing on a big grass hummock, wondering if I could step across a particularly deceitful looking bit of water, half ditch, half sluggish stream, to secure a plant of blue fringed gentian that branched like a magnificent candelabra with cups of lapis lazuli; — and this Sandpiper flew from an opposite tussock and gave its plaintive cry. Seeing that I did not stir, it walked unconsciously along the edge of the ditch, mincing and balancing in a curious way, jerking its body in see-saw fashion, which has given it the name of "Teeter." Every few minutes it flew to the grass, whispering to itself as it fed.

The Spotted Sandpiper possesses all the delicacy and beauty of a Song-bird, and it seems as much an act of cruelty to hunt it down for sport as if it was a Thrush or Oriole. It does not live in flocks.

ORDER PALUDICOLÆ: CRANES, RAILS, ETC.

FAMILY RALLIDÆ: RAILS, GALLINULES, COOTS.

Clapper Rail: *Rallus longirostris crepitans.*

Salt-water Marsh Hen.

Length: 14–16 inches.
Male and Female: General colouring *sand-gray, with no reddish tinge.* Above variegated ash and olive-brown; no decided mottlings. Below, yellowish brown whitening on the throat; wings and tail dull brown. Bill longer than the head and yellowish brown; feet the same colour.

Season: Common summer resident from Connecticut southward. May winter.

Breeds: In dense marshes, most abundantly in the Carolinas.

Nest: A collection of grasses and reeds; on the ground, barely out of the reach of water.

Eggs: Numerous, 6–12, cream-white, speckled with reddish brown.

Range: Salt-marshes of the Atlantic coast of the United States, from New Jersey southward; resident from the Potomac southward, casually north to Massachusetts.

The Clapper Rail is one of the noisiest of most obstreperous of Shore-birds. It straggles to the Massachusetts coast in summer, and is at times quite plentiful, but irregularly so. This is the species that is killed in great numbers among the salt-marshes in the neighbourhood of Atlantic City, N.J. It takes its name—*longirostris*, long bill, and *crepitans*, crepitating, clattering—from the extra length of its bill and the incessant noise that it makes, especially in the breeding-season. These Rails have a most ludicrous gait, tipping forward as they run.

Virginia Rail: *Rallus virginianus.*

PLATE 67. FIG. 2.

Length: variable, 8.50–10.50 inches.

Male and Female: General tone streaky and reddish. Above dark brown plainly streaked with olive, a white line from the bill extending over the eye. *Throat white.* Below bright reddish; wings dark brown; coverts chestnut; tail dark brown barred with white.

Season: A common summer resident, breeding on the salt-marshes. Sometimes winters.

Breeds: Northward from Pennsylvania.

Nest: A slight mat of grasses in a clump of reeds near water, usually in an inaccessible place.

Eggs: 6–8, resembling those of the last species.

Range: North America, from the British Provinces south to Guatemala.

A very pretty species, having a general ruddy tint and being abundant both in fresh and salt marshes. It is

PLATE 67.

1. WILSON'S SNIPE.

Length, 10.50–11.50 inches.

2. VIRGINIA RAIL.

Length, 8.50–10.50 inches.

known locally as the Little Red Rail and is a perfect copy, in miniature, of the King Rail, which only visits us casually, but is well known from the Middle States southward. The Virginia Rail is very shy and will always hide, if possible, instead of flying, and it has the faculty of running across water upon a few floating sticks and bits of litter.

Dr. Coues, in his "Birds of the Northwest," in describing a night scene in Arizona near the Mojave River, where he suffered many hardships, speaks of the haunts of the Rail thus: "At nightfall some Mallard and Teal settled into the rushes, gabbling curious vespers as they went to rest. A few Marsh Wrens appeared on the edge of the reeds, queerly balancing themselves on the thread-like leaves, see-sawing to their own quaint music. Then they were hushed, and as darkness settled down, the dull, heavy croaking of the frogs played bass to the shrill falsetto of the insects. Suddenly they too were hushed in turn, frightened may be, into silence; and from the heart of the bullrushes, 'crik-crik-rik-k-k-k,' lustily shouted some wide-awake Rail, to be answered by another and another, till the reeds resounded. . . . The Rails are, partially at least, nocturnal. During such moonlight nights as they are on the alert, patrolling the marshes through the countless ways among the reeds, stopping to cry, 'all's well' as they pass on, or to answer the challenge of a distant watchman. That they feed by night, as well as by day, cannot be doubted. Their habit of skulking and hiding in the most inaccessible places they frequent renders them difficult of observation, and they are usually considered rarer than they really are."

Sora: *Porzana carolina.*

Carolina Rail.

Length: 8–9 inches.

Male and Female: Bill only $\frac{3}{4}$ inch long, straight and stout. Above olive, brownish, and black, many feathers having white edges and with black and white barring on the flanks. Breast slate-colour, with some black on the centre of the throat. Tail dusky brown, darkest in centre, and almost pointed.

Season: Summer resident.

Breeds: Freely from the Middle States northward; in brackish and salt marshes.

Nest: In reeds, near water; a slight mat of marsh-grass, etc.

Eggs: Distinguishable from other species by the distinct drab ground-colouring.

Range: Temperate North America, but most common east of the Plains. South, in winter, to the West Indies and northern South America.

The common Rail of gunners, a little larger than the moulted Bobolink or Reedbird, with which it is closely associated in the southern marshes, sharing with it the name of Ortolan.

The flesh of this Rail is tender and sweet, but rather tasteless, unless an artificial flavour is imparted to it in the cooking. Its value as an article of food, as in the case of many Reedbirds, depends upon the curiously enthusiastic taste of gourmands, and, as with the Bobolink, it seems a waste of powder, as well as of exuberant life, to kill them, the edible result being a pitiful mouthful of gritty, shot-filled flesh, stabbed through by a skewer, and merely serving to lengthen some weary dinner where a collection of animal and vegetable bric-à-brac takes the place of satisfactory nourishment.

Florida Gallinule: *Gallinula galeata.*

Blue Rail; Red-billed Mud Hen.

Length: 12–14 inches.

Male and Female: Head and neck bluish gray, back olive-brown, wings and tail dark. Beneath dark gray, grading to white on belly. *Bill and frontal plate red.*

Season: Summer resident of the Housatonic River. Twelve eggs taken at Stratford June 25, 1891, by Mr. W. H. Lucas.

Breeds: Through its range, but only casually in the northern part.

Nest: A platform of broken and matted reeds, built up to form a hollow nest, seeming oftentimes to rest on the water, as it is moored to shifting reeds.

Eggs: Numerous; often 14.
Range: Temperate and tropical America, from Canada to Brazil and Chili.

This Gallinule, which inhabits both salt and fresh marshes, is called Blue Rail by sportsmen because, at a little distance, the various tints of its plumage merge in a grayish blue. A feature of the family of Gallinules (which is a sub-family under Rails) is the bare horny shield upon the forehead and the very large, *unwebbed* feet.

American Coot: *Fulica americana.*

White-billed Mud Hen; Crow Duck.

Length: 14–16 inches.
Male and Female: Dark slate above, head and neck almost black. Whole edge of wing and tips of some quills white. Below paler gray, tail dark brown. Bill flesh-white with a slight rusty black mark at the tip. Feet pale dull green.
Season: Abundant spring migrant.
Breeds: Locally all through range, in marshy spots near sluggish creeks and rivers.
Nest: Like that of the last species.
Eggs: A dozen or more, shaped like Hen's eggs, ground gray with dark brown spots from the size of a pinhead to the size of a pea.
Range: North America, from Greenland and Alaska southward to the West Indies and Central America.

A bird of like appearance to the Florida Gallinule, having a similar but smaller frontal plate. The feet, however, are constructed for swimming, all the toes being supplied with flaps.

Its nesting-habits are very interesting, being akin to those of the Grebes, and Dr. Coues writes graphically of them in his "Birds of the Northwest."

ORDER HERODIONES: HERONS, ETC.

FAMILY ARDEIDÆ: HERONS, BITTERNS, ETC.

American Bittern: ***Botaurus lentiginosus.***

Stake Driver.

PLATE 68.

Length: Exceedingly variable, from 23–34 inches. (Coues.)

Male and Female: Above yellowish brown, much streaked and mottled with different shades of brown, from dark to light. Below buffy white, the feathers striped and edged with brown. Tail brown, small, and rounded. Bill yellow, edged with black; legs yellow-green.

Note: Several harsh sounds and a note resembling the blow of a mallet in driving a stake, hence its name Stake Driver.

Season: Summer resident; May to November. Not common.

Breeds: Through range north of Virginia. In pairs, not in colonies.

Nest: A rude affair on the ground.

Eggs: 3–5, grayish brown.

Range: Temperate North America, south to Guatemala and the West Indies.

This is the solitary Heron, of whom Hamilton Gibson says, "many have heard the Stake Driver, but who shall locate the stake?" It inhabits the loneliest bogs and marshes and is the Booming Bittern to which Thoreau so often refers.

Except in the breeding-season, it is an entirely solitary bird, and utterly averse to companionship. One of its habits, when disturbed in its reedy hiding places, is to stand motionless with its bill pointing skyward, thus merging completely with the surrounding marsh growth.

The American Bittern is not a nocturnal feeder, though his retiring habits lead people to think so; he probably migrates by night, but that is all. He seems to be a rather sluggish, selfish character, mysterious to us; simply because we cannot fathom his plan of existence. He eats and drinks,

PLATE 68.

AMERICAN BITTERN.

Length variable, 23–34 inches.

but is never merry, and maintains a stoical silence even, in the midst of a bog of plenty; a table fairly overladen with the frogs, lizards, snakes, etc., that his appetite craves. His long legs, which trail awkwardly behind him in flight, are said to act as a rudder to direct his course.

Least Bittern: *Ardetta exilis.*

Length: 11–14 inches.

Male: Top of head, which is slightly crested, and back rich, greenish black. Back of neck chestnut brown, also wing coverts and the edges of some quills. Tail like back. Below muddy yellow, with dark brown patches on sides of breast, and some white around the throat. Bill, eyes, and toes yellow.

Female: Purplish chestnut above.

Season: Summer resident, breeding near Stratford on the Housatonic.

Breeds: Through range in marshes in company with the Rails.

Nest: On a mat of old rushes a foot or two above ground.

Eggs: Usually 4, of a livid hue.

Range: Temperate North America, from the British Provinces to the West Indies and northern South America.

The Least Bittern, the smallest of its family, has a curiously hybrid appearance, and is not easy to place; it is shy and always hiding in the reeds, and even when you catch a glimpse of it, the resemblance to a Rail is confusing. You may startle them when looking for Marsh Wrens' nests, and, as they shoot up from the reeds for a moment, before settling again, you will have your best chance of identifying them. After being once disturbed, and seeing the cause, they remain wisely in seclusion, and no amount of poking and thrashing will drive them out.

As with the majority of Shore and Water Birds, it is almost impossible to go afoot to their breeding-haunts. A canvas duck boat, easily carried, hip boots, and a water and mosquito proof disposition are necessary for anything more than the most casual study of these birds in their haunts.

Great Blue Heron: ***Ardea herodias.***

Blue Crane.

PLATE 69.

Length: 42–50 inches.

Male and Female: Long, black crest, the two longest feathers of which are shed in the summer moult. Upper parts and tail bluish slate, below black and white streaked, forehead and crown white. Feathers about neck long and loose. Bill yellow and dusky; legs and feet dark. This Heron can be recognized by its great size and *bluish slate* back; it is not distinctly *blue* at all.

Season: Common, nearly resident, may breed. (Averill.)

Breeds: Locally through range.

Nest: Usually a rude pile of sticks in a tree.

Eggs: 3, large, and of a dull bluish green.

Range: North America from the Arctic regions, southward to the West Indies and northern South America.

Without question the Great Blue Heron,[1] locally called the Blue Crane, is one of the most picturesque birds that we have in New England, and only divides the honours with the Bald Eagle and the Great Horned and Snow Owls. In many places they appear in small flocks, but I have never seen them here except as individuals or occasionally in pairs. They are wild, suspicious birds, and yet, if they think themselves unobserved, they will stand almost motionless by the side of a small stream or pond half a day at a time, only bending the long neck at intervals to seize some frog or other edible. You may stand by a smooth mill-pond walled by trees that hang into the water. Through many gaps the distant meadows stretch, almost as smooth as the pond, but of a different hue; it is a lovely, placid scene, but needs a bit of life to draw it to a focus. Look a second time; upon the muddy edge of one of the little islands, in bold relief, sphinx-like, stands a solitary Blue Heron, and you at once understand why Egypt gave reverence to the Ibis. Deliberately it spreads its wings that winnow six feet of air, and flies slowly across the water, its legs hanging like twin reeds with clawing roots.

[1] The White Heron or Egret, "The Bonnet Martyr," is cousin of this bird.

GREAT BLUE HERON. Length, 42–50 inches.

Green Heron: ***Ardea virescens.***

Poke.

Length: 16–18 inches.

Male and Female: Head with lengthened crest. Above dark glossy green, sometimes with an iridescence. Edging of wing coverts reddish. Neck a rich shade of chestnut, with a purplish wash, white streak at the throat, and under parts whitish, shading to ash below. Legs and bill yellowish.

Season: Common summer resident.

Breeds: Through its North American range.

Nest: Of sticks in a tree, seldom high up.

Eggs: 3–6, pale green.

Range: Canada and Oregon, southward to northern South America and the West Indies; rare in the arid interior.

That this Heron is the commonest and best known of its family, is attested by the numerous local names it bears. "Fly-up-the-creek," "Chalk-line," and "Chuckle-head" being a few of the list to which every small boy feels it his duty to add one, usually of a very uncomplimentary nature.

When seen in the breeding-season, at short range, the plumage of these Herons is very lustrous and beautiful, but when on the wing the iridescence of the feathers is invisible and the receding head, accentuated by the long crest, and the poking bill give the birds an idiotic expression.

In many places they breed in communities called Heronries; but here usually in single pairs, in the wooded strip that runs from the marsh lane to the eastward of Wakeman's Island. The Green Heron is a great believer in ventilation, and its nest always reminds me of the boy's definition of a sieve, which he said was "a sort of round thing made mostly of holes." The sticks of the nest are so few and far between that one would imagine the current of air passing between would prevent the eggs from hatching. I saw a nest last spring that had listed so that one of the eggs lay broken on the ground, and there is a very good story told about a nest that was such a shaky concern that every time the old birds jarred it a stick fell off, and the structure grew smaller and smaller, until the day when the young were ready to fly there were but three sticks left; finally these parted and the little Herons found themselves perching on the branch that once held the nest!

This species feeds upon frogs, small fish, insects, the larvæ of the dragon-fly, etc. They are not strictly nocturnal, but feed largely at dawn and dusk.

Black-crowned Night Heron: *Nycticorax nycticorax nævius.*

Qua Bird; Quawk.

PLATE 70.

Length: 23–26 inches.

Male and Female: Above either dull or greenish black; tail, wings, and neck grayish. Throat and forehead whitish. Below livid white. Crest of three long, white feathers rolled into one. Bill black; legs yellow.

Season: Common summer resident; April to October.

Breeds: Southward from New Brunswick.

Nest: Nest not large, built in a very slovenly manner in treetops, usually in communities.

Eggs: 3–4, pale sea-green.

Range: America, from the British Provinces southward to the Falkland Islands, including part of the West Indies.

Another common Heron, only second to the Green, in abundance. Here it frequents inland ponds in preference to the salt-marshes, and, though I have not found its nests, I have seen the birds all the way from Mill River to Redding under circumstances that point to their breeding in single pairs.

They are nocturnal, as the name indicates, and when you come upon them in their roosts by daylight they are dazed and sleepy, and use an effort to pull themselves together, but at twilight their heavy, dark bodies may be seen flying overhead, identified beyond question by the cry, "quok-quok," uttered at regular intervals. The sound is much like that emitted by the kid bellows of a child's toy rooster, and is the gazoo of the night orchestra. The skirl and boom of the Nighthawk have an eery sound, and the Whip-

PLATE 70.

BLACK-CROWNED NIGHT HERON.

Length, 23–26 inches.

poor-will's cry is filled with vague foreboding; the Night Heron's merely suggests that he has half swallowed a particularly unappetizing frog, and wishes to unswallow it.

This is the most gregarious of all the Herons. Dr. Wood tells of a swamp some miles from East Windsor, Conn., which was the breeding-place of thousands. Samuels knew of a Heronry near Dedham, Mass., where a hundred pairs were collected in the space of an acre, and he at once realized the force of Wilson's comment on a like congregation, that, "The noise of the old and the young would almost induce one to suppose that two or three hundred Indians were throttling each other."

As the birds resort, year after year, to the same crowded breeding-grounds, it can be easily imagined that these Heronries are not the most attractive places for ornithological research.

I had very much doubted the present existence of such extensive colonies in populous regions, but Mr. Chapman in his "Guide to the Birds found near New York," which has been mentioned before, says, "There is a colony containing about one thousand pairs not far from New York City."

ORDER ANSERES: LAMELLIROSTRAL SWIMMERS.[1]

FAMILY ANATIDÆ: DUCKS, GEESE, ETC.

SUB-FAMILY MERGINÆ: MERGANSERS.

American Merganser: ***Merganser americanus.***

Fish Duck.

Length: 23.50–27 inches.

Male: Bill toothed, chiefly red. Head slightly crested, and with upper neck very dark glossy green; upper half of back black. Below, breast and part of the neck white, belly salmon. Wings largely white, banded with black.

[1] Term derived from the plan of bill, which is *lamellate*, signifying that the mandibles are furnished with a series of *laminar* or saw-toothed projections fitting into each other.

Female: Smaller. Above brown and ash-gray, slightly crested.
Season: "Common winter resident from November to April." (Averill.)
Breeds: North of the United States.
Range: North America generally.

"In buying a Duck notice the bill, that it be not cylindrical, hooked, or saw-toothed." This is good advice, for the mission of the Wild Duck, as far as society in general is concerned, seems to be the epicure's table, where it appears in various stages of rawness, according to the name under which it has been sold. There are many Ducks that are totally unfit for food, and the Merganser is one of these, being a "Fishing Duck," and able to follow its prey under water. It is a gluttonous bird, gorging itself with such quantities of fish, frogs, etc., as to render its flesh exceedingly rank. It is beautifully feathered, however, and frequently figures in dining-rooms on the ornamental panels of stuffed Game-birds.

Another species associating with this is the Red-breasted Merganser, which hardly differs from it save in the redness of the upper breast and in having a long, pointed crest. Both species inhabit the vicinity of fresh and salt water alike.

SUB-FAMILY ANATINÆ: RIVER DUCKS.[1]

Mallard: *Anas boschas.*

PLATE 71.

Length: 24 inches.
Male: Bill greenish yellow; head and upper part of neck brilliant, glossy green, a white colar dividing it from the chestnut-brown of the lower neck. Under parts and sides pale gray, waved with darker. Back reddish brown at top, growing dull near tail. Tail coverts black; tail mostly white; wings gray, white, and black. *Speculum*[2] shaded purple, bordered with black. Feet orange-red.

[1] Ducks feeding largely upon juicy vegetable matter, and not diving for their food. Feet smaller than those of the Sea Ducks, and more suited for walking.

[2] The secondary quills of the wings of Ducks usually exhibit patches of varied or iridescent colour; this coloured patch is called the *speculum*.

PLATE 71.

MALLARD.

Length, 24 inches.

Female: Dull; under parts yellowish, blotched faintly with dusky; above back, brown; some feathers with rusty edges. Head and neck mottled like under parts.

Season: A wandering visitor, taken occasionally in the autumn on the Housatonic at Stratford.

Breeds: Northward from the Northern States, more frequently in the interior.

Nest: Of dry grass, weeds, and feathers, on the ground near the water.

Eggs: 8–10, yellow, gray.

Range: Northern part of Northern Hemisphere. In America south in winter to Panama and Cuba.

A very handsome and notable game Duck, living chiefly on vegetable diet, and having delicate flesh; plentiful around the Great Lakes.

Black Duck: *Anas obscura.*

Length: 22 inches.

Male and Female: Bill greenish yellow. Above dusky, but not black; feathers edged with rusty brown. Neck, throat, and sides of head streaked with grayish and dark. Below brownish. *Speculum* violet and black; in the male tipped with white. Legs red.

Season: A resident, but more plentiful in the migrations.

Breeds: From New Jersey to Labrador.

Nest: A mat of marsh grasses on the ground.

Eggs: 8–10, a drab yellow.

Range: Eastern North America, west to Utah and Texas, north to Labrador.

This Black Duck (which is not black) is a great favourite among sportsmen, on account of its delicately flavoured flesh. It is plentiful about the larger ponds all through the autumn, and I have seen it on the mill-pond in December when there was thin ice on the margin.

The late Dr. Charles Slover Allen gives a delightful account of its breeding-habits on Plum Island, in *The Auk* of January, 1893, from which the following is a paragraph: —

"Early in the morning, May 27 (1888), I saw a Rail dodge into a little clump from the water's edge, and in trying to find it I stepped into the Duck's nest, flushing the bird and partly breaking one of the eleven eggs it contained. They were uncovered, though embedded in down, and several were already pipped. The old bird soon came back to the marsh and suddenly appeared in the clear water from behind some bushes and tried to entice me away. After cutting away some of the branches concealing the nest, I started back along the causeway so as to bring my camera from the lighthouse. I had gone but a hundred yards or so when another Black Duck appeared swimming in a clear patch of water far out in the centre of the marsh. It vanished behind a grassy ridge and then took wing. Although I had no boots I waded out and examined a tuft of bushes and grass far back in the direction from which the Duck was swimming. This bird had undoubtedly been startled by the outcries of the first, and had quietly left her nest, only showing herself when at a distance. In this nest, fairly covered with down, were four young already hatched and not dry as yet, and six eggs rapidly hatching in the hot sun. When I returned to this nest with the camera an hour later, every egg had hatched and nothing but the empty shells remained. I could find nowhere the slightest trace of the birds, young or old."

Green-winged Teal: *Anas carolinensis.*

PLATE 72.

Length: 14 inches.

Male and Female: Slightly crested. Head and neck rich chestnut, with a band of green on either side behind the eyes. Above waved bars of black and white. Wings dull gray. *Speculum* half purplish black and half a rich green, other wing feathers having chestnut, white, and purplish markings. Below whitish, turning to pale brown on the breast, clouded with distinct black spots; throat and sides waved black and white, like the back. Bill black; feet grayish. Female with less green on the wings and no crest; mottled brownish above.

Season: Common fall migrant about the Housatonic at Stratford; September and October.

Breeds: Chiefly north of the United States.

Range: North America; migrates south to Honduras and Cuba.

The Teal Ducks are two very small species, with beautiful plumage and sweet, delicate flesh, which latter quality is accounted for by the fact that their food is mainly vegetable, — the seeds of numerous grasses, sedges, and other aquatics, small fruits and berries. They also eat grasshoppers and many other insects, and tadpoles as well. They are preferably fresh-water Ducks.

PLATE 72.

GREEN-WINGED TEAL.

Length, 14 inches.

Samuels has seen the Green-winged Teal associate with the Ducks in a farmer's yard or pond, and has known them to come into the barnyard with tame fowls and share the corn thrown out for their food. Every fall I have seen them flying over the garden by twos and threes, evidently making their way from the interior toward the coast, which they follow very closely in their migration. Oftentimes they fly so low that the peculiar reedy whistling of their wings can be plainly heard.

Blue-winged Teal: *Anas discors.*

PLATE 73.

Length: 15–16 inches.

Male and Female: Bill blackish. Head and neck purplish lead-colour, black crown, small white crescent before each eye. Back variegated dark brown and yellowish brown, and rump dark greenish brown. Wing coverts dull sky blue. *Speculum* beautiful green, between white bars. Below violet-gray, spotted with black on the breast and barred on the flanks. Feet light-coloured. Female much the same, the head being dusky, but retaining the bright wing markings. Other markings less distinct.

Season: Common in the fall migration with last species.

Breeds: From the northern United States northward.

Range: North America in general, but chiefly east of the Rocky Mountains; north to Alaska and south to the West Indies and northern South America.

Resembling the last species in general habits, but in this vicinity it is neither as tame nor as plentiful. Though it prefers fresh ponds, it is more frequently found about salt creeks than the Green-winged. It has been known to breed in New England, and Giraud notes it as breeding on Long Island also.

Pintail: *Dafila acuta.*

Sprig-tail.

PLATE 79. FIG. 1.

Length: Variable; sometimes 30 inches, according to the development of the tail.

Male: Bill bluish black. Head and half of neck greenish brown; black and white stripe on either side of neck. Back and sides waved with soft gray and black. Wings generally gray ; *speculum* purplish green between white, a bar in front, and a black and white bar behind. Tail long, black and gray. Below whitish, with black wavings on the sides. Feet lead-blue.

Female: Wing markings faint, only a trace of the *speculum;* tail shorter; generally mottled above with black and yellowish brown; below pale ochre-brown.

Season: Migrant; not rare at Stratford, Conn.

Breeds: Northward from the northern United States.

Nest: Of litter on the ground.

Eggs: 6–12, greenish clay colour.

Range: Northern Hemisphere ; migrates south to Panama and Cuba.

Very graceful Ducks of trim build and beautifully mottled feathers, long body and well-poised head. Their flesh is excellent, and they are much sought after by the sportsmen who go southward for the late fall shooting.

According to Wilson, it is a bird of mud flats and shallow, fresh-water marshes; and, unlike other Ducks, which when alarmed scatter in different directions, the Sprig-tails mount, clustering confusedly together, and thus give the sportsmen a good opportunity of raking them.

Wood Duck: *Aix sponsa.*

Summer Duck.

PLATE 3. PAGE 21.

Length: 18–20 inches.

Male: A sweeping crest of golden green like the head, sides of head with much purple iridescence. White stripe from reddish bill to the eye, and from behind eye to throat. Front of neck and upper breast ruddy, with white specks, other lower parts white; a black and white crescent before the wings, sides more or less waved with black, white, and yellowish. Above brilliant iridescent hues, — purple, bronze, green, etc.; *speculum* green. Feathers on flanks lengthened, and variegated black and white. Legs and feet yellowish.

Female: Crest slight or wanting. Gray head and neck, below mottled gray, brown, and white, above glossy brown. Wings like the male, but the contrasts much reduced.

Note: "Peet-peet, oe eek! oe eek!"

Season: A summer resident.

PLATE 73.

BLUE-WINGED TEAL.

Length, 16 inches.

Breeds: Through its range.
Nest: Usually a feather-lined hollow in a partly decayed tree, near water and often at a considerable distance from the ground.
Eggs: A dozen or more, varying according to the age of the bird, either greenish, clay-coloured, or pale buff, and smooth.
Range: North America, wintering in the Southern States.

This is the most beautiful of the native Ducks, taking its specific name, *sponsa*, betrothed, from the richness of its plumage, which gives it a bridal or festive appearance. It is a fresh-water Duck, and exclusively so in the selection of its breeding-haunts.

It arrives from the first to the middle of April, and locates either in deep woods near water, or in narrow wooded belts that follow the course of small rivers. Sometimes a hole in a horizontal limb is chosen for the nest that seems far too small to hold the duck's plump body; occasionally it utilizes the hole of an Owl or Woodpecker, the entrance to which has been enlarged by decay. Many stories are told of their attachment to their breeding-places, but an incident which happened a dozen miles from here illustrates it as well as any. For several years a pair of Wood Ducks had made their nest in the hollow of a hickory which stood on the bank, half a dozen yards from Mill River. In preparing to dam the river near this point in order to supply water to a neighbouring city, the course of the river was diverted, leaving the old bed an eighth of a mile behind. The water might move if it chose, but not the Ducks, who continued to breed in the old place.

The young are frequently carried in the bill of their parents from the nest to the water's edge,—if the nest is not directly over the water, where the little birds, who leave the nest as soon as hatched, can easily drop to it, breaking their fall by extending their wings.

Audubon says that when the nest is forty yards or more from water, the young are led in the right direction by their parents. This must have been the way that the Ducks I mentioned regained the diverted stream; for the height and density of the trees between it and the nest would have made it impossible for the parent to fly with a duckling in her beak.

The drake does not assist in the labours of incubation and the female is left in the lurch in the same manner as the Partridge.

Sub-family Fuliguline: Sea Ducks.[1]

Redhead: *Aythya americana.*

American Pochard.

Plate 74.

Length: 20–23 inches.

Male: Not crested, head and neck a warm chestnut; bill dull bluish with black terminal band. Above ash waved with black lines, giving a silvery hue. Below white, waved with black; lower neck, fore parts of body and lower tail coverts blackish. Tail grayish brown. Wings gray with white specks; *speculum* whitish ash, bordered with black.

Female: "Wholly brown forehead and cheeks tinged with red."

Season: A migrant; rare at Stratford according to Mr. Averill, but I have seen it several times on the Fairfield marsh-meadows.

Breeds: Northward from California and Maine.

Range: North America.

The common Wild Duck of our markets which often, when deprived of its identifying feathers, goes masquerading as the Canvasback, with whom it associates.

Canvasback: *Aythya vallisneria.*

Length: 20–22 inches.

Male: Bill blackish, 2½ inches long, or not shorter than the head. Above waved black and white, head tinged with black in front, and a rich glossy chestnut neck and back to head. A brownish black collar across upper breast, below whitish; sides dusky. Tail slatish, feathers pointed. *Speculum* white.

Season: Rare fall and winter migrant.

[1] Feet fully webbed, large flap on hind toe, rapid swimmers, but awkward on land. Feed largely upon animal food, and their flesh, with a few notable exceptions, is rather coarse if not as rank as the fish-eating species.

REDHEAD.

Length, 20–33 inches.

Breeds: From the Northern States northward to Alaska.
Range: Nearly all of North America, wintering from the Chesapeake southward.

The favourite Duck of dinner parties and suppers, where it divides the honours with diamond-backed terrapin. The particular flavour of its flesh, when at certain seasons it feeds on *vallisneria*, or wild celery (which is not celery at all, but an eel-grass) won its fame. But as this eel-grass is a local plant, not growing all through the range of the Canvas-back, and as when the celery is lacking it eats frogs, lizards, tadpoles, fish, etc., a certificate of residence should be sold with every pair to insure the inspiring flavour.

The biography of this Duck belongs rather to the cook-book than a bird list, and in fact even its most learned biographers refer mainly to its eatable qualities, and Dr. Coues even takes away its character from that standpoint, saying, "There is little reason for squealing in barbaric joy over this over-rated and generally underdone bird; not one person in ten thousand can tell it from any other duck on the table, and only then under the celery circumstances."

American Scaup Duck: *Aythya marila nearctica.*

Broad-bill.

Length: 20 inches.
Male: Heavy, broad, bluish bill. No crest. Above, upper back glossy black with washes of green and purple. Below white, with black wavings near the vent. Lower part of back waved with black and white; *speculum* white. Bluish feet; claws black.
Female: Head and fore parts rusty brown, upper parts rusty black, with some white wavings. Below white, and a conspicuous white patch on forehead.
Season: A migrant; common in March and April, October and November, sometimes wintering.
Breeds: Inland, north from Manitoba.
Range: North America in general.

An abundant Duck, visiting the bays in great flocks, being especially abundant about the Chesapeake. As it does not eat fish, and subsists to some extent upon seeds and tender aquatic plants, its flesh is edible, and is prized next to that of the Canvas-back Duck.

American Golden-eye: *Glaucionetta clangula americana.*

Whistler.

Length: 17–20 inches.

Male: Head with puffy feathers, and neck glossy green. Above blackish; below generally whitish. Much white on the wings. *Iris golden yellow*, a round, white spot before the eye. Feet orange-coloured; bill black, tipped with yellow.

Female: Head snuff-brown, upper parts brownish, lower parts marked with grayish; less white on wings.

Season: Common winter resident.

Breeds: From Maine northward.

Range: North America, in winter south to Cuba.

The American Golden-eye and the three following species are Sea Ducks whose rank and fishy-smelling flesh excludes them from the list of Game Ducks. They are seen about the creeks and beaches at a time when there is little bird life present, and are interesting on this account. The Whistler is a title the Golden-eye receives, from the loud noise made by its wings during flight, which is accomplished with wonderful velocity.

Bufflehead: *Charitonetta albeola.*

Length: 12.75–15 inches.

Male: Above black, neck, shoulders, and all below white. Head puffy, purplish green, with a large white patch on the nape extending to front of eyes. Wings largely white; tail black. Bill short, about 1 inch.

Female: Above blackish with white streak on each side of head, below whitish.

Season: Winter resident; November to April.

Breeds: From Maine northward through the Fur Countries to Alaska.

Range: North America, south in winter to Cuba and Mexico.

A handsomely plumed Duck with a puffy head; to be found by inland ponds and rivers that remain unfrozen, as

PLATE 75

OLD SQUAW.

well as on the coast. It is a cunning diver, and obtains its food in this way: it is said, that the Bufflehead, like the Grebes and Loons, will dive at the flash of a gun, and remain under water with its bill alone visible.

Samuels writes that, "When several of these birds are together, one always remains on the surface, while the others are below in search of food, and, if alarmed, it utters a short *quack*, when the others rise to the surface, and on ascertaining the cause of the alarm, all dive and swim off rapidly to the distance of several hundred feet."

Old Squaw: *Clangula hyemalis.*

The Old Wife.

PLATE 75.

Length: Depending on the tail development, up to 23 inches.

Male: *In winter*, head and neck white, with gray cheeks; above varied with black and white. Breast blackish; belly white. Four middle tail feathers blackish and very long. Wings grayish; no *speculum*. Bill black, tipped with orange; feet dark.

Female: Dusky brown, paler on throat, whitish below. White patch around eye and on side of neck.

Season: Common winter resident.

Breeds: Far north.

Range: Northern Hemisphere; in North America south to the Potomac and the Ohio.

A clamouring, noisy Duck, but also having a sonorous musical voice. It has the same habit of diving as the Bufflehead, and is even less particular about its food than the last two species. It locates usually on the reedy creek bars and inlets from Long Island Sound. Dr. Coues says it frequents large inland waters; and Professor Koch, that it is a visitor on the Susquehanna River in April.

American Scoter: *Oidemia americana.*

Booby; Sea Coot.

Length: 17-20 inches.

Male: Entire plumage blackish, the back and neck being more or less glossy. Bill tumid or bulging at base, and parti-coloured.

Female: Dingy brown, some white on the sides of head, below dirty white. Dark feet; bill not swollen.
Season: Fall migrant, staying well into winter.
Breeds: From Labrador northward.
Range: Coasts and larger lakes of northern North America; south, in winter, to New Jersey, the Great Lakes, and California.

This Coot has no beauty of plumage either in male or female, is wonderfully tough and inedible, and is often sold by unscrupulous gunners to ignorant housewives as Black Duck. I know of a young housekeeper who bought a pair under these circumstances. The difficulties began when the Coots were plucked, every feather offering separate resistance. The legs and wings seemed held firm by brass rivets, and were immovable, and the cook made sceptical remarks, which, however, passed unheeded. But when the "*Black Ducks*" appeared nicely browned on the table, the illusion was broken; it was impossible to carve them; even the breast yielded only a creaking chip. The next day the dog tried one of them, and used it as a plaything for some time, shaking it, and occasionally giving it a hopeless gnaw. Then it was removed with the swill, being still intact, and the man cut it in half with an axe, to see if it could be done.

All this unscientific research goes to prove that the American Coot is a strongly built and most muscular bird, and that his use in the world is best known to himself, but that as a table delicacy he is a failure, and that in one household the mention of his name is prohibited.

Sub-family Anserinæ: Geese.

Canada Goose: *Branta canadensis.*

Wild Goose.

Plate 76.

Length: 3 feet or more.
Male and Female: Dark ash; head, neck, and tail black; cheeks and throat white; bill and feet black. Short, rounded tail of pointed feathers. Wings dark brownish, with paler edges. Below a dirty white. Bill and feet black. Female paler.

PLATE 76.

CANADA GOOSE.

Length, 3 feet or more.

Season: Familiar winter resident, but most common in the fall migration, when numbers remain until very cold weather, and return all through the early spring.

Breeds: Chiefly northward, but sometimes in the northern United States.

Range: Temperate North America, south in winter to Mexico.

This Wild Goose, even when only seen casually, is easily identified by its great size, being almost twice as large as the Brant, the only other common species. Its distinctive mark, other than size, is a broad, white band that extends like a handkerchief folded cornerwise under its chin and tied on the top of its head.

The flight of the Goose is heavy, but very impressive. Geese usually form in two columns, meeting in front on either side of the experienced leader, forming a wedge. In the late autumn of 1892, I saw this flock-formation take place near Weston Mill Pond shortly before dark. The Geese arose in a straggling column from some cat-tail flags, in what, to me, seemed the greatest state of confusion, but before they had gone a hundred feet the line had divided into the wedge shape, though it was rather irregular. The *honking* call seemed to come from several individuals, and not from the leader alone.

Upon other occasions I have seen small flocks fly over the meadows in almost a straight line. The honking of Geese is a strange, unbird-like sound, and when they pass over at night and you hear the fanning of their wings it seems as if some sleeping cloud-goblin had awaked himself with a sudden snore. As these Geese feed mainly upon vegetable food their flesh is good, and they are perpetually harried by gunners.

Brant: *Branta bernicla.*

Length: About 24 inches.

Male and Female: Head, neck, shoulders, and upper breast dark ash, white patch on each side of the neck. Back with a brownish cast, much white in the tail. Under parts brownish gray with some white. Bill and feet black. Female smaller.

Season: A common coastwise migrant, and in mild seasons a winter resident along Long Island Sound.

Breeds: In Arctic regions.

Range: Northern parts of the Northern Hemisphere. In North America chiefly on the Atlantic coast; rare in the interior or away from salt water.

This small Goose, hardly larger than the Red-headed Duck, is the common species of the Atlantic coast. It is not so well known among amateurs as the Canada Goose, but this may be accounted for by its sometimes being mistaken for a Duck. Its distinguishing mark is the small, *white patch on either side of the top of its glossy, dark neck.* The food of the Brant is like that of the Canada Goose, but anything older than a bird of the year makes a very muscular article of food, only to be enjoyed by a jaw that has grown strong by much arguing, like that of Old Father William, according to the version of the ballad given in "Alice's Adventures in Wonderland."

ORDER TUBINARES: TUBE-NOSED SWIMMERS.

FAMILY PROCELLARIIDÆ: FULMARS AND SHEARWATERS.

Wilson's Petrel: *Oceanites oceanicus.*

Stormy Petrel.

Length: 8 inches.

Male and Female: Bill black. Above sooty brown, blackening on wings and tail; upper tail coverts white. Long black legs, the foot-webbing spotted with yellow.

Season: A summer resident; from May to late September.

Breeds: In the South Sea Islands, in January and February, according to Mr. F. M. Chapman.

Range: Cosmopolitan.

The commonest Petrel of the Atlantic coast, from Delaware Bay northward; it is the most plentiful of the three "Mother Carey's Chickens." The Petrels seldom visit the mainland in this locality, but are often seen about lighthouses. They seem like the very spirits of wind and waves, dropping and whirling, resting a moment in the trough of the sea, and then off again, tirelessly following in the wake of vessels. Mr. Judson, the keeper of the Stratford light, kept one of these Petrels, which he caught, in captivity for some time.

Another species, Leach's or the White-rumped Petrel, is common off the New England coast, where it is resident on some of the islands, off the coast of Maine. It lays a single egg in a ground burrow. This species is of the same size and general appearance as Wilson's, but has much longer legs.

ORDER LONGIPENNES: LONG-WINGED SWIMMERS.

FAMILY LARIDÆ: GULLS AND TERNS.

Kittiwake Gull: *Rissa tridactyla.*

Length: 16–18 inches.

Male and Female: Bluish gray above (darker in winter), head and neck gray, and bill light yellow. Under parts pure white. Black feet, black tips to tail quills.

Season: Winter and late fall visitor in the Middle States. In New England common off the coast all winter.

Breeds: Gulf of St. Lawrence, Labrador coast, and casually off the Maine coast.

Nest: By choice on rocky ledges over the water.

Range: Arctic regions, south in eastern North America, in winter, to the Great Lakes and the Middle States.

The Kittiwake may be regarded as a winter migrant or visitor along the shore, where it comes in small numbers early in December, associating with the Herring Gulls, but it is plentiful from Massachusetts and Rhode Island northward.

American Herring Gull: *Larus argentatus smithsonianus.*

Winter Gull.

PLATE 77. FIG. 1.

Length: 24–25 inches.

Male and Female: Winter dress: above pure light gray, head and neck streaked with dusky, under parts and tail white, the latter having an imperfect dusky bar; wing coverts mottled with gray. Bill yellow.

Season: Common winter resident, coming in late August and remaining until March.

Breeds: From the Great Lakes and Maine northward.

Nest: Hollow in the ground lined with a little grass or a few seaweeds.

Eggs: 2–3, ground colour dirty white, tinted with pale blue or green deepening to brown, with numerous brown and black spots and markings.

Range: North America generally, in winter south to Cuba and lower California.

The common Gull, both of coast and interior, seen in great flocks about the beaches, and on the flats and sand bars at low water. From middle autumn until the birds in general are returning in the spring, these Gulls enliven the solitude of the shore with their chatter, and their shrill, high-keyed voices can be heard above the waves and storm.

Beside being beautifully plumed and decidedly picturesque objects in the marine picture, they have an economic value which appeals even to the most unsentimental minds. They are excellent scavengers, taking from creeks, bays, and rivers, as well as from the lakes and open sea, much refuse that becomes unsavoury if washed ashore and left to decompose.

Laughing Gull: *Larus atricilla.*

Length: 16.50 inches.

Male and Female: Head and neck dark slate; bill carmine. Back slate-colour, divided from the head by the white of the neck. All under parts white; also tail coverts. Legs and feet dull reddish. Young, upper parts gray tinted with various browns,

PLATE 77.

2

1

1. AMERICAN HERRING GULL. Length, 24–25 inches.

2. COMMON TERN. Length, 14.50 inches.

mingled with the slate-colour of the adults on the wings, and clouded with gray on the breast.

Season: A summer visitor; once a common summer resident on Long Island, but now rare.

Breeds: Off the Atlantic coast, from Maine to Florida.

Nest: Of dried sea grasses and beach-grass stubbs.

Eggs: 2–3, shaded olive, spotted and splashed irregularly with dull reddish purple, and black-brown.

Range: Eastern tropical and warm temperate America, chiefly along the sea-coast, from Maine to Brazil; Pacific coast of middle America.

This Gull, taking its name from the peculiar quality of its cry, which is like a peal of laughter, belongs more commonly to the coast south of New York than to New England. It breeds, however, on Muskeget, and Mr. George H. Mackay gives an account of its habits in *The Auk* of October, 1893. He says that formerly they were much more plentiful than to-day,—the same sad story of all the soft-hued Water-birds who have been hunted even from their sea-bound homes. But this abuse is somewhat abating,—at least, so all bird-lovers hope,—and there are fewer of our native birds seen in millinery, and the feathers, other than Ostrich-plumes, that are used now are largely dyed and baked chicken feathers, twisted into many contortions, or queer birds with celluloid beaks, ugly enough to make bird-wearing unfashionable. Many tropical birds, however, are still used in making up these grotesque adornments.

Bonaparte's Gull: *Larus philadelphia.*

Length: 14 inches.

Male and Female: Head and upper neck dark lead-colour; bill black; back "gull-blue." Rump and tail white; also under parts. Wings white and gull-blue. In winter the head is white, with dark spots. Legs and feet light red.

Season: Common migrant in spring and fall, and sometimes winters.

Breeds: Mostly north of the United States.

Range: Whole of North America; south, in winter, to Mexico and Central America.

A very handsome little Gull, with a darting, skimming flight, resembling that of the common Tern or Sea Swallow. It passes up the Sound in scattering flocks in early spring (Mr. Averill having noted large flocks April 21, 1888), and is frequently seen in the autumn, while individuals appear at intervals during the summer. It feeds upon insects and large beetles, as well as marine food.

Common Tern: *Sterna hirundo.*

Sea Swallow.

PLATE 77. FIG. 2.

Length: 14.50 inches.

Male and Female: Bill long, coral-red at base, black toward end and tipped with yellow. Upper head and back of neck black. Entire back and wings light gray with a bluish wash. Tail coverts, most of tail, and wing linings white; belly and sides of breast grayish white; other lower parts white. Legs and feet light red.

Season: Summer resident, breeding about the eastern part of Long Island Sound.

Breeds: From the Arctic coast, somewhat irregularly to Florida and Texas.

Nest: None; eggs laid on the sand and indistinguishable from those of other species.

Range: Greater part of the Northern Hemisphere. In North America chiefly confined to the Eastern Province, and wintering from Texas and Florida to southward.

The characteristics of this Tern are the black cap, coral-red bill, legs, and feet.

The Terns are not distinctly different from the Gulls, the size of some being identical; but the Terns have a more trig, thoroughbred build, and bear the same relation to the more ponderous Gulls that a yacht does to a trading-craft of equal tonnage. The Terns have long, sharply pointed wings that give them a Swallow-like dash in flying either over the surface of the water when fishing, or above the reed beds when searching for insects, some species being partly insectivorous. This free, angled flight has given this species the name of Sea Swallow.

When flying over the water in fishing, they hold their beaks at right angles with their bodies, instead of poking them forward like the Heron's, which attitude makes them, Dr. Coues says, "curiously like colossal mosquitoes."

Terns were very plentiful twenty years ago, but the persecution for millinery purposes has thinned the ranks pitifully; and the survivors keep more and more aloof, until it seems as if an absolute change in the bird's range will be the result.

Muskeget Island, northeast of Nantucket, is a breeding-place for these Terns, as well as many other Water-birds, and there is a guardian on the island to see that they are protected, especially in the breeding-season. A friend who visited Muskeget last July, told me that everywhere on the sand there were eggs in groups of two and three, and young Terns in various stages of growth, who were so tame that they allowed him to handle them as readily as kittens. The heat of the sun keeps the eggs warm in the daytime, and as soon as they are hatched the young birds go down to the water's edge and feed upon a glutinous substance that is washed up. The adults go in enormous flocks to Nantucket every morning and spend the day in the harbour and little bays, feeding upon the wastage of the island, returning to Muskeget at dusk.

Roseate Tern: *Sterna dougalli.*

Length: 14–15 inches.

Male and Female: Bill black, yellow at tip, and reddish at base. Black cap, and long head feathers; back of neck white, also entire under parts white with a rosy wash. Wings varied, gray, tail pearl-gray. Feet and legs yellowish red.

Season: A rare summer resident.

Breeds: Casually along the Atlantic coast to Maine.

Range: Temperate and tropical regions, north on the Atlantic coast of North America to Massachusetts, and casually to Maine.

A rarely beautiful species, not often seen north of New England, but breeding with the Common Tern at Muskeget, and hardly daring to show its rosy breast to the vandals in unprotected lands. I quote the following, relative to the protection of these birds, from Mr. F. M. Chapman: "Through the efforts of a number of bird-lovers, who raised a sum of money for the purpose, permission has been obtained from the Lighthouse Board to have the light-keeper on Little Gull Island appointed a special game-keeper, whose duty it shall be to protect the Terns on Great Gull Island." A few days later, in reading a copy of *Our Animal Friends* for December, 1894 (the humanizing monthly magazine of the American Society for the Prevention of Cruelty to Animals), I saw the ensuing statement, which supplements Mr. Chapman's very opportunely: —

"We have received a report from Mr. Dutcher,[1] which lies before us and contains much interesting information. Mr. Dutcher says: 'I take pleasure in reporting that, during the season of 1894, protection was given to the colony of Terns on Great Gull Island, New York, during the breeding-season. In 1886 the island was visited, and a colony of from three to four thousand Terns was found there, but it was a common practice for persons to visit the island and shoot the birds, taking the eggs for various purposes, principally, however, for eating. Subsequently it was ascertained that the colony was decreasing year by year, and the necessity of protection became apparent if it was not to be entirely destroyed, as many others have been on the Long Island coast.' In a letter, dated October 4, Captain Field reports the result of one single year's protection to be most satisfactory. The increase of the Tern colony at the close of the season is estimated to have been from one thousand to fifteen hundred birds, or, in other words, the colony has been increased by one-half."

[1] Mr. William Dutcher, through whose efforts mainly the Terns were taken under protection of the A. O. U., the Linnean Society, and the A. S. P. C. A.

Least Tern: ***Sterna antillarum.***

Length: 9 inches.

Male and Female: Legs and bill yellow. Crown black; black wings; tail, and rump gull-blue. A few outer wing feathers black; below white.

Season: A migrant, formerly a summer resident along the Atlantic coast.

Breeds: Casually through its range.

Range: Northern South America northward to California and New England and casually to Labrador.

The smallest of the Terns, living upon fish and insects. It flocks about inland waters as well as on the Atlantic and some parts of the Pacific coast. It is a rather southerly species, but was once a common summer resident along the eastern shore. Its eggs are laid in the sand like those of other species, and differ from them in sometimes having the spots wreathed around the larger end, while the smaller is almost plain.

ORDER PYGOPODES: DIVING BIRDS.

FAMILY ALCIDÆ: AUKS, PUFFINS, MURRES, ETC.

Dovekie: ***Alle alle.***

Sea Dove; Little Auk.

Length: 8–9 inches.

Male and Female: Short, thick, black bill. Above dark brown with some white on wings; below generally whitish.

Season: A winter migrant of varying rarity.

Breeds: In the Arctic regions.

Range: Coasts and islands of the North Atlantic and eastern Arctic oceans; in winter North America south to New Jersey.

An off-shore bird of heavy build and singular appearance, to be seen about lighthouses and barren bits of coast from New Jersey north. It is properly a coastwise bird, but there are accounts of its being driven far inland by storms.

FAMILY URINATORIDÆ: LOONS.

Loon: *Urinator imber.*

Great Northern Diver.

PLATE 78.

Length: 31–36 inches.

Male and Female: Head, throat, and neck iridescent green, blue, and purplish. Triangular patches of black and white streaks on either side of the throat, almost joining at the back and narrowing in front. Above spotted black and white. Breast streaked on sides with black and white; under parts white. Bill dark yellowish green.

Season: Winter resident; most common, however, in the migrations September to May.

Breeds: Northward from the northern tier of States.

Range: Northern part of Northern Hemisphere; ranges, in winter, south to the Gulf of Mexico.

This Loon appears here more as a wandering visitor than a winter resident, for those who remain after the general migration are constantly shifting about. Its plumage is very rich and velvety, though, as in the case of so many Water-birds which we see only in the autumn and winter, the fully plumed adult males are in the minority, and the more dully feathered young predominate.

The Loon dives and swims in the same manner as the Grebes. It only inhabits the interior while the lakes and rivers remain unfrozen.

Red-throated Loon: *Urinator lumme.*

Length: 25 inches.

Male and Female: Blue-gray forehead, chin, upper throat, and sides of head; crown and general upper parts dull black, with a glossy greenish wash and streaked and mottled with white. A triangle of rusty red on the front of neck. White below. Bill black.

Season: Winter resident; fairly common.

Breeds: In high latitudes.

Range: Northern part of Northern Hemisphere; migrating southward in winter, nearly across the United States.

LOON.

Length, 31–36 inches.

Smaller than the Great Diver, having a reddish brown throat patch as a mark of identification, which, however, is lacking in the young of the year. This Red-throated Loon is the species most usually seen here, but it is neither a particularly handsome or conspicuous bird.

FAMILY PODICIPIDÆ: GREBES.

Horned Grebe: ***Colymbus auritus.***

Length: 14 inches.

Male and Female: In spring, prominent crests forming two yellow-brown horns; rest of head puffy and glossy black. Above dark brown, with edgings of gray and black. Neck, upper breast, and sides rusty brown; some white on wings. Young without horns; neck and lower parts whitish. Bill black, with yellow tip.

Season: A winter resident, and a plentiful migrant in spring and fall.

Breeds: North from the northern United States.

Nest and Eggs: The buffy white eggs are deposited on decayed reed-beds, and sometimes on floating masses of reeds.

Range: Northern Hemisphere.

These curiously constructed birds are expert swimmers, but very helpless on land. They have no tails to speak of, and in the breeding-season wear variously feathered head-dresses which give them a ludicrous appearance, and make them veritable caricatures. But if you presume upon this apparent stupidity, and try to approach them, you will be very much surprised at the speed with which they slip from the shore and dive out of sight; not with a splash, but sinking like lead, and escaping by swimming under water, with the head alone visible. When inhabiting the coast the Grebes live upon fish, but when inland they subsist upon fresh-water newts, frogs, insects, and sometimes the seeds of grasses.

Pied-billed Grebe: *Podilymbus podiceps.*

Dipper; Dabchick.

PLATE 79. FIG. 2.

Length: 13 inches.

Male and Female: Some bristling frontal feathers, but no regular horns. Above dark brown, showy black markings on chin and throat. Breast and lower throat yellowish brown, irregularly spotted and barred, on the upper parts, lower parts glossy white. Wings brown, gray, and white. Bill spotted with blue, white, and dusky, and crossed by a black band, hence Pied-billed.

Season: Common migrant, on Housatonic River in September and October.

Breeds: Through range.

Nesting: Habits similar to the last species.

Range: British Provinces, southward to Brazil, Buenos Ayres, and Chili, including the West Indies and the Bermudas.

The most common Grebe on the eastern coast, and, though said to breed through its range, is not noted as a resident hereabout. It frequents fresh water, even more freely than salt, and Dr. Langdon gives an interesting account of its inland breeding-habits in his "Summer Birds in an Ohio Marsh": "The little floating island of decaying vegetation, held together by mud and moss, which constitutes the nest of this species, is a veritable ornithological curiosity. Imagine a 'pancake' of what appears to be mud, measuring twelve or fifteen inches in diameter, and rising two or three inches above the water, which may be from one to three feet in depth; anchor it to the bottom with a few concealed blades of 'saw grass,' in a little open bay, leaving its *circumference entirely free;* remove a mass of wet muck from its rounded top, and you expose seven or eight soiled, brownish white eggs, resting in a depression, the bottom of which is less than an inch from the water; the whole mass is constantly damp. This is the nest of the Dabchick, who is out foraging in the marsh, or, perhaps, is anxiously watching us from some safe corner near by. . . . During

PLATE 79.

1. PINTAIL.

Length, 26–30 inches.

2. PIED-BILLED GREBE.

Length, 13.50 inches.

the day we invariably found the eggs concealed by a covering of muck as above described; but as we ascertained by repeated visits at night, and in the early morning, they are uncovered at dusk by the bird, who incubates them until the morning sun relieves her of her task."

KEY TO THE BIRDS.

(The descriptions in this key are of the male bird in spring plumage, except in the case of those birds that we see only in winter. The variations of the female are noted in the detailed biographies.)

SECTION I. LAND BIRDS.

A. BIRDS CONSPICUOUSLY RED, BRICK, OR ORANGE.

1. Entire breast and belly pale brick-red. Above olive-gray, head black. Wings dark brown; tail black, with white spots on the two outer quills. Throat streaked with black and white, white eyelids. Bill yellow, dusky at tip; feet dark.

   American Robin. See page **64**.

2. Above brilliant blue-black, white belly, sides of body and wing linings orange-salmon. Bill and feet black.

   American Redstart. See page **115**.

3. Rich scarlet, wings, tail, and feet black.

   Scarlet Tanager. See page **131**.

4. Above strawberry-red with some gray fleckings; wings and tail brown; heavy blackish bill; feet dark. Winter bird.

   Pine Grosbeak. See page **133**.

5. General colour Indian-red; wings and tail brownish. *Beak distinctly crossed at tip.* Winter bird of pine trees.

   American Crossbill. See page **137**.

6. Red, conspicuously crested. Black throat and band around beak. Beak light red ; feet brown.

Cardinal. See page **161**.

7. Black head, throat, and upper half of back. Wings black, larger coverts tipped and inner feathers edged with white. Middle tail quills black, *everywhere else orange-flame.* Feet and bill slatish black.

Baltimore Oriole. See page **172**.

8. *Throat and breast orange-flame colour*, lower parts tinged with yellow. Black head striped with flame ; black wings and tail with white markings, black streaks on breast. Bill and feet dark.

Blackburnian Warbler. See page **102**.

9. *Breast rose-carmine, which colour extends under the wings.* Above black ; belly, rump, three outer tail quills, and two spots on wings white. Heavy brown bill.

Rose-breasted Grosbeak. See page **162**.

10. *Crown, chin, and throat bright red.* Above black, white, and yellowish ; below greenish yellow. Tail black, white on the middle feathers, white edge to wing coverts. A tree-creeper. Bill pointed, about as long as head.

Yellow-bellied Sapsucker. See page **198**.

11. *Head, neck, and throat crimson.* Back, wings, and tail bluish black. White below, much white on wings, and white rump. A tree-creeper. Bill horn-coloured.

Red-headed Woodpecker. See page **199**.

B. BIRDS CONSPICUOUSLY BLUE.

1. *Azure-blue above.* Wings blue with blackish tips, upper breast brick-red, lower parts white. Bill and feet black.

Bluebird. See page **66**.

2. *Deep blue, in some lights having a greenish cast.* Wings and tail washed thinly with brownish. Bill dark above.

Indigo Bunting. See page **164**.

3. *Lead-blue above ;* head finely crested ; *wing coverts and tail bright blue*, barred with black. Below grayish white with a black collar.

Blue Jay. See page **177**.

4. *Above lead-blue*, variegated with black. Below whitish, two dull blue bands across breast. Long crest ; straight bill longer than head.

Belted Kingfisher. See page **204**.

C. BIRDS CONSPICUOUSLY YELLOW.

*** WARBLERS. — Small wood-birds with slender bills, much varied plumage, and (as a rule) weak voices.**

1. *Forehead and under parts clear yellow.* Dark stripe through eye; bill bluish black. Above olive-green; wings slaty blue with white bars. Feet dark.

   Blue-winged Warbler. See page **90**.

2. *Clear yellow below,* which remains constant all the season. Above olive-green, brightening on the rump and shoulders. Slate-gray head and neck. No bars on wings or tail, which are brownish. Bill and feet dark.

   Nashville Warbler. See page **91**.

3. Above slate-blue, triangular spot of greenish yellow back of shoulders. *Chin and throat yellow.* Wings brownish with two white bars, two white spots on tail. White belly, reddish brown band across breast. Bill dark above, flesh-coloured below; feet light.

   Parula Warbler. See page **93**.

4. *Above rich olive-yellow, breast and under parts golden yellow.* Breast streaked with cinnamon-brown. Bill lead-coloured; feet light brown.

   Yellow Warbler. See page **94**.

5. *Crown, sides of breast, and rump yellow.* Above slate colour, striped and streaked with black; below whitish; upper breast black. Bill and feet black.

   Myrtle Warbler. See page **96**.

6. *Rump and under parts rich yellow,* the latter streaked with black on the breast and sides. Above dark olive, wings barred with white. Bill and feet dark.

   Magnolia Warbler. See page **97**

7. *Back and crown bright olive-yellow, sides and front of head clear yellow.* Throat and upper breast black, black continued in a stripe down the sides. White below. Bill and feet dark.

   Black-throated Green Warbler. See page **102**.

8. *Above bright yellowish olive, clear yellow below* with dark streaks on sides.

   Pine Warbler. See page **103**.

9. *Under parts clear yellow* with bright chestnut streaks on the sides. *Chestnut crown.* Brownish above. Rump yellowish. Bill and feet dark.

   Yellow Palm Warbler. See page **104**.

10. *Under parts rich yellow*, yellow streak running from nostril back of eye, and two yellow wing bands. Colours much mixed above, — olive, green, or yellow; chestnut streaks forming patch across back; sides of neck and body streaked with black.

Prairie Warbler. See page **105**.

11. *Rich yellow lower breast and belly.* Decidedly marked gray head and neck, the rest of upper parts yellowish olive. Throat and upper breast usually black, veiled with ash-gray. Wings and tail glossy olive-green. Upper mandible dark, lower mandible and feet flesh-coloured.

Mourning Warbler. See page **110**.

12. *Under parts, including wing and tail coverts, yellow*, grading to white on middle of belly. Above olive, *head masked with black.* Bill black; flesh-coloured feet.

Maryland Yellow-throat. See page **110**.

13. *Brilliant yellow throat, breast, and wing linings.* Olive-green above; strong, curving blue-black bill; feet lead-coloured. (Larger than the preceding species, voice strong.)

Yellow-breasted Chat. See page **112**.

14. *Yellow face, and under parts;* black hood, chin, and upper breast; above rich olive. Bill black; feet light.

Hooded Warbler. See page **113**.

15. Above olive-yellow; *under parts rich yellow*, shading to olive on the sides. *Black cap.* Bill dark above, lower mandible and feet light.

Wilson's Warbler. See page **114**.

16. Above ash-blue, crown spotted with arrow-shaped black marks blending on the brow. *Below pure yellow with a showy necklace of black longitudinal streaks on the breast.* Yellow line over eye, black patch under it. Bill dark; feet flesh-coloured.

Canadian Warbler. See page **114**.

** Birds with thicker sparrow-like bills.

17. *Body*, all but wings, tail, and frontlet, *clear gamboge yellow.* Frontlet black; wings black, varied with white.

American Goldfinch. See page **140**.

*** Large ground-feeding birds.

18. *Under parts bright yellow, black throat crescent.* Much variegated above, general colour brown. Bill stout and straight, strong legs, a walker. A ground feeder and meadow bird.

Meadowlark. See page **170**.

D. BIRDS CONSPICUOUSLY BLACK, DUSKY, OR DARK GRAY.

1. *Above olive-gray; head black.* Wings dark brown; tail black, with white spots on the two outer quills. Entire breast and belly pale brick-red. Throat streaked with black and white; white eyelids. Bill yellow, dusky at tip; feet dark.

American Robin. See page **64**.

2. *Gray above;* wings brownish gray, white spot on outer edge. Breast grayish white; tail brownish, three outer quills white. Night singer.

Mockingbird. See page **76**.

3. *Clear, deep slate above;* under parts light gray. Crown and tail black; vent rust-red.

Catbird. See page **78**.

4. Dark bluish slate all over, except lower breast and belly, which are grayish white, and form a vest. Several outer tail feathers white, which are conspicuous in flying. Bird of autumn and winter.

Slate-coloured Junco. See page **155**.

5. Head, neck, breast, back, and middle tail feathers black. Belly and spots on outer tail feathers white. Sides light bay. Red eyes, black bill, light-brown feet.

Towhee. See page **160**.

6. *Above black;* belly, rump, three outer tail quills, and two spots on wings white. *Breast rose-carmine*, which colour extends under the wings.

Rose-breasted Grosbeak. See page **162**.

7. *Above bluish ash*, lighter on the rump and shoulders; below light gray, waved with darker lines. Black bar on each side of head; wings and tail black, outer quills of latter white-tipped. Blackish beak; legs bluish black. Winter bird.

Northern Shrike. See page **122**

8. *Black head, chin, tail, and under parts.* Buff patch on back of neck; also buff edges to some tail feathers. Rump and upper wing coverts white. Bill brown. Meadow bird.

Bobolink. See page **165**.

9. Body flat and compact. Above slate-blue; *top of head and nape black.* Wings blackish, edged with slate; belly white, growing rusty toward vent. Bill dark lead colour; feet dark brown. Tree-creepers: most conspicuous in autumn and winter.

White-breasted Nuthatch. See page **73**.

10. *Above striped black and white.* Breast white in middle, black stripes on sides. Wings and tail black, with white markings; bill and feet black. Small tree-creeping bird.

Black-and-white Creeper. See page **88**.

11. *Above black and white; white stripe on middle of back, red crescent on back of head.* Under parts grayish white; wings black and white. Bill sharp, stout, and straight, nearly as long as head. Tree-creeping bird.

Hairy Woodpecker. See page **196**.

12. Closely resembling the last species, but smaller. Wings and tail *barred* with white. A tree-creeper.

Downy Woodpecker. See page **198**.

13. *Whole head and neck, tail, and part of wings black.* Breast, rump, and shoulders chestnut-brown. Whitish wing band, and some feathers edged with white. Rounded black tail, edged with lighter. Bill and feet bluish black.

Orchard Oriole. See page **171**.

14. Small birds, feeding among tree branches. *Crested, with black frontlet.* Above ash-gray, wings and tail darker, sides of head dull white. Under parts whitish with brownish wash on sides. Bill lead-black; feet lead colour.

Tufted Titmouse. See page **71**.

15. Feeding as last species. Conspicuous bird of autumn and winter. No crest; above gray with a brownish tinge; *crown, throat, and neck black. Cheeks white.* Below white, shading to gray with a brownish wash. Wings and tail gray with white edgings. Bill and feet lead-black.

Chickadee. See page **72**.

16. *Black cap,* grayish white cheeks, general upper parts striped gray, black, and olive. *Breast white with black streaks.* White spots on outer tail feathers.

Black-poll Warbler. See page **101**.

* Typical Blackbirds.

17. Head, throat, and shoulders glistening, dark brown; all other parts iridescent black. A walker. Bill dark brown; feet rusty black.

Cowbird. See page **167**.

18. Rich blue-black; scarlet shoulders, edged with yellow.

Red-winged Blackbird. See page **169**.

19. In breeding plumage, glossy, black with metallic glints, and a rusty wash. In autumn rust-coloured. Bill and feet dark.

Rusty Blackbird. See page **175**.

20. Glossy, metallic black, iridescent tints on head, tail, and wings. Tail long; feet black.

Purple Grackle. See page **175.**

20 (*a*). Metallic green and purple feathers, above tipped with buff. Bill yellow in summer; dark in winter.

English Starling. See page **180.**

** Crows.

21. Large bird, glossy, purplish black. Wings appear saw-toothed in flying, tail extending beyond wings. Bill and feet black.

American Crow. See page **178.**

22. Smaller than last species. Glossy, purplish black, chin unfeathered.

Fish Crow. See page **179.**

*** Birds of the air, dashing from their perch to seize insects.

23. Above dark ash; head, wings, and tail black; orange-red streak on poll. Beneath grayish white, darkest on breast, tail terminating in a white band.

Kingbird. See page **182.**

**** Birds of the air, feeding on the wing.

24. A sooty-brown, swallow-like bird, building in chimneys. Wings longer than tail, which is nearly even, the shafts of the quills ending in sharp spines.

Chimney Swift. See page **193.**

E. BROWN OR BROWNISH BIRDS, OF VARIOUS SIZES AND MARKINGS.

* Brown or olive backs; rather long, slender bills. Lightish breasts, more or less speckled. All fine songsters, running or hopping on the ground.

1. Above *tawny-brown, deepest on head;* whitish eye ring. Sides of throat light buff, middle of throat, breast, and belly white, sprinkled on the sides with heart-shaped dark brown spots. Bill dark brown; feet flesh-coloured.

Wood Thrush. See page **57.**

2. *Above evenly tawny. Throat buff*, flecked on sides with fine arrow-shaped brown spots. Under parts white; *no eye ring;* feet light.

Wilson's Thrush. See page **58.**

3. Head and back uniform olive-brown. Throat buff and slightly speckled; sides dull grayish white. *Cheeks gray; no eye ring.* Bill slender.

Gray-cheeked Thrush. See page **60.**

4. Above olive-brown. Buff breast and throat, deepening in colour on the sides, and speckled everywhere but on the centre; breast with blackish spots. *Yellowish eye ring.* Dark bill; feet pale brown.

Olive-backed Thrush. See page **61**.

5. Above olive-brown, *reddening on the rump and tail.* Throat, neck, and sides of breast washed with buff and thickly sprinkled arrowheads. Under parts white; *yellowish eye ring.* Bill blackish above, lower mandible light; feet light brown.

Hermit Thrush. See page **62**.

6. Long bird. Above reddish brown, beneath yellowish white, with brown spots on breast and sides. *Very long tail;* two light bars on wings. Bill black, lower mandible yellow at base; feet light.

Brown Thrasher. See page **80**.

7. Above dark olive-brown. Tail and wings brownish black; several outer tail feathers partly or wholly white. White eye ring, and line over the eye. Under parts whitish, with washes of various shades of brown. Bill dark; feet brown. A bird of fields and waysides, seen in late autumn and spring.

American Pipit. See page **87**.

8. Olive-brown above; *whitish eye ring;* two brown stripes on head, enclosing a dull orange crown. White below, with brownish spots in the centre of breast running into streaks on the sides. Brown bill; legs and feet flesh-coloured.

Ovenbird. See page **106**.

9. Above, including wings and tail, plain olive-brown. Under parts sulphur-yellow, speckled everywhere, except a space in the middle of belly, with dark brown. Bill and feet dark.

Water Thrush. See page **108**.

10. Above grayish brown, with a brown crown, and white line over the eye. Creamy white breast sparingly streaked with brown. Peculiarly heavy dark bill; legs light.

Louisiana Water Thrush. See page **108**.

**** Brownish birds of very small size, with slender bills. Backs usually barred with browns and grays. Tails held erect.**

11. Chestnut-brown above, wings and tail barred with clear brown. Under parts buffy. Bill straight and dark, same length as head; feet dusky flesh colour.

Carolina Wren. See page **82**

12. Dark brown above, minutely barred with blackish. Under parts gray, with brownish wash and faint bandings. Fairly long tail. Bill black above, lower mandible light; feet brown.

House Wren. See page **83**.

13. Colour similar to last species, except the under parts, which are rusty and dimly, but finely, barred with dark. Tail and bill short; the latter dark and slender.

Winter Wren. See page **84**.

14. Above brown. Crown and part of back streaked with black and white. White beneath, washed with rusty across breast and along sides. Wings and tail barred. Very short bill.

Short-billed Marsh Wren. See page **85**.

15. Above clear brown, whitish line over eye, neck and back streaked sparingly with white. Wings and tail brown; the latter barred. Bill nearly as long as head.

Long-billed Marsh Wren. See page **86**.

*** **Sparrow-like birds, with stout bills. General plumage brown, gray, or rusty, much streaked and spotted, and occasionally washed with reddish purple. One species has a white throat and one a white crown.**

Finch Family. See page **133**.

**** **Birds with soft, Quaker-coloured plumage of browns and drabs; not barred, striped, or spotted.**

A. *Crested; short, blunt, broad, black bill.*

16. Black frontlet. Crest, breast, throat, wings, and tail purplish ash. Secondary wing quills tipped with waxy red points. Tail feathers banded with yellow, and sometimes tipped with red, like the wings.

Cedar Waxwing. See page **124**.

B. *Not crested; head about the same length as long curving bill. Tail long.*

17. Powerful bill; lower mandible yellow. Above olive, with gray and metallic tints. Two middle tail feathers olive, outer quills black, with conspicuous white spots. Wings washed with bright cinnamon. Under parts grayish white.

Yellow-billed Cuckoo. See page **202**.

18. Above general colouring same as last species. Black bill, red eyelids. White spots on tail inconspicuous.

Black-billed Cuckoo. See page **203**

******* Mottled brown and black birds (other than true Hawks and Owls) flying and feeding chiefly at twilight and night.**

19. A long-winged bird of twilight and night. Large mouth, fringed with bristles. Plumage dusky and Owl-like, much spotted with black and gray. Wings mottled with shades of brown. Lower half of outer tail quills white.

Whip-poor-will. See page **190**.

20. A bird of day, as well as of night. Mottled black and rusty above; the breast finely barred and with a V-shaped white spot on throat. Wings brown, a large white spot extending entirely through them, conspicuous in flight. White bar on tail.

Nighthawk. See page **191**.

F. DAINTILY PLUMED SMALL BIRDS FEEDING ABOUT THE BRANCHES AND TERMINAL SHOOTS OF TREES.

1. Tiny bird of autumn and winter. Flame-coloured crown spot, edged with yellow and enclosed by black line. Above olive-green and yellowish olive, which is more decided on wings, rump, and tail. Whitish line over eye; under parts yellowish gray. Bill and feet black.

Golden-crowned Kinglet. See page **68**.

2. Small bird with vermilion spot on crown. Ash-gray head; back olive-gray, yellower on tail. Breast and under parts yellowish gray. Edges of eyelids whitish. Bill black; feet dark brown.

Ruby-crowned Kinglet. See page **69**.

3. Head yellowish brown; black stripe on each side of crown, also back of eye. Above greenish olive; under parts buffy. Bill and feet light.

Worm-eating Warbler. See page **89**.

4. Yellow crown and wing coverts. Above bluish gray. Chin, throat, and eye stripe black. Below slaty white tinged with yellowish. Bill and feet blackish.

Golden-winged Warbler. See page **90**.

5. Top of head yellow. Black stripe running through the eye, and a black spot in front of it. Back and wing coverts streaked black and yellow. Throat and breast white with chestnut stripe, starting at the black mustache and extending down the sides. Bill black; feet brown.

Chestnut-sided Warbler. See page **98**

6. Above bluish slate rather than blue, lighter on forehead. Black throat, terminating in a line down the sides. White spot on wings; outer tail feathers white spotted. White beneath. Bill and feet dark.

Black-throated Blue Warbler. See page **95**

7. Above streaked with black and grayish olive. Forehead, cheeks, and sides of head black, enclosing a chestnut patch. Chin, throat, and upper breast, and a streak along the sides dull chestnut. White cross-bars on wings, and white spots on tail. Bill and feet dark.

Bay-breasted Warbler. See page **99**.

*** Birds with bills slightly hooked at tip; plumage olive above and white or yellowish below; feeding in the trees; loud and constant singers.**

Vireo Family. See page **116**.

G. TREE-CREEPING BIRDS OF VARIOUS SIZES, SEEN UPON THE TRUNKS AND BRANCHES, FEEDING UPON INSECTS AND THE LARVÆ IN THE BARK.

1. Body flat and compact. Above slate-blue, head and hind neck black. Wings blackish, edged with slate. Belly white, rusty toward vent. Most conspicuous in autumn and winter.

White-breasted Nuthatch. See page **73**.

2. Above lead-coloured, brownish on wings and tail. Crown and sides of head and neck black. Under parts rust-red. Bill lead colour, feet lead-brown. Bird of autumn and winter.

Red-breasted Nuthatch. See page **74**.

3. Above brown and white striped, the brown being of several shades, growing reddish on rump. Throat, breast, and belly grayish white; tail pale brown. Slender, curving bill. Bird of late autumn and winter.

Brown Creeper. See page **75**.

4. Small bird. Above striped black and white. Breast white in middle, black stripes on sides. Wings and tail black, with white markings. Bill and feet black.

Black-and-white Creeper. See page **88**.

5. Above black and white, white stripe on middle of back, red stripe on head. Under parts grayish white; wings black and white. Bill blunt, stout, and straight, nearly as long as head.

Hairy Woodpecker. See page **196**.

6. Closely resembling the last species, but smaller. Wings and tail *barred* with white.

Downy Woodpecker. See page **198**.

7. Above black, white, and yellowish; below greenish yellow. Tail black, white on the middle feathers, white edge to wing coverts. Crown, chin, and throat bright red. Bill about as long as head, more pointed and slender than last species.

Yellow-bellied Sapsucker. See page **198**.

8. Head, neck, and throat crimson. Back, wings, and tail bluish black. White below, much white on wings and white rump. Bill about as long as head.

Red-headed Woodpecker. See page **199**

9. Above golden brown, barred with black. Black crescent on breast, red band on back of head. Round black spots on belly; black cheek patch. Wing linings gamboge-yellow, rump white. Bill slender, curving, and pointed.

Flicker. See page **200**.

H. WINTER BIRDS OF MEADOWS AND UPLANDS.

1. Soft brown and white plumage; bill and feet black. Birds seen in large flocks, feeding upon seed-stalks that rise above the snow.

Snowflake. See page **142**.

2. Top of head black, edged with rusty; black above, with feathers all edged with white. Below grayish, with faint black markings. Legs and feet black, with a long hind claw or spur. Birds of meadows, stubble-fields, and the shore.

Lapland Longspur. See page **144**.

3. Upper parts with a pinkish cast, most marked on neck and rump. Black crescent on breast; black bar in front of head, extending to side of head, forming two tufts or horns. Frontlet, throat, and fore-neck pale yellowish. Below whitish, streaked with black.

Horned Lark. See page **181**.

4. Head, breast, and rump washed with rich crimson over a ground of gray and brown. Back, wings, and tail dusky; dusky white beneath. Tail short and forked; wings long and pointed. Crimson wash not conspicuous as the bird flies.

Redpoll. See page **138**.

I. BIRDS OF THE AIR, CONSTANTLY UPON THE WING AND FEEDING AS THEY FLY.

* With plumage more or less iridescent or tinted with metallic colours.

a. Birds flying over low meadows, streams, and beaches; tails more or less forked; wings sharply pointed. Bills dark, widely triangular.

Swallow Family. See page **125**.

b. Very small birds, feeding about flowers; bill long and needle-like. Metallic green above, grayish below; glistening ruby throat, and deeply forked tail.

Ruby-throated Hummingbird. See page **194**.

** Plumage not iridescent or metallic, but sooty brown, olive, or grayish above, and white, gray, or yellowish below.

c. A Swallow-like bird, building in chimneys. Deep sooty brown. Wings longer than the tail, which is nearly even, the shafts of the quills ending in sharp spines.

Swift Family. See page **193**.

d. Birds of small and medium size, with plumage ranging through browns and olive, with yellow or gray breasts, with and without erectile crests. Perching with drooping tail and wings vibrating and suddenly dashing into the air in pursuit of insects.

Tyrant Flycatchers. See page **182**.

SECTION II. BIRDS OF PREY.

A. STOUTLY BUILT BIRDS, WITH LARGE HEADS, FACIAL EYE DISKS, ETC.

*** No feathered horns.**

1. Above tawny yellow, ash, and white, with black and white spots; below whitish, speckled with dark. Dark bars on tail and wings. Legs long, and feathered. Small, bluish black eyes; bill light. Face disk heart-shaped.

Barn Owl. See page **206**.

2. Mottled dark brown, rusty, and grayish. Striped on breast with dark brown. Face feathers white tipped; wings and tail barred with brown. Legs and dark feet fully feathered. Bill ivory-coloured; eyes blue-black.

Barred Owl. See page **209**.

3. Smallest United States Owl. Above brown, spotted more or less with lighter brown and white. Striped beneath with rusty-brown. Legs feathered with yellowish white. Bill black; claws dark.

Saw-whet Owl. See page **210**.

4. Plumage varying from pure white to white barred and spotted with brown and black. Legs and toes thickly feathered. Bill and claws black.

nowy Owl. See page **213**.

** Horned Owls.

5. Above finely mottled with brown, ash, and dark orange. Long, erect ear tufts. Complete facial disk reddish brown with darker inner circle; dark brown, broken band on wings and tail. Breast pale orange with long, brown stripes. Legs and feet completely feathered. Bill and claws blackish.

American Long-eared Owl. See page **207**.

6. Inconspicuous ear tufts, facial disk with a dark ring enclosing a lighter one. Plumage varied from bright orange to buffy white with bold stripes of dark brown. Darker above, and more mottled below, growing whiter toward vent. Legs feathered with plain buff. Bill and claws dusky blue-black.

Short-eared Owl. See page **208**.

7. Conspicuous ear tufts, bill light horn colour. Plumage either grayish or rust-red and mottled; tail and wings equal. Feet covered with short dark feathers. Claws dark. A small common Owl.

Screech Owl. See page **211**.

8. Large heavy Owl. Long ear tufts, feathers mottled irregularly, buff, tawny brown or whitish. Feet and legs feathered; bill and claws black.

Great Horned Owl. See page **212**.

B. DIURNAL BIRDS OF PREY, WITH SMALLER HEADS THAN THE LAST GROUP, CONSPICUOUSLY HOOKED BILLS AND CLAWS, NO HORNS OR PERFECT FACIAL DISKS. FLIGHT GRACEFUL AND RAPID; PLUMAGE PLAIN, STREAKED OR MOTTLED.

* Plumage brightly coloured or much varied.

1. Tail long. Eyes reddish brown. Above bluish gray, deepest on head. Beneath whitish, barred on the sides and breast with rusty and dark brown. Small head, long legs, slender feet. Flight dashing.

Sharp-shinned Hawk. See page **216**.

2. Similar to last species, but larger. Tail rounded and barred with dusky or rufous. Feet rather stout, greenish yellow.

Cooper's Hawk. See page **217**.

3. *Tail rust-red*, with a black band near end. Above dark brown variegated with white, gray, and tawny; below whitish and buff, streaked below with brown. Bill horn-coloured.

Red-tailed Hawk. See page **218**.

4. *Shoulders rust-red.* Above reddish brown, the middle of the feathers darker than the edges. Head and lower parts rusty, barred with whitish; tail black with white bands. Feet bright yellow.

Red-shouldered Hawk. See page **219**.

5. Small, brightly coloured Hawk. Above reddish, with or without black spots and bars. Top of head bluish slate with a red crown patch. Below varying from whitish to reddish, with or without dark spots. Wings narrow and pointed.

American Sparrow Hawk. See page **222**.

** Plumage dark brown, gray, or whitish, not red or rusty.

1. Above bluish gray; below white, mottled with brown. Wings brownish, long, and pointed. Tail long; upper tail coverts white. Bill and feet black. A summer Hawk of moist lands.

Marsh Hawk. See page **215**.

2. Very large bird. *Head, neck feathers, and tail pure white.* Beak yellow and abruptly hooked. Plumage dark brown; legs feathered only half-way down; feet yellow.

Bald Eagle. See page **220**.

3. A fishing Hawk seen flying over large bodies of water. Plain dark brown above, the tail having a white tip and a band of dark brown. Head, neck, and lower parts white; breast plain, or sometimes spotted faintly with brown. Bill bluish black; feet grayish.

American Osprey. See page **223**.

SECTION III. GAME, SHORE, AND WATER BIRDS.

A. WOOD DOVES, WITH DELICATELY SHADED AND OFTEN GLOSSY PLUMAGE, ETC.

1. Upper parts bluish gray; reddish brown below, fading to whitish toward vent. Wings dark, with a few spots; tail quills dark blue at the base and white at tips. Bill black; feet lake-red.

Passenger Pigeon. See page 225.

2. General colouring bluish fawn. Above olive-brown, varying to bluish gray; neck and head washed with metallic tints. Below a dull purplish, changing to reddish brown. Bill black; feet lake-red.

Mourning Dove. See page 226.

B. BIRDS WITH MOTTLED FEATHERS, ETC.

(Seen Scratching on the Ground like Barnyard Fowls.)

1. Crown slightly crested. White forehead, eye line, and throat patch, edged with dark. Above variegated reddish brown. Below whitish, warming on the sides to reddish, with dark bars. Bill rusty black; legs not feathered.

Bob-white. See page 227.

2. Slightly crested head, yellowish eye stripe, and neck mottled with reddish and dusky brown. Back variegated chestnut; lower parts lighter, with dark bars. Long tail, which spreads fan-like. Neck ruff of dark feathers; feathered legs.

Ruffed Grouse. See page 229.

C. SMALL AND MEDIUM-SIZED BIRDS, WITH STOUT BODIES, BULLET-SHAPED HEADS, ETC., SEEN IN THE VICINITY OF BOTH SALT AND FRESH WATER.

1. Shore birds of medium size, seen turning over stones on beaches as they feed. Above patched with black, white, red, brown, and gray, a calico pattern. Below white with black breast. Much white on wings and tail. Bill black, shorter than the head, and slightly recurved; feet orange.

Turnstone. See page 231.

2. Above mottled with black, gray, and yellowish. Beneath mostly black. Bill long and black; feet black.

Black-bellied Plover. See page 232.

3. Above mottled with black and greenish yellow; whitish below. Axilliary feathers ashy brown. Bill and feet black. This Plover is subject to great variations of plumage. A popular game-bird.

Golden Plover. See page 233.

4. Gray-brown, washed with olive above; rump variegated with all shades of orange and reddish brown. White frontlet, and red eyelids. Below white, collar and breastlet black. Bill black; legs light.

Killdeer Plover. See page 233.

5. Bill, and half-webbed feet, yellow, bill having a black tip. An orange ring around eye. Above ash-gray; below white with a black band across the breast.

Semipalmated Plover. See page 234.

6. Above light gray. Coloured eye ring; bill yellow; partial white collar on back of neck, and a partial dark band on throat. Below white.

Piping Plover. See page 235.

D. SMALL AND MEDIUM-SIZED BIRDS OF BOGGY MEADOWS, ETC., SLENDER BILLS, USUALLY MUCH LONGER THAN THE HEAD.

1. Eyes large, set in upper corner of head. Short, thick neck, and compact body. Above variegated with brown, black, tawny, and gray; below brown, ranging from buff to tawny. Legs very short. Bill longer than head, straight and stout.

American Woodcock. See page 236.

2. Straight greenish gray bill, two and a half inches long. Eyes set far back as the last species. Above reddish and dark brown, sides of head and neck buff. Dark, plain wings

margined and tipped with white; tail bay and black, outer feathers soiled white with brown bars. Feet greenish gray.

Wilson's Snipe. See page **237**.

3. Bill long and slender like the last species, which it greatly resembles. "Rump and tail white, the former spotted, the latter banded with black." Winter plumage ash-gray above and whitish below. Bill and feet greenish black.

Dowitcher. See page **238**.

4. Straight bill an inch and a half long. Above black, white, ash, and reddish; crown gray, streaked with black; nape of neck reddish. Below rich chestnut; legs short and thick.

Knot. See page **239**.

5. Bill straight, half as long as head, flesh-coloured, tipped with black. Above black and reddish, with stripe over eye; neck short. Below whitish, washed on neck and breast with dusky, broken by brown lines. Rump black; wings dusky; some tail feathers tipped with white. Feet dusky greenish.

Pectoral Sandpiper. See page **240**.

6. Above dark brown, feathers edged with ashy and reddish. Neck ash-gray spotted with black. White eye stripe. Wings dusky, rump and tail coverts black. Below grayish white. Bill black; legs dull green.

Least Sandpiper. See page **241**.

7. Long, thin, yellow legs; bill greenish black, over two inches long. Above dusky, spotted with black and white. Below white, streaked sparsely with gray on the neck. Rump white, also the tail feathers, which are barred with brown.

Greater Yellow Legs. See page **242**.

8. Long, slender, dark bill. Dark brown above with an olive wash. Head and neck streaked with white, rest of upper parts spotted with white. Below white with some streaks on the throat. Legs dull greenish.

Solitary Sandpiper. See page **243**.

9. Short bill, but little longer than the head. Above gray, tinged with reddish. Below varying from white to buff, dark lines on breast and spots on belly. Outer tail quills white, barred with black. Feet dirty yellow.

Bartramian Sandpiper. See page **244**.

10. Slender, flesh-coloured bill tipped with black, longer than the head. Above Quaker gray, with an iridescent lustre, spotted and streaked with black. White eye line. White below, dotted with black; feet flesh-coloured.

Spotted Sandpiper. See page **244**.

E. BIRDS WITH STRONG LEGS AND LONG TOES; SUBDUED PLUMAGE; INHABITANTS OF REEDY MARSHES.

1. General colouring sand-gray, with no reddish tinge. Wings and tail dull brown. Bill longer than the head, yellowish brown; feet the same colour.

Clapper Rail. See page **245**.

2. General tone streaky and reddish. Above dark brown, plainly streaked with olive, a white line from the bill extending over the eye. Throat white. Below bright reddish. Wings dark brown, barred with white.

Virginia Rail. See page **246**.

3. Bill only three-fourths of an inch long, straight and stout. Above olive, brownish, and black, many feathers having white edges, and with black and white barring on the flanks. Breast slate-coloured, with some black on the centre of the throat. Tail dusky brown, darkest in centre and almost pointed.

Sora. See page **247**.

4. Bill and frontal plate red. Above, head and neck bluish gray, back olive-brown, wings and tail dark. Beneath dark gray, grading to white on belly.

Florida Gallinule. See page **248**.

5. Dark slate above, head and neck almost black. Whole edge of wing and tips of some quills white. Below paler gray; tail dark brown. Bill flesh-white, with a slight rusty black mark at the tip. Red frontal shield. Feet pale dull green.

American Coot. See page **249**.

F. LONG-LEGGED, LONG-NECKED, LONG-BILLED, LARGE BIRDS; LIVING IN WOODED SWAMPS.

1. Above yellowish brown, much streaked and mottled with different shades of brown, from dark to light. Below yellowish white, the feathers edged and striped with brown. Tail brown, small and rounded. Bill yellow, edged with black; legs yellow-green.

American Bittern. See page **250**.

2. Top of head, which is slightly crested, and back, rich greenish black. Back of neck chestnut-brown; also wing coverts and the edges of some quills. Tail like back. Below muddy yellow, with dark brown patches on sides of breast, and some white around the throat. Bill, eyes, and toes yellow.

Least Bittern. See page **251**.

3. Long black crest, the two longest feathers of which are shed in the summer moult. Upper parts and tail bluish slate, below black and white streaked, forehead and crown white. Bill yellow and dusky; feet and legs dark. (Very large Heron, often four feet long.)

Great Blue Heron. See page 252.

4. Head with lengthened crest. Above dark glossy green, sometimes with an iridescence. Edging of wing coverts reddish. Neck a rich shade of chestnut, with purplish wash ; white streak on the throat ; under parts whitish, shading to ash below.

Green Heron. See page 253.

5. Above either dull or greenish black; tail, wings, and neck grayish. Throat and forehead whitish. Below livid white. Crest of three long white feathers often rolled into one. Bill black ; legs yellow.

Black-crowned Night Heron. See page 254.

H. OFF-SHORE BIRDS.

* Legs long.

1. A tube-nosed swimmer. Bill black. Above sooty brown, blackening on wings and tail; white rump. Long black legs, the foot-webbing spotted with yellow. One of "Mother Carey's chickens."

Wilson's Petrel. See page 268.

** Legs short.

2. Bluish gray above, bill light yellow. White below. Black feet and tip to tail.

Kittiwake Gull. See page 269.

3. Above grayish blue or "gull-blue,"[1] head and tail lighter ; white below. Bill yellow, feet flesh colour.

American Herring Gull. See page 270.

4. Head and neck dark slate ; bill carmine. Back slate-coloured, divided from the head by the white of the neck. All under parts white, also tail coverts. Legs and feet dull reddish.

Laughing Gull. See page 270.

5. Head and upper neck dark lead colour ; bill black ; back "gull-blue." Rump and tail white, also under parts. Wings white and gull-blue. Legs and feet light red.

Bonaparte's Gull. See page 271.

6. Bill long, coral-red at base, black toward end, and tipped with yellow. Upper head and back of neck black. Entire back and wings light gray with a bluish wash. Tail coverts, most

[1] A peculiar shade of bluish gray.

of tail, and wing linings white; below white and gray. Legs and feet light red.

Common Tern. See page 272.

7. Bill black, yellow at tip, and reddish at base. Black cap and long head feathers; back of neck white, also entire under parts white with a rosy wash. Wings varied gray; tail pearl-gray. Feet and legs yellowish red; claws black.

Roseate Tern. See page 273.

8. Legs and bill yellow. Crown black; back, wings, tail, and rump gull-blue. A few outer wing feathers black; below white.

Least Tern. See page 275.

I. STOUT-BODIED DIVING BIRDS OF FRESH AND SALT WATER.

1. Short, thick, black bill. Above dark brown with some white on wings; below generally whitish. A small off-shore bird seldom seen near land.

Dovekie. See page 275.

2. Bill black, edged with yellowish. Head, throat, and neck iridescent green, blue, and purplish. Triangular patches of black and white streaks on either side of the throat, almost joining at the back, and narrowing in front. Sides of breast streaked with black and white; under parts white.

Loon. See page 276.

3. Bill black. Blue-gray forehead. Upper parts generally dull black, streaked and mottled with white; a triangle of rusty red on the front of neck. White below.

Red-throated Loon. See page 276.

4. Prominent crest, forming two yellow-brown horns, rest of head puffy and glossy black. Above dark brown with edgings of gray and black. Neck, upper breast, and sides rusty brown; some white on wings. Bill black with yellow tip. These birds are expert swimmers but practically helpless on land. In winter, horns lacking.

Horned Grebe. See page 277.

5. Some bristling, frontal feathers, but no regular horns. Above dark brown, showy black markings on chin and throat. Breast and lower throat yellowish brown, irregularly spotted and barred on the upper parts; lower parts glossy white. Wings brown, gray, and white. Bill much spotted.

Pied-billed Grebe. See page 278.

INDICES.

INDEX OF ENGLISH NAMES.

INDEX OF LATIN NAMES.

INDEX OF LATIN NAMES.